"One of the great documents of the human spirit . . . the story of an American legend that speaks to the winner in all of us. This is more than a book; this is a testament, a call and a challenge. It should be required reading for all Americans."
—Rev. Jesse L. Jackson

"A probing insight into the triumphs and tragedies of a Black businessman with a vision, a solid business objective and a social agenda. . . . Johnson's tone is candid, yet down-to-earth. He has woven a story, laced with witty anecdotes, that describes his relationships with some of the most powerful leaders in American history."
—Black Enterprise

"Truly inspiring. . . . A fascinating history, not only of Johnson's enterprises but their role in the great Black awakening of the '50s, '60s and '70s."
—Chicago Sun-Times

"Johnson's business autobiography is about integrity, hard work, and the American dream."
—Venture

"An enthralling and engaging autobiography from a world-class capitalist who happens to be Black. . . . While not without its sorrow, Johnson's success story (which he relates with notable gusto) transcends race in many respects. A winner's tale, then, and an immensely readable and inspiring one to boot.
—Kirkus Reviews

"Johnson offers a book that is both genial and truly inspirational. It deserves widespread attention from readers who applaud up-by-the-bootstraps success."
—Booklist

# Succeeding Against the Odds

## JOHN H. JOHNSON

### with Lerone Bennett, Jr.

**Amistad**

New York, New York

Grateful acknowledgement is given for permission to reprint "The Negro Speaks of Rivers," by Langston Hughes. Copyright 1926 by Alfred A. Knopf, Inc. Renewed 1954 by Langston Hughes.

Amistad Press, Inc.
Time-Life Building
1271 Avenue of the Americas
New York, New York 10020
Distributed by
Penguin USA
375 Hudson Street
New York, New York 10014

First published in May 1989 by Warner Books as an Amistad Book.
First issued as an Amistad Press, Inc. trade paperback with a new Fiftieth Anniversary Statement in January 1993.
10 9 8 7 6 5 4 3 2 1
Printed in the United States of America

**Library of Congress Cataloging-in-Publication Data**

Johnson, John H. (John Harold), 1918–
    Succeeding Against the Odds

    Johnson, John H. (John Harold), 1918–      2. Publishers and publishing—United States—Biography. 3. Afro-American periodicals—Publishing—History—20th century. 4. Afro-American business enterprises—History—20th century. 5. Executives—United States—Biography. I. Bennett, Lerone, 1928–      II. Title.
Z473J75A3 1989      070.5'092'4  B      88-40571  ISBN: 1-56743-002-3

*Book design: H. Roberts*

FOR MY MOTHER
GERTRUDE JOHNSON WILLIAMS
without whom
this story would not
have been possible

# FOREWORD

Nobody succeeds alone or writes a book alone.

My life and the book that tells the story of my life would not have been possible without the help and encouragement of many people. And I want to thank the people, Black and White, living and dead, the subscribers, advertisers and employees, who supported the *Ebony* idea and helped me survive with honor.

This is also their story.

I am especially indebted to my wife, Eunice, and my daughter, Linda, who lived this story with me and never faltered in their support. Both read sections of the manuscript and made valuable suggestions.

*Succeeding Against the Odds* is also Eunice's story and Linda's story.

A special thanks is due my personal secretary, Della L. Palmer, my cousin Willie Miles Burns and Nathaniel Hayes of Arkansas City, Arkansas.

I am also grateful to Johnson Publishing Company Librarian Pamela Cash Menzies and Photo Editor Basil O. Phillips for research assistance. Charles F. Harris of Amistad-Warner Books went beyond the call of duty in facilitating publishing arrangements.

I am indebted finally to the thousands of people who insisted that I write this book and who would not let me rest until it was finished.

—John H. Johnson
Chicago, 1989.

# FIFTIETH ANNIVERSARY STATEMENT

Half a century ago, I had the good fortune of founding Johnson Publishing Co., which immediately became the largest Black-owned publishing company in the world . . . a position it has held now for 50 years.

I have been told by people who keep records that no other magazine or institution has been the undisputed leader in its field for that long, and I am indebted to all Americans, Black and White, living and dead, and especially employees, subscribers and advertisers, who supported the JPC Dream and made us No. 1 for 50 straight years. For 50 straight years, we have increased the profits and influence of American businesses, and our publications still reach the largest number of Black men, Black women, and Black professionals.

We are proud of this record and of our unique relationship with Black America. And this 50th Anniversary of Johnson Publishing Company is a celebration not of Johnson Publishing Co. alone, not of our employees alone, not even of Blacks alone. This is a celebration of a triumph of the American spirit, and it tells us, among other things, that despite the real and continuing problems, the American Dream is still alive and well and working in America.

And it is important to note that on Nov. 1, 1942, when I founded my first magazine, *Negro Digest*, Jim Crow ruled the North and the South and nobody, or almost nobody, believed that it was possible to elect a Black governor in Virginia, or to put a Black man into a uniform of the Brooklyn Dodgers. The world and Virginia and the Brooklyn Dodgers have changed since then, and some analysts have been kind enough to say that *Negro Digest* and its successors, *Ebony, Jet, Black World* and *EM,* played a role in that change.

Since the founding of *Negro Digest,* the Johnson Publishing Co. Dream has expanded to eleven countries on two continents. Despite the success of the Company, neither my principles nor ideals have changed.

I still believe in the silent power of the possible.

I still believe that there is no defense against an excellence that meets a public need and that nothing—neither racism nor sexism nor ignorance—can permanently deny a Mae Jemison, or a Bill Cosby, or a Colin Powell who performs a better experiment or creates a better TV show or a better army.

That's my creed and my faith.

I believe today, as I believed in the beginning, that it is better to light a candle than to curse the night.

More than that, deeper than that, I believe—and this book is my evidence—that there is nothing we can't dream or dare or do here if we keep the faith of our fathers and mothers and put our hands to the plow and hold on.

It is in that spirit, and with that hope, that we present on the 50th Anniversary of Johnson Publishing Company this special edition of *Succeeding Against the Odds.*

—John H. Johnson
Chicago, 1992.

# CONTENTS

Prologue: View From the Mountaintop

## ROOTS AND RIVERS

## MY KIND OF TOWN

## WORDS

## WORDS AND PICTURES

## THE COLOR OF SUCCESS

## THE COLOR OF CHANGE

# Prologue: View From the Mountaintop

EVERYBODY told me no at first, including my wife.

I turned the nos into yeses and the disadvantages into advantages.

In the process, I made hundreds of millions of dollars and discovered how to succeed against the odds.

I was asked many times to publish my story, but I refused because circumstances made it impossible to tell the unvarnished truth. Circumstances have changed, and I can now tell the true story of how I rose from the welfare rolls to the roll of the 400 richest Americans.

My story, a story addressed to dreamers and long shots everywhere, begins where all good stories begin—at the beginning, with my first real November.

## NOVEMBER 1, 1987
### 5:45 A.M.

It's Sunday in November, and I'm a long way from home and wide-awake.

1

I'm in the Presidential Suite of Los Angeles's Century Plaza Hotel—I'm here for the taping of one of my TV shows—but the big screen of my mind is a life and a world away.

Forty-five Novembers ago, in another America, in another world, I borrowed $500 on my mother's furniture and started a new magazine.

The first issue of that magazine—*Negro Digest*—was published forty-five years ago today.

And what amazes me and makes chills run down my spine is that I did the same thing on that Sunday that I did on this one: I got up at dusk of dawn to inspect my fortifications and to help the sun rise.

It's difficult to tell a person who hasn't been there what that first November meant to me.

It was Christmas, July Fourth, Graduation Day, and Emancipation Day all wrapped up into one.

An explorer who sights an uncharted land, a poet who finds a new rhyme, a diver who goes down into the deep and returns with a black pearl of priceless value knows the blood-rushing, gut-wrenching feeling of exhilaration—and terror—that I felt on the first day of my *first* November.

*November 1, 1942.*

I remember that Sunday as if it were yesterday.

I was twenty-four years old, a recent migrant from Arkansas, lost and found in the big city of Chicago. Like millions of other young men, I was waiting for my number to come up in the draft. Unlike so many others, I had another number on the big board of dreams. And the performance of that number was a matter of life and death to me.

I'd lived all my life on the edge of poverty and humiliation. People say a lot of foolish things today about poverty. But I *know*—I've been there. It's not so much pain in the belly; it's pain in the soul. It's the wanting and not having, the eyes that see you and don't see you, and, all the while, just out of reach, on the other side of the glass bars of your cell, the sweets, the lights, the goodies, and the somebodyness.

I tell you, I *know*—I've been there and back.

In 1942, my mother and I were recent graduates of the relief rolls. And I'd decided that I was never going down that road again—*never*. I was willing to go anywhere. I was willing to do anything, or almost anything, to get some of the good things of this life.

You understand what I'm saying? I'm saying that *I had decided once and for all. I was going to make it, or die.*

The new magazine was a down payment on that dream. It was my stake at the big table of people who made deals and drove big cars and lived on Lake Shore Drive and migrated to Palm Springs when Lake Michigan froze over.

Would the new magazine take me there?

Would it even make enough money to finance a second issue?

And how was I going to pay back the printer and the loan company and the people I had persuaded to extend credit?

Most important of all, and most frightening of all: *Would I disgrace my mother before her friends?*

That was the question.

Would the sheriff take my mother's furniture and put us out on the cold and mean streets?

The odds against me on that day were at least $200 million—that's what people *say* I'm worth—to 1. And that's not counting the handicap of race.

But I beat the odds.

I proved that long shots *do* come in.

The magazine I published on that faraway November day opened a vein of pure black gold. And in tribute to the god of November I made November my signature month.

On November 1, 1945, I started *Ebony.*

On November 1, 1951, I started *Jet.*

In other Novembers, in other years, I founded Fashion Fair Cosmetics and Supreme Beauty Products, and bought controlling shares in Supreme Life Insurance Company, where I started my career as an office boy and a gofer.

Today I own the biggest Black-oriented corporation in America, and I sit on the boards of some of America's biggest corporations.

What a difference forty-five years make!

On November 1, 1942, I was poor, ambitious, and scared to death.

On November 1, 1987, I'm rich, ambitious, and scared to death.

That's why I got up at five o'clock this morning.

That's why I'm still running.

I'm scared somebody will pinch me and wake me up.

I'm scared somebody will take the office building in Chicago's Loop, the condominium on Lake Shore Drive, and the home on Palm Springs's highest mountain.

That's what I'm scared of.

I'm scared I'll find out I've been dreaming and that people were right when they said it was impossible for a Black boy—or any other boy—to rise in one generation from poverty to *Forbes* magazine's roll of the 400 richest Americans.

### 6:45 P.M.

We're in Hollywood, and we're surrounded by superstars and supersymbols.

Magic Johnson of the Lakers, Bea Arthur of *Golden Girls*, Benjamin Hooks of the NAACP, heavyweight champion Mike Tyson, singer Luther Vandross, Mario Van Peebles, Spike Lee, Robert Townsend, Marla Gibbs, Clifton Davis, Jackée, Chicago postmaster Janet Norfleet—to name a few—are on hand for the taping of the ninth annual American Black Achievement Awards show.

ABAA, as we call it, is in many ways the most extraordinary awards show on television. Founded to recognize Black greatness and to inspire future greatness, it recognizes not only athletes and entertainers but also professionals, artists, politicians, and entrepreneurs. As the sponsor of the show, I tell the honorees and award recipients that this is the forty-fifth year of the dream.

"For all these forty-five years," I say, "for forty-five Novembers, we have maintained that excellence knows no boundary and that the man or woman who builds a better mousetrap or sings a better song or preaches a better sermon cannot be ignored or denied."

## NOVEMBER 2, 1987
### 12:15 A.M.
Loaded down with Sunday newspapers, I catch the "Red-eye Special" for the return trip to Chicago. We're over the Rockies when I finish the last newspaper, and my pockets are bulging with newspaper clips and notes.

### 7:05 A.M.
The sun is rising over Soldier Field when I arrive at Johnson Publishing Company headquarters at 820 South Michigan, three doors down from the Chicago Hilton and Towers. One of the striking features of this building is the driveway that lets me enter the building from Michigan Avenue without leaving my car.

No other office building on Michigan Avenue has a private Michigan Avenue driveway, and I'm proud of it. It required a special dispensation from Mayor Richard Daley when Daley was at the height of his power.

It's 7:10 when I reach my desk on the eleventh floor, which is set aside for my exclusive use. The floor contains offices, a private apartment, kitchen, dining room, exercise room, and barber chair.

I'm the first employee to arrive on this first working day after the anniversary, and that gives me a certain amount of pleasure.

A reporter asked me once why I never take a real vacation, and I told him, "Work is my vacation."

There's no celebration, or even mention, of the forty-fifth anniversary of the founding of the biggest Black-owned and Black-oriented corporation in America.

We celebrate the old-fashioned way: *We work.*

**12:16 P.M.**

I sign a stack of checks and dash for the airport. The plane leaves for New York in precisely forty-six minutes. Raymond Grady, one of my employees, drives, and I navigate. I arrive at the gate in forty-five minutes and fifty-eight seconds, two seconds before the door closes. This is November— this is my lucky month.

**8:00 P.M.**

The Grand Ballroom of the New York Hilton.

Black tie.

The reigning names of the publishing industry are on hand to induct ten persons into the Publishing Hall of Fame. Henry Luce of *Time-Life* and De Witt and Lila Wallace of *Reader's Digest* have already been inducted. To-night a great-grandson of slaves is going to be inducted, along with (posthumous citations) William Randolph Hearst, and Richard Simon and Max Schuster, founders of Simon and Schuster.

This is, as we used to say in Arkansas, high cotton, and I'm moved. I speak for a few minutes extemporaneously, telling the audience that this honor is not a tribute to me personally but to the dream that unites us all.

"For it is the most enduring element of our faith," I say in conclusion, "that men and women are limited not by the place of their birth, not by the color of their skin, but by the size of their hope."

## *NOVEMBER 3*

**7:00 A.M.**

I catch the first plane out of La Guardia, and I'm in my office at 8:45.

I go first to the cashier's cage and check the cash flow. I

always tell new entrepreneurs: Check the money first, and check it personally.

I next riffle through the mail and walk through two or three departments.

That's my style.

I'm a hand-on, hands-in, hands-wrapped-around manager. Both hands.

I delegate freely and I check, double-check, and triple-check.

More to the point, I'm a details man.

I try to know more about the details of an operation than anyone else. I have been known to spend a whole day double-checking the seat assignments for guests and executives in the huge Arie Crown Theater of McCormick Place, where we hold the annual Ebony Fashion Show. I asked Mayor Richard Daley once what was the secret of his success.

"I take care of the details," he said, "and the big picture takes care of itself."

Details.

All day long, from nine to five, executives and senior employees come to the eleventh floor with details, status reports, and problems. I tell them if there's a problem they can't solve, bring it to me, and I'll solve it. That's my job. I've made mistakes in my life. But God knows I've never been at a loss for a solution, even when it was wrong. A good general, I say, *always* has another plan.

**10:56 A.M.**

Two or three times a day, I call executives of selected divisions to status conferences in the "fishbowl" conference room on the ninth floor.

The first conference of the day is with the Supreme Beauty Products Division.

I chair the conference, and I sit as usual at the head of the big oak conference table, with my daughter, President and Chief Operating Officer Linda Johnson Rice, at my right.

Supreme, which manufactures and distributes hair products, including Duke and Raveen, for men and women, is in trouble. What are we going to do about it?

I'm sentimental about Supreme, which is a spin-off of my first nonpublishing venture, Beauty Star Cosmetics. Beauty Star started as a mail-order firm in 1946. When the big money, and the respectability, started coming in, I tried to kill it. But it refused to die. The orders continued to come in, even when the ads stopped, and it was reborn in 1960 as Supreme Beauty Products. Then, in 1987, White corporations openly threatened to drive Black hair-care manufacturers out of the field, and I was confronted with a challenge I couldn't refuse.

That was several months ago. The problem I face this morning is that the field is changing and nobody knows where it's going. A related and equally difficult problem is shelf space and distribution. The answers I get from the Supreme executives are confused and confusing.

What am *I* going to do about it?

My answer is clear. I draw a line in the dust. If the executives don't solve the problem, I'm going to find new executives.

### 11:37 A.M.

WJPC, a radio station I bought in 1973, is losing money, like most AM stations. My FM station, WLNR, is moving up in the ratings with a "soft touch" adult-music format.

What can we do to turn the AM station around?

I ask for suggestions and comments and get public relations answers—the kind of answers that made it possible for outsiders to take over our electronics industry and to make inroads in steel and car manufacturing. I tell the staff to cut out the crap and tell the truth.

The answers vary. Cut the staff, change the format, get out of AM while getting out is good.

I listen, I make mental notes. But I've already decided. I already know what I'm going to do.

**12:45 P.M.**

A luncheon with Fashion Fair executives in the Executive Dining Room on the tenth floor. The waiters distribute drinks, lobster, and steak, and I ask for status reports on the largest Black-owned cosmetics operations in the world. When I first started the division in 1973, I decided to bypass mass distribution outlets and concentrate on high-line stores like Neiman-Marcus and Marshall Field's.

They told me a Black line couldn't be marketed that way. We lost $1 million a year for five years, but we finally turned it around. The reports I hear today say we're now the largest Black cosmetics line in the world, and we rank in the top ten among all cosmetics lines sold in department stores.

**2:00 P.M.**

There is a crisis on *Jet*. A hot story has broken in Atlanta, and the magazine is locked up. I call the plant and tell them to hold the form for a new story and a new head.

**2:45 P.M.**

The *Ebony* editorial board meets, and I approve covers for the next three months. I reject one cover suggestion and tell the senior staff to ask for additional ideas from the staff. There's a brief discussion of a letter which said that the magazine is too entertainment-oriented.

I recall the wisdom of my mother, who persuaded me to take castor oil by putting it in orange juice. The entertainment in *Ebony*, I tell the editors, is orange juice—the medicine that cures is castor oil. But you can't cure people if they don't read the magazine.

How do you persuade people to read the magazine? You lure them with entertainment. When you get their attention, you try to educate and uplift and grapple with the serious issues of the day.

Della Palmer, one of my three secretaries, brings a stack of checks, and the meeting continues while I sign them.

**8:47 P.M.**

The building is dark; the last employee has gone. I say good night to the Pinkerton guard, get into my car, and drive out of the building into the Michigan Avenue traffic.

The night is clear, cold, and dark, and the stars are shining. I'm reminded suddenly of something Mary McLeod Bethune, the great woman leader, told me: The darker the night, the brighter the stars.

## NOVEMBER 5, 1987
**9:00 A.M.**

Everything you've heard about Lee Iacocca is true.

He's dynamic, charismatic, shrewd. He's selling America, and his greatest asset is that without which a salesperson is a mere puppet: He believes in his product. If the pride is back or on the way back, America owes a lot to Lee Iacocca.

Lee is in the chair at the Chrysler board meeting at the Chrysler Building in New York City, and he's in commanding form. Everybody is talking about the stock market crash, but Lee is bullish on America. He tells a story about his daughter, who asked how a pension fund could lose $250 million in one day.

"Where did the money go?" she asked. Lee says he told her: "It was never *there* in the first place."

If you don't understand that point, the calculus of high finance is beyond you.

The stock market crash didn't affect me greatly. Most of my investments are in companies I own or control.

## NOVEMBER 7
**9:30 A.M.**

Today is Saturday, and I'm up early, visiting newsstands and drugstores and checking the sales of my magazines and products. Michael Jackson is on the cover of *Jet*, and the magazine is selling. Prince is on the cover of *Ebony*, and they're down to their last copies at newsstands at the corners of Chicago and Michigan and Randolph and Clark streets. There are long lines at the Fashion Fair counters at Carson Pirie Scott and Marshall Field's. But there are problems at the drugstores and convenience stores. Duke and Raveen, the two major products of Supreme Beauty, aren't moving fast enough. To help things along, I place $200 and $300 orders at several stores. This is a pump-priming maneuver designed to clear the shelves and force store managers to reorder.

## NOVEMBER 18
**9:45 A.M.**

The three members of the executive committee of the Greyhound Corporation meet at Greyhound Towers in Phoenix, Arizona. Greyhound is no longer in the bus business, but you can still leave the driving to us. Especially in the areas of food service, bus manufacturing, and consumer products, like Dial and Purex. The major discussion this morning is on the details of the purchase of the Dobbs House chain.

## NOVEMBER 19
**10:00 A.M.**

The full board convenes in Greyhound Towers. CEO John Teets chairs the meeting and reports quarterly gains. I'm proud of Teets's leadership for two major reasons. First, I was a member of the committee that selected him. Secondly, and equally important, he represents a new breed of up-from-the-ranks managers who could be the salvation of our embattled economy.

I am, as usual, the only Black at this meeting. This happens so often now that I seldom take note of it. But this doesn't mean that all problems have been solved. When I first started operating at this level, some directors—not at

Greyhound—announced decisions that had been made earlier at parties or social gatherings.

"You remember, John," they'd say, "we decided at Ralph's place."

But I didn't know Ralph, and I'd never been to his place. The whole thing was funny, for they seemed to be genuinely surprised—and embarrassed—that I wasn't at Ralph's, like everybody else in the "in" crowd. I finally told them to cut me in or cut me out, and the situation changed. I'm now on key committees of the boards of Continental Bank, Chrysler, Zenith, and other Fortune 500 corporations.

It is encouraging, incidentally, to see more women on major boards. Ten years ago, when Princess Grace and I were on the Twentieth Century-Fox board, we jokingly and ironically called our end of the board table "the minority caucus."

## NOVEMBER 24
**11:00 A.M.**

The White House is calling.

The social secretary says President Reagan wants to know if Mr. and Mrs. Johnson will accept an invitation to a state dinner for General Secretary and Mrs. Mikhail Gorbachev. That's the way the White House and Fortune 500 companies operate. An aide calls first to see if you'll accept the invitation if it is extended.

In this case, the answer is in the question. Billionaires and political and cultural legends are fighting for invitations to one of the biggest social events of the decade.

Will I attend if invited?

I consider the question gravely, from all angles, for one whole second, and I say, "Of course."

I tell my secretary to make a reservation at a hotel. "Which one?" she asks. I tell her any good nearby hotel, except the Shoreham. In the late forties, a Shoreham clerk told me that the hotel didn't rent rooms to Negroes. The

Shoreham has changed since then, but I haven't—and I haven't forgotten.

## NOVEMBER 30
**11:53 A.M.**

One of the perks of my position is that I almost always have a front seat at the theater of history.

For five days now, I've watched with awe as millions of Black and White Chicagoans filed past the bier of Harold Washington, the first big-city Black mayor to die in office.

I knew Harold—everybody called him Harold—and supported him. I gave $63,000 to his critical 1983 campaign and was the largest single financial contributor.

Now, after four short dazzling years, I'm one of 5,000 national and community leaders crammed into the 4,000-seat Christ Universal Temple for the funeral.

Harold would have loved this. Political heavyweights from all over, including large delegations of his enemies, sitting shoulder-to-shoulder, weeping and commiserating.

As I sit here, with tears flowing, I realize suddenly that a Harold Washington would have been inconceivable fifty-four years ago when I came to Chicago.

I realize also that the only way to preserve his legacy is to provide the economic ballots that make political ballots meaningful. Mayor Andrew Young of Atlanta is right: "We struggled in the fifties to integrate the schools. We struggled in the sixties to integrate the lunch counters and ballot boxes. Now we've got to struggle in the eighties and nineties to integrate the money."

## DECEMBER 1
**2:01 P.M.**

The White House is calling.

A social secretary says Nancy Reagan wants to know if Mr. and Mrs. John H. Johnson will join a small group of distinguished Americans for coffee and orange juice before going outside to welcome the Gorbachevs to the White House and America.

Same answer as above, after the same lengthy deliberation.

## DECEMBER 8
**8:30 A.M.**

A long black limousine drops me off at the East Gate of the White House.

Security is tight, and I have a moment to savor the occasion. I've visited this house forty or fifty times in the last forty-five years, and I've dined here with seven presidents. But I never approach these columns without a sense of time warp, without a sense of wonder that a Black boy who walked barefooted in Mississippi River mud could be driven up to the White House, in the same time period, in a black limousine.

Perhaps the most satisfying moment of my life was the time I brought my mother, Mrs. Gertrude Johnson Williams, to this house and introduced her to a real live president. I think she thought on that day that her sacrifices had not been entirely in vain.

I carry all these memories and a cloud of witnesses, Black and White, into the room where politicians, billionaires, and cultural icons are sipping coffee and waiting for the leader of Soviet Russia.

There are twenty, maybe thirty people in the room—David Rockefeller and the Reverend Billy Graham among them. We chat for a moment, then move to the Rose Garden and stand in a special, roped-off section for the nationally televised welcome for the Gorbachevs.

My driver and I are separated in the confusion following the ceremony. David Rockefeller passes by and gives me a ride in his limousine.

David Rockefeller and I are old friends—we were founding members of the International Executive Service Corps in 1965—and we talk about old times and the meaning of the

Gorbachev visit. We're both impressed by the charm and toughness of the Soviet leader. We agree that the new generation of Soviet technocrats poses a new challenge to American industry and leadership.

**1:45 P.M.**

Instead of going back to my hotel, I stop at my Washington office, about a half block from the White House. Then, on an impulse, I decide to do a little market research. For almost an hour, I walk the streets of Washington, studying the people and newsstands.

Then, suddenly, at the corner of Eleventh and G streets, it hits me. Most of the young men are wearing short hairstyles and using old-fashioned hair pomade. We've spent thousands of dollars on market research, and my executives have made scores of field trips. Why hasn't somebody zeroed in on these facts?

I hail a cab and return to my hotel, rejuvenated physically and financially by my little walk. I've solved one aspect of the Supreme Beauty Products puzzle.

We're two blocks from my hotel when I solve the other by deciding to pay more than the traffic will bear for one of the best executives in the field.

**6:30 P.M.**

"Mr. and Mrs. John H. Johnson!"

The Marine Guard puts some extra spin on the announcement, and my wife and I enter the East Room and mingle with the guests.

I look around the room, for I'm more than a little curious. If you have to invite 125 people out of a pool of 240 million, how do you choose? I notice that Roger B. Smith, the chairman and CEO of General Motors, is here. So are Donald Petersen, the chairman and CEO of Ford, and James Robinson, the chairman and CEO of American Express.

There are, surprisingly, no mayors or governors present. But Joe DiMaggio, Mary Lou Retton, James Stewart, and

Billy Graham are among the guests. I count six Blacks, in addition to the Johnsons: General and Mrs. Colin Powell, Mrs. Ralph Bunche, Pearl Bailey, and Mr. and Mrs. Meadowlark Lemon. Lemon made his mark with the Harlem Globetrotters, a popular attraction in Russia. Race apart, I'm the only publisher here, and we're the only guests from the city of Chicago and the state of Illinois.

I'm surprised that I recognize most of the dignitaries. More surprising, many seem to recognize me. The women, of course, are elegantly gowned. My wife, Eunice, who is the director of the Ebony Fashion Fair and a force in the fashion world, more than holds her own in that department.

There is a sudden fanfare, and the Reagans and Gorbachevs arrive for the traditional receiving line. The president greets me warmly and passes me on to the Russian leader, saying, "This is John Johnson, one of our distinguished citizens." If the Russian leader is surprised to find me here, he doesn't betray it. He looks straight into my eyes and says, through an interpreter, that he's pleased to meet me.

An interesting man, a tough man, a *cool* man.

I tell myself that he'd make a formidable business opponent and a dangerous poker player.

As usual, Eunice and I are seated at different tables. My place card is at a table next to the table of the president and Raisa Gorbachev. My dinner companions include former Defense Secretary Caspar Weinberger, and the president's daughter, Maureen Reagan. I know Weinberger; he's visited our offices. I've never met the president's daughter, who turns out to be both charming and witty. She tells us that she has known Weinberger for a long time.

"I even remember," she says, "when he was a Democrat."

Weinberger says he has known the Reagans longer. "I even remember when your daddy was a Democrat."

I am tempted to say that I have a longer memory. I remember when most Blacks were Republicans.

The president's daughter asks about my career and background, and I relate a few anecdotes. She tells me that I should write a book.

After dinner, we return to the East Room, where Van Cliburn plays the piano and joins the Gorbachevs in an impromptu rendition of a Russian song, "Moscow Nights."

The irrepressible Pearl Bailey, who's an old friend of the Reagans, tells me that something strange and wonderful is happening in this room.

"I went over to the president," she says, "and I told him: 'Mr. President, there's a lot of love in this room tonight.'"

We pass Pearl and her White husband, Louis Bellson, on the way out. She tells me that the president came up to her at the end and said, "Pearl, you're right. There *is* a lot of love in this room tonight."

## DECEMBER 22
**2:00 P.M.**

Secret Service agents leap from cars and fan out over the Johnson Publishing Company Building.

They're followed by Jesse Jackson, the charismatic presidential candidate, and an entourage of aides and family members.

"Godfather," Jesse says—he always calls me "Godfather" —"I've never missed visiting you in the Christmas season. I just wanted to come by and touch bases with you and my second family."

The gesture surprises and pleases me. I've known Jesse for a long time. In fact, I provided his first job when he came to Chicago, penniless, unemployed, and unknown. He was a particular favorite of my late mother.

He reminds me of that now, saying that the Christmas season always reminds him of the spirit and reach of "Miss Gertrude." Without warning, he starts preaching, saying that America has forgotten the true meaning of Christmas, "which is not about gifts, not about toys. It's about a poor mother and her child, it's about Mary and her baby and no room in the inn, it's about poor people eating out of garbage cans and sleeping on park benches—that's what Christmas is about. It's about Miss Gertrude coming to Chicago in the thirties with young John Johnson and no money and a lot of hope and faith."

He continues in this vein for four or five minutes, the rich biblical cadences rolling out of him, making our little conference room a chapel. When he finishes, there is not a dry eye in the room.

We walk him to the elevator. On an impulse, I pull an *Ebony* editor aside and tell him: "Scrap the March cover. I don't care what it costs, I don't care what people say. I'm going to put Jesse on the cover, not only because it's news but because it's right—and it's what my mother would have wanted me to do."

## DECEMBER 26
**1:00 P.M.**

Guess who's coming to dinner?

It's not dinner, really—it's lunch. And it's a working lunch for financial advisers to the superstar. But Michael Jackson is definitely coming. And the couple who manage our Palm Springs home are in a tizzy.

There's no reason for concern. Michael eats little or nothing, and is the essence of gentility as we sit at a table overlooking our pool, discussing high-yield bonds, residuals, and the Beatles. Michael and his accountant, Marshall Gelfand, are here to bring me up to date on the last meeting of his financial committee, made up of Gelfand, Michael's attorney, John Branca, and two outsiders, producer David Geffen and me. Geffen and I serve without pay.

I'm on the committee because Michael called one day and asked for advice, saying he didn't want to end up broke like so many athletes and entertainers. I told him to avoid uncertain investments—no restaurants, no vacant land. To maintain a certain level of liquidity, and to look for investments that could serve as an annuity, such as the Beatles catalog.

That's the same advice I offer today. Michael, always the soul of courtesy, listens as we state our opinions. Then he quietly and firmly makes his own decision.

From time to time, I've broadened my advice beyond the field of investments. At this point, Michael is taking a public relations beating, with a flurry of cruel and false stories about his life-style. I suggest that he confront this vicious campaign head-on by letting the public see the real Michael and by giving back some of the good fortune he has enjoyed. He responds positively, and we discuss his commitment to the United Negro College Fund and the additional Blacks he plans to hire for his operation.

After the conference ends, I remain at the table for a few minutes, enjoying the view from our Palm Springs mountaintop. I recall the words of a writer who said I'd climbed a lot of mountains and asked if I had any unfulfilled ambitions. I told him, "I don't want to climb any more mountains—I just want to stay on top of the one I'm on."

## JANUARY 2, 1988
**6:00 P.M.**

Bob Hope, who lives up the street on the same mountain, is guest of honor at the dedication of the $20-million Bob Hope Cultural Center in Palm Desert. The dedication brings out President and Mrs. Reagan and the leading citizens of Palm Springs. Hope, sharp as ever, breaks up the crowd. He says if he'd known he could get this many people to pay $5,000 a ticket for a dedication without a Hope performance, he would have been doing "dedications" a long time ago.

An old friend, emboldened by liquor, pulls me aside and tells me that I'm the only Black who consistently operates at this level.

"How," he asks, consciously playing on Martin Luther King's phrase, "is the Black view from the mountaintop?"

The same, I say, almost before the words leave his mouth, as the White view—clear, heady, clean, but a little lonely and a little disappointing when you discover that *that's all there is* and that you have the same joys and fears on the top that you had on the bottom.

"Does this mean," he asks, moving in closer, "that the struggle wasn't worth the candle?"

By no means, I say, adding:

"I've been in the ditch, and I've been on the mountaintop, and, believe me, being on the mountaintop is better."

We laugh the laugh of those who know and then tackle the last mountaintop taboo.

Is there racism after the first $100 million?

I tell him there are minor irritants, like invitations that never come, and being passed over for inner-circle clubs, but that one of my major problems comes from people who assume that I'm the chauffeur when I get out of one of my Rolls-Royces.

There was, for example, the problem I had when Eunice and I were one of forty couples who paid $25,000 a couple to attend Ambassador Walter H. Annenberg's benefit party for Prince Charles and his favorite charity, Operation Raleigh.

Eunice and I drove up in our brown Rolls, and two men, one on each side, opened the doors. The man on my side, who didn't see Eunice, automatically assumed that I was the chauffeur, like every other Black he'd seen that night.

"Park the car over there, boy," he said, pointing to an area reserved for chauffeurs.

"I'm no boy," I said with embellishments from Eddie Murphy and Richard Pryor. "I'm a guest."

"Yeah," he said, "and I'm the president."

We discussed the matter, and he agreed reluctantly that a $25,000 ticket and an owner-operated Rolls-Royce made me a guest.

Ambassador Annenberg, incidentally, who made the largest contribution of any living person to Howard University and who has made major contributions to the UNCF and other Black organizations, knew nothing about this incident and wouldn't have tolerated it had he known.

The story shocks my friend, and I tell him that this was not an isolated incident.

"Sometimes," I say, "when I'm sitting on top of the mountain, looking down into the valley, past my tennis court, my swimming pool, hot tub, and fruit trees, I think maybe I'm a White man. Then, when I leave the mountaintop and go down into the valley, the first White person I meet in effect calls me a nigger.

"Whenever, for example, there's a new clerk at the grocery store, where I have my account, he invariably asks, 'Who do you work for?' I can't get mad with the clerks, for most of the Blacks who come into the store do, in fact, work for white people.... So I don't let it bother me. If I let things like that bother me, I'd be in a rage all the time."

I could have added and should have added that the closer I get to the top the more I realize that I'm never going to be fully accepted on merit and money alone. And that a different generation of Blacks—and a different generation of Whites—will know the final victory.

### JANUARY 11
**2:45 P.M.**

Ninth-floor conference room.

Chicago headquarters, Johnson Publishing Company.

After several weeks of negotiations, I solve the WJPC crisis by deciding to use the same staff and the same musical input for WJPC-AM and WLNR-FM.

### JANUARY 16
**8:33 P.M.**

This is the third national celebration of the Martin Luther King, Jr., holiday.

I knew Dr. King, supported him, and employed him briefly as an *Ebony* columnist. And it's an honor to participate in the "Salute to Greatness" dinner, one of the high-lights of the week-long celebration of the Martin Luther King, Jr. Center for Nonviolent Social Change.

David C. Garrett, Jr., former chairman and CEO of Delta Air Lines, and I are the 1988 recipients of the "Salute to Greatness" awards. The dais of the Marquis Ballroom of Atlanta's Marriott Marquis Hotel is loaded down with polit-ical and economic heavyweights, including Georgia Gover-nor Joe Frank Harris, Mayor Andrew Young, and Ford Chairman and CEO Donald E. Petersen.

Greyhound Chairman John Teets and *Black Enterprise* publisher Earl Graves speak on my behalf. Then Coretta Scott King, the keeper of the King flame, and Jesse Hill, president and CEO of Atlanta Life Insurance Company, present the plaque "in appreciation of your commitment to fulfill Dr. King's Dream."

In response, I recall the Dream of an Arkansas mother and son:

"As a young boy growing up in the segregated town of Arkansas City, Arkansas, where Blacks could only work as domestics or laborers on the Mississippi River levee, *I never thought there would be a night like this.*

"Watching my mother work as a cook in a levee camp for five years so we could get money to go to Chicago, where I could attend high school because there was no Black high school in Arkansas City, *I never thought there would be a night like this.* [Applause.]

"My mother never went beyond the third grade. Yet she was the best educated person I ever met. She was daring, she was caring, she believed you could do anything you wanted to do, if you tried. She gave me that faith and that hope, and that has guided my life.

"I couldn't fail her...for she had sacrificed too much for me....

"She worked as a domestic, but when her money ran out and she couldn't even find work as a domestic, my whole family went on welfare for two long years. I know you know that during those difficult years *I never thought there would be a night like this.*"

## JANUARY 19
**6:14 A.M.**

I get up early and go to the window to look at Lake Michigan, a stone's throw from our Lake Shore Drive condominium.

The water reminds me.

Today is my birthday. I no longer celebrate or count the years, but this is a big zero which can't be ignored or denied.

Seventy years ago, I was born in a tin-roofed house near the Mississippi River levee in Arkansas City, Arkansas.

How did I get from there to here, from a shotgun house on the banks of the Mississippi to a condominium on the banks of Lake Michigan?

What is the meaning and message of my journey from poverty to wealth?

And can others, regardless of their color, profit from the lessons of my life and make the same journey?

# Roots _____

# and _____

# Rivers _____

# 1

## *Two Against the Tide*

WE were running.

That's my first sharp memory.

We were running for our lives, and every living thing around us—man, woman, and child, dog, cat, and chicken, Black and White—was running, too.

The levee had broken, and the Mississippi River was on the rampage.

This was the message that greeted my mother and me as we emerged from St. John Baptist Church on Sunday, April 24, 1927.

We didn't know it then, but this was the beginning of the worst flood in American history, and more than 800,000 Americans were running with us.

The first message said that the levee at Pendleton, twenty-five miles up the river from Arkansas City, had broken and that we should grab our pets and valuables and run to the Arkansas City levee.

The second message, minutes later, said: Forget the valuables and the pets. Run for your lives!

And now we were running and the water was coming behind us and dogs were barking and people were screaming and my mother was gripping my hand so hard I thought it would come off.

Would we make it?

Or would the rampaging water roll over us, as it was rolling over the mules and chickens behind us?

For a terrifying moment, the issue was in doubt. Then my mother shifted into a higher gear, lifting me almost off the ground, and we scrambled up the slippery incline of the levee.

*Hands.* I remember the hands—black, white, brown, yellow hands—reaching out to us, pulling us to safety. And I remember, as if it were yesterday, the shock as I opened my eyes on a scene of interracial bedlam.

By this time, six or seven hundred people and almost as many dogs were huddled together on the ridge, integrated in muddy misery. From time to time rabbits, quail, deer, and even foxes emerged from the water and scrambled over the man-made hills of furniture and clothes.

I stood for a moment, befuddled, shaking with excitement and fear.

I was nine years old, and I was standing in deep water that defined, annealed, baptized, and washed away.

But none of that was clear to me, or even relevant, as I lifted my face to the rain and willed a dry tomorrow.

*Survival.*

Above everything else, above dignity and happiness and the future of Arkansas City, was the question of survival.

Personal survival.

We were two—a Black boy and a Black woman—against the tide, and battalions of hostile men were arrayed against us. Would we—could we—survive against such odds? And what would happen to me if my mother and I were separated or—God forbid—if she suffered some mishap?

The question was a nightmare that pressed in on me, like a load of sandbags, and interfered with my breathing and made the ground shake beneath my feet. There were other fears, more immediate, more pressing. The fear, for example, I shared with almost everybody, the fear of the big nasty slithering snakes—moccasins and blue runners—that oozed out of the water and hid in the bundles and tents, waiting for someone to step on their tails or heads.

This was one side of the coin. The other side—the lure of excitement and adventure—also pressed in on me. And I soon perceived that there were things to be seen on this levee that a nine-year-old boy had never seen.

With the help of Blacks and Whites, who paid no attention to our color, we settled on the island of the levee, where we lived for six weeks. On one side was "Ol' Man River," not the romantic river of the song but an arrogant monster, constantly probing and looking for a weak spot in the circle of sandbags. On the other side was a new body of water where Arkansas City used to be.

From the vantage point of the levee, I watched the water cover the tin roof of our home.

It is one of the peculiarities of the mind that it magnifies trivialities in moments of tragedy. I was overwhelmed at that moment by the thought that my favorite toy was gone and that I would never see it again. It didn't occur to me until later that we were naked in the world and that everything we owned—our clothes, our furniture, and the few dollars we'd saved—was gone.

This, then, was the beginning of a new beginning.

We were new people in a new world, Noahs without arks.

I looked around and wondered what tomorrow would bring.

So did Frederick Simpich, a writer for the *National Geographic* magazine.

"At noon," he wrote, "the streets of Arkansas City were dry and dusty. By 2 o'clock, mules were drowning in the main streets of that town faster than they could be unhitched from wagons. Before dark the homes and stores stood six feet deep in water."

Another and more poetical witness was singer Bessie Smith, whose "Backwater Blues" was recorded during the Great Flood of 1927.

*When it rains five days and the skies turn dark as night,*
*When it rains five days and the skies turn dark as night,*
*Then trouble's takin' place in the lowlands at night.*

*Back-water blues done caused me to pack my things and go.*
*Back-water blues done caused me to pack my things and go.*
*'Cause my house fell down and I can't live there no more.*

Before it was over, twenty feet of water covered Arkansas City, and parts of seven southern states were inundated in what Herbert Hoover called "the greatest peace-time disaster in our history."

Red Cross officials rushed to the scene in motorboats and seaplanes, bringing shovels, tents, bedding, No. 2 cookstoves, food, drinking water, and medical supplies. They distributed the supplies without regard to race. This made me a permanent fan of the American Red Cross.

The situation on the levee was not, all things considered, the best school for a nine-year-old Black boy. But it was a perfect setting for studying the human condition. A whole city brought to its knees, turned upside down, and forced to reinvent itself in daylight on a levee between two bodies of water. Men and women stripped of all pretensions and reduced to the essentials: bread, water, shelter, sex.

I kept my eyes and ears open, captivated by what I saw. This was, in part, a by-product of my situation. The weak and the oppressed everywhere develop sharp and knowing eyes as a technique of survival. They see not to see but to survive. And I was a born survivor. And a born reporter.

Even then I had a nose for news. I was fascinated by gossip and rumors and reports. I wanted to know what moved people, why they did what they did, why they wanted what they wanted. Business associates and employees say today that I have a thousand eyes and that I know everything that happens in my businesses and on the floors of my building. The boy on the levee was the father of the man and the publisher.

I was too young to understand all of the implications of what I saw. But it was a revelation to me that the Mississippi River, more powerful than the Fourteenth Amendment, more powerful even than the churches of Jesus Christ, had washed away the sin of division, and that Blacks and Whites were working together and fighting the Mississippi together, shoulder-to-shoulder.

There was something else, something so big and obvious that it had never registered on my mind: The Negroes of Arkansas City, my family among them, were the best workers, manning the shovels, throwing the sandbags, patching the cuts, pacing themselves, measuring themselves, pleasuring themselves by the steady, rhythmic beat of their songs.

*I'm so glad*—hunh!
*That trouble don't last always.*

It lasted long enough.

And when we picked our way through the mud, keeping a sharp eye out for snakes, to the site of our house, we found another trouble. The house was gone, and that pleased us. The authorities had promised to build new homes for families who couldn't find their old houses. But we were unlucky. We found our old house, battered and full of dirt and nameless things that crawled and slithered, three blocks away.

And so it started again, the rhythm of our lives.

My parents and my parents' parents had lived in this valley for generations, building the levees to contain the

River, fleeing in panic after the inevitable flood overturned years of hard work, cleaning up and starting over after the flood, building new homes, new lives, new dreams, and waiting, waiting, waiting, always waiting and living on the edge for the next warning, the next flood, and the next rush to high ground.

This was the rhythm of my people, of the Johnsons and the Jenkinses, who'd lived on the banks of the Mississippi for generations.

They knew the River, the Johnsons and Jenkinses.

They loved it, hated it, feared it.

The River was in their souls.

It was their destiny, their fate, their curse.

I never hear Langston Hughes's poem without wondering about that long line of Johnsons and Jenkinses and the inner resources that made it possible for them to survive their struggle with the River that dominated and controlled their lives.

*I've known rivers:*
*I've known rivers ancient as the world and older than the*
*flow of human blood in human veins.*

*My soul has grown deep like the rivers.*

*I bathed in the Euphrates when dawns were young.*
*I built my hut near the Congo and it lulled me to sleep.*
*I looked upon the Nile and raised the pyramids above it.*
*I heard the singing of the Mississippi when Abe Lincoln*
   *went down to New Orleans, and I've seen its muddy*
   *bosom turn all golden in the sunset.*

*I've known rivers:*
*Ancient, dusky rivers.*

*My soul has grown deep like the rivers.*

# 2

---

# *The Heritage of a Survivor*

THE Johnsons and Jenkinses were old southern families who came to America from Africa.

By the time of the Great Flood of 1927, they had known rivers, blood, sweat, tears, joy, slavery, and emancipation.

This saga of survival was too personal, too *real* to my mother, who never talked about it. It would become fashionable in later years to say—and my magazines would help spread the idea—that a people without roots is a people without a future. But to the children and grandchildren of slavery, slavery was pain in the flesh, horror in the mind, nightmares in the night.

*They were still living it.* They were bound hand and foot by the infamous sharecropping system. And survivors of slavery, like King Banks, my mother's stepfather, were living reminders. It is no wonder, then, that they didn't talk about it and that the children of the third generation of freedom had to find their own road to the past and to the future.

I found my own way and distilled a vague and yet painfully sharp image of the Johnson-Jenkins past. Somewhere in a vague place called Africa—I had no idea, in my youth, where it was or how to get there—the first Johnson-Jenkins—let's call him or her X—was captured, chained, branded, and put into the hold of a slave ship for the trip to America.

Millions of X's fellow citizens—they were Africans, sons and daughters of the builders of the Pyramids and great empires—died on the slave ships, where they were packed so close together that they couldn't move, and on the plantations, where they worked from sunup to sundown for two hundred years. But millions more, the Jenkinses and Johnsons among them, survived. And, surviving, they ensured the survival of Arkansas and America.

I am their son and descendant.

And I am a survivor, too.

Survival is in my blood. It's in my nerves and muscles. For I am a descendant of people who were so tough that nothing—neither slavery, nor segregation, nor the River—could destroy them.

In the end, by some mystery no historian can truly explain, the first Johnson-Jenkins not only survived but prevailed and was reborn on the banks of the Mississippi River in the person of Gertrude Jenkins, who came into this world on Tuesday, August 4, 1891, in Lake Village, Arkansas. Her parents were two young Arkansans, Will and Malinda Jenkins. They were born after slavery. My mother therefore was of the second generation of freedom.

This was not a good time for a Black girl to be born. The 1890s were, by all accounts, the low point on the graph of Black life in America. This was the decade of *Plessy* v. *Ferguson* and Jim Crow laws and almost daily lynchings.

During this decade and the first decades of the twentieth century, the Ku Klux Klan and other violent organizations reversed the Fourteenth and Fifteenth amendments and drove Black businessmen from downtown sections in Little Rock. At the same time, violent men destroyed the electoral foundation of politicians like R. C. Weddington, who represented Desha County and Arkansas City in the Arkansas legislature in 1891.

They would write books about this in the twentieth century—and I would publish some of them—but it was no theory to young Gertrude Jenkins, who lived the death of Black hope. By means we can only imagine, she completed the third grade. She was then driven—by poverty, by need, by want—into the fields and kitchens of the Mississippi Valley. But she always lived in a valley on the other side of oppression. Her body was in the fields and kitchens but her mind was in another sphere, in the first-class section.

(I am her child and heir.)

Always hopeful, always cheerful, she settled in Arkansas City, where she worked as a domestic and became active in the church and service organizations.

Arkansas City, which is 101 miles from Little Rock, 146 miles from Memphis, and 654 miles from Chicago, is a backwater today, with a population of some six hundred divided almost equally between Blacks and Whites.

In the first decades of the century, however, Arkansas City was a growing, rip-roaring Mississippi River town built around a thriving sawmill. In those days, the city was a transportation terminal, and people came from Little Rock, from Pine Bluff, from all over, to catch the ferry to Mississippi.

Overshadowing Front Street, which was a single row of business houses, and the two major buildings, the Desha County Courthouse and the three-story Desha Bank, was the towering Mississippi River levee. There were separate-but-equal honky-tonks on the riverfront in the Yellow Dog red-light section, and separate-but-equal whorehouses.

For churchgoing people and culture lovers, there were

excursions on the Mississippi and a theater on the corner of Front Street. Out on Highway 4 there was an arena which seated some 2,500 people. In 1924, Jack Dempsey, the heavy-weight champion of the world, fought here in an exhibition.

The major town landmark was the big clock on the tower of the Desha County Courthouse. The courthouse and the clock had a tragic and ghostly history. According to stories that were told over and over in Black households, a Black was lynched on the courthouse grounds in the first decade of the century.

The victim maintained his innocence to the end. Before he died, he put a curse on the courthouse, saying that the clock would never tell the correct time again. To the dismay of Whites, the clock began to display erratic tendencies. The hands finally stuck at five o'clock, where they remain to this day.

In this setting, in the shadow of the clock, Gertrude Jenkins met and married Richard Lewis and gave birth to her first child, a daughter named Beulah. The marriage didn't work, and "Miss Gert," as almost everybody called my mother, later married Leroy Johnson, a handsome la-borer who worked in the sawmill and helped out on the levee.

I was born to this couple on Saturday, January 19, 1918, shortly after midnight, in a shotgun, tin-roofed house about three blocks from the river. My mother didn't name me John, as is commonly believed. I was christened "Johnny" Johnson because my mother had promised a close friend, Johnnie Ford, that she would name her next child Johnny (or Johnnie), whether she had a boy or a girl.

The year of my birth was a year of ferment in America. The White population was 95.5 million and the Black popu-lation was 10.9 million, 10 percent of the total population. There were roughly 1,200,000 Whites and 470,000 Blacks in Arkansas. The state had nine cities with 2,000 or more Blacks. Little Rock, the largest city, had a Black population of 14,500.

By a quirk of fate, I was born in the last year of World War I, and I founded *Ebony* in the last year of World War II. But my life is defined not by wars but by critical turning points in history.

World War I, the one that made the world safe for democracy, triggered the Great (Black) Migration to the North and changed Black and White America forever.

In the first years of my life, an armistice ended World War I, the first Pan-African Congress met, Madame C. J. Walker died, Liberty Life Insurance Company was incorporated, and troops put down the Chicago riot. These were also the launching years of Model T and Model A Fords, the Charleston, the Black Bottom, flappers, jazz, movies, and the radio.

It was in this America, in a segregated and restricted environment bounded by the Mississippi River and the St. John Baptist Church on the east and the Arkansas City Colored School on the west, that I spent the first fifteen years of life.

They were years of struggle, wonder, and growth, cushioned by a close-knit family and a close-knit community. One of the ironies of our situation is that progress, urbanization, and decades of unemployment destroyed the foundations of the strong Black community that enabled Blacks to survive slavery and segregation.

I was lucky.

I was born into a strong family and reared in a strong community where every Black adult was charged with the responsibility of monitoring and supervising every Black child. I was reared in a community where every Black adult was authorized to whip me, if I needed whipping, and to send me home for a second whipping from my mother, whether I needed it or not.

Sixty years later, I attended a meeting of the Advisory Board of the First Commercial Bank of Little Rock with, among others, Sam Moore Walton, the richest man in America. We discovered with surprise and delight that we had six things in common. We were nonsmokers and nondrinkers who were born into poverty. We grew up in small southern towns and were reared by strong and loving parents who spared neither hugs nor rods.

Is there a message in this?

Yes. The message is that we've strayed in Black America—and in White America—from the values of family, community, and hard work. And we've got to go back to that future. We've got to go back to the time when being an adult was a dangerous vocation that required a total commitment to the community and every child in it.

My mother was a disciplinarian who used a "switch," as she called it, to emphasize her teaching. At bottom-line time, she'd make me go out into the backyard and cut a switch or branch from a tree. I always cut a small one, and she always sent me back to get a bigger and stronger branch. In later years people asked me why I never smoked cigarettes or drank whiskey. I never smoked or drank because my mother caught me smoking behind the house when I was ten and gave me a beating that I remember to this day.

But we must be careful here. For beating alone will not improve the manners of mules or men. The solution here and elsewhere is toughness leavened by the dough of love.

I didn't have a lot of toys. I didn't have a lot of clothes. But I had a lot of love.

I spent most of my formative years as the only child in a two-parent household. My half sister, Beulah, who was fourteen years older, left home to teach school in a neighboring town when I was small. My mother's cousin, Willie Miles, stayed with us a year or two, but she, too, moved on to Little Rock and institutions of higher learning.

I was reared in two-parent households, but there was never any doubt: My mother was the dominant force in the household and in my life. She was a short, forceful woman then, not quite five feet, with the family bowlegs and a big smile and a will of steel. She walked straight up, her head held high, a woman of stature and quality. She had known pain and discouragement and fear. Out of all this came a special kind of dignity. The dignity of a person who'd seen a lot and survived and wasn't afraid of the future.

In another day, my mother would have been a politician or a leader. She was always organizing clubs and service organizations. And she excelled in the most difficult of all American politics, the politics of the Black church. The churches she belonged to were always fussing and fighting about the election of pastors and the distribution of church property, and she almost always ended up on the winning side.

My father, on the other hand, was an outgoing man who didn't, according to my mother, take family responsibilities seriously. He was about five feet eleven with dark brown skin. He had a beautifully groomed mustache which I admired and which I emulate to this day.

I never really knew him. He traveled a lot, following the levee camps up and down the Mississippi. He was killed in a sawmill accident when I was eight. The next year, the year of the flood, my mother married James Williams, who delivered groceries for a bakery shop. He was a good stepfather, and we never had a cross word.

This was, in part, the doing of my mother. She told us if we had anything pleasant to say to each other we should communicate directly. But if we had anything unpleasant to say, we should tell her and she, in turn, would tell the offending party.

Even if we were in the same room, I would say, "Mother, tell Mr. Williams to stop doing that." And he would say, "Gertrude, tell Johnny I don't like that."

Some people thought this routine was funny. The only thing I can say is that it worked—for thirty-four years.

# 3

## Race and the First Picture Show

I WAS a working child.

I learned how to work before I learned how to play. When most children were experimenting with their first toys, I was hard at work in the real world, helping my mother and stepfather.

My stepfather, like my real father, moonlighted on the Mississippi, following the levee camps and pitching in during floods. My mother oftentimes accompanied him, washing and ironing clothes for the laborers and cooking in the levee kitchens. I tagged along and learned at an early age how to cook and how to wash and iron clothes. Even when my mother did day work, I tagged along and ran errands.

Despite or perhaps because of this early labor, I was, in the words of my mother, "a hell-raiser." I loved a prank, a good joke, and a fish fry. I also had an eye for girls. But Arkansas City, unfortunately, was not fertile ground for fantasy or, given the close watch of my mother and other adults, experimentation. Most of the boys had a secret crush on Willie B. Frazier, the daughter of the town's richest Black, but she paid little or no attention to us.

Was I happy?

The question has no meaning. Happiness is a concept based on a comparison. And we had no basis for comparison. Arkansas City was our whole world. There was the sawmill factory and the levee and the Mississippi River, and beyond that—nothing. There were no newspapers or radios. We thought the way we lived was the way people were supposed to live.

We didn't have money, but we weren't—crucial distinction— poor. Our poverty, in other words, couldn't be compared with the soul-crushing poverty in the slums of modern America.

I was never hungry. When my mother worked as a domestic, she cooked more than she served, and White families let her bring food home. She usually worked for families with children, and I got their old clothes.

Did this bother me? Not at first. I had been conditioned to believe that this was the way things were supposed to be. I had shoes and pants. In the winter we had heat. In the summer the iceman brought ice. On hot Sundays, we cranked the old freezer and made ice cream and sat on the front porch and fanned ourselves.

It was not a *completely* bad life. The only problem, dim at first but constantly growing clearer, was a feeling that we were not in control of our destiny, that a word or a frown from a White person could change our plans and our lives.

What we now call race relations were generally peaceful. Blacks and Whites lived next door to each door, and there were few instances of outright brutality in my youth. We were right across the river from Mississippi, and we heard horror stories about lynchings. There was one story in particular about a Black man who was lynched for winking at a White woman. We didn't believe that sort of thing could happen in Arkansas City. But to prevent any misunderstanding we made a conscious effort not to blink our eyes in the presence of a White woman.

My mother, like the mothers of other southern Black sons, shielded me from segregation and discrimination. She was always saying, "Don't do that!" "Don't say that!" As a result, I never really confronted the system. Yet I always knew that I was different, and that I was in danger.

I was ten or eleven when I came face to face with the bared fangs of the system. My mother was working for a wealthy doctor, who sent me to the drugstore to pick up a prescription. When I got to the store on a hot Saturday afternoon, one of the clerks asked, "What do you want, nigger?"

He put so much venom into the word that I ran, crying, to my mother. She told the doctor, who went downstairs and gave the clerk a beating and said, in effect: "Don't you call *my* nigger a nigger."

It was important in that era for a Black family to have a kind of "protective custody" relationship with a strong and important White family. If you worked for such a family, the head of the family would protect you from other Whites. He didn't always protect you from himself or members of his family, but he protected you from others.

The funniest—and saddest—incidents of this period grew out of attempts to control the laughing of Black people. When the first picture show came to town, the first floor was reserved for Whites, and Blacks were assigned to the balcony. Blacks were also told, in so many words, that we could only laugh when White people laughed.

If, as often happened, a scene set off an uproar in the Black section, someone would say, "You niggers, cut out that laughing." The laughing would die down, with a few impudent snickers, until a scene struck the fancy of the

White audience and there was a general license for Blacks to laugh along with the Whites.

But it never really worked. For Blacks, as a form of defiance or film criticism, always laughed too long and too loud, bringing forth the command "You niggers, cut out that laughing!" I'm glad there were no Richard Pryor movies in that era, for some Blacks would have literally laughed themselves to death.

# 4

## *Many Thousands Gone*

DESPITE the usual racial problems, Arkansas City was a cut above the typical southern town. A Black doctor, John A. White, had an office in the main office building. Another Black, Dallas Patterson, operated a barbershop in the same building.

One of my early heroes was Paris Frazier, a levee contractor and carpenter who dominated the building trade and constructed houses for Blacks and Whites. Frazier, who was the first Black in town to own a car, lived in a house that was palatial by Arkansas City standards. The house had an indoor toilet, an unheard-of luxury in that day. When we went to play with his daughter, Willie, we used to flush the toilet and wonder where the waste went.

I decided that I wanted a house like that and a shiny car that kicked up dust in the road and an indoor toilet that flushed.

We arrive here, by means of an indoor toilet, at a

crucial educational principle. For people are pretty much the same everywhere. Black, white, brown, yellow, magenta, they only see what they see. They only reach for what they can reach. They only struggle, to paraphrase Frederick Douglass, when there is a reasonable chance of whipping somebody or some thing. It takes an unusual person like my mother to believe what can't be seen and to stake everything on a card that has never fallen.

I shared my mother's faith.

I believed in the plastic power of the possible.

I believed with her that the possible, the thing that can be, is greater than the actual.

But a little hard evidence never hurt any true believer. And Paris Frazier's car and indoor toilet were concrete motivations that were more persuasive than a thousand lectures and sermons.

All through this period, all through the late twenties, as America moved toward the stock market crash and the Depression and the New Deal, I was looking for somebody or some thing that could help me reach my goal. I didn't even know then what I wanted. The only thing I knew was that I wanted something different from the dirt, sweat, and pain around me.

Almost all Arkansas City Blacks worked hard, wore overalls, sweated—and were poor. I made a survey and noticed that the people with money and power wore suits and didn't sweat or work hard physically. I decided on the basis of this unscientific survey that it was better to wear a suit and supervise people who worked hard and wore overalls and sweated.

For two or three years, I played a private game, putting on different robes and roles. I abandoned the Paris Frazier model, not because of the overalls, but because I knew nothing about carpentry and saw no immediate chance to learn. I was attracted, however, to the ministry for a lot of nonministerial reasons.

The minister was one of the few Blacks in our community who wore a suit and had the respect of Blacks and Whites. He also had the pick of the chicken pieces at Sunday dinners, and, according to unverified rumors, the support of certain sisters.

One day, after hours of hard work in a blazing hot sun, I had some sort of vision which seemed to say that I had been "called." To further my calling, I studied the preacher, imitated his movements, and listened carefully to the sermons, hoping one day to duplicate what he was doing.

Since I spent all day Sunday in church, it was easy to pursue my studies. My mother took me to Sunday School on Sunday morning and we stayed for church. After dinner, we returned for BYPU, Baptist Young People's Union, and the night services.

There was a strict line of division in Arkansas City between the "good" people who attended church and frowned on drinking and honky-tonking, and the "bad" people who gambled and visited the hot spots.

My mother was on the good side. My father and stepfather were ecumenical. My vote was cast by proxy by my mother and her switch.

I decided finally that I had misinterpreted my "vision" and that my long-range hope was in the Arkansas City Colored School. The school was run by a legendary principal, C. S. Johnson, a graduate of Atlanta Baptist College (now Morehouse), and his wife, M. J. Johnson, a graduate of Spelman.

Professor Johnson, like most of the pioneer Black teachers, taught everything: reading, writing, arithmetic, manners. He inspected our clothes in the morning to make sure we were neat and clean. And he insisted on polished shoes and correct behavior. He was, in fact, an extension of the home. Like my mother, like almost all Arkansas City parents, he carried a big stick and used it.

Although the four-room school was somewhat primitive by modern standards, it stressed excellence and brought better results than most contemporary schools. There was no nonsense in this building. We knew that education for us was a matter of life and death, and that certain graduates of this school, including my half sister, Beulah, and my cousin, Willie, had climbed out of their dungeons on a ladder of words.

Always, everywhere, by word, by example, by the carrot and stick, Professor Johnson pressed this message: What they did, you can and *must* do, too, or go to the wall.

The only problem was that the Arkansas City Colored School System stopped at the eighth grade. If I intended to get out of my dungeon, I had to find a new or a longer ladder.

This was the consuming passion of my life in the late twenties and thirties. In 1930, when work ran out in Arkansas City, my stepfather joined a levee camp upriver, and my mother took me to Vicksburg, Mississippi, to live with a family she knew. I went to St. Mary's Catholic School for a year and then returned to Arkansas City for the eighth and final grade.

By this time, cracks were developing in the towering levee of race. You could see this clearly in the militant *Chicago Defender* newspapers that Black Pullman porters smuggled into nearby McGehee. These newspapers, which reported the opportunities that were developing in Chicago and other northern cities, gave me an intellectual and physical thrill. I loved to touch the newsprint and to trace the contours of the screaming red headlines. I didn't know it until later, but I had been called—and found.

There were other cracks in the dam. One of my mother's childhood friends, Mamie Johnson, had migrated to the big city of Chicago. Like millions of other Blacks, she sent letters to friends and relatives. One of her letters to my mother said that armies of Blacks were flocking to Chicago and that education, good jobs, and freedom were ours for the asking.

This was a historic movement similar in tone and

texture to the nineteenth-century flight of the slaves, who sang a famous song:

> *No more peck of corn for me.*
> *No more, no more.*
> *No more peck of corn for me.*
> *Many thousands gone.*

*Many thousands were gone and going.* This was a new and interesting fact, and I looked at myself and my world with different eyes.

I took this new thing that was stirring in me up to the levee and looked out over the Mississippi River and wondered what was happening in the great world beyond and whether God had a place in it for me.

# 5

## *The Advantage of the Disadvantage*

THERE'S an advantage in every disadvantage, and a gift in every problem.

My disadvantage—a disadvantage that carried me to unprecedented wealth—was that Arkansas City didn't provide a high school education for Blacks.

I've thanked fate for that gift many times.

For if there had been a high school for Blacks in Arkansas City, I would have attended it, and I would not have left for Chicago and a multimillion-dollar empire and a mountaintop in Palm Springs.

My second disadvantage was an economic crunch, stemming from the Great Depression. This crunch eliminated the traditional Black option of sending a boy or girl to boarding school in Pine Bluff or Little Rock.

These two disadvantages were simply brute facts which couldn't by themselves motivate anybody. They became a problem when they were integrated into the lives of a boy and his mother, who decided that they were challenges to be overcome and not facts to be passively accepted.

It was this problem that transformed my life. For, from my perspective, God, history, fate, life—choose a word—was challenging me, *testing* me, offering me prizes beyond my wildest imagination when I was faced with a crossroads problem that couldn't be solved by traditional means.

There was nothing magical or unique about this situation. There comes a moment in every person's life when he or she stands at an intersection of two roads, one of which leads up and the other down. And the choice he makes at that moment defines him forever.

There were two choices, and two choices only, before me, and I had to choose. The choice, as usual, was between security and insecurity, between the known and the unknown. I had to decide whether I was going to hang on to the devil I knew or whether I was going to turn loose, without a safety net, and free-fall to danger, destiny, wealth, or death.

I've believed ever since that living on the edge, living in and through your fear, is the summit of life, and that people who refuse to take that dare condemn themselves to a life of living death.

With the help of my mother, who instinctively understood all this, I chose danger, destiny, and wealth. The choice was not easy. For when I entered the last grade of the Arkansas City Colored School in the fall of 1931, it seemed that I had exhausted all my options and that I was condemned to live a life of drudgery on the banks of this river in the shadow of a clock that had stopped running.

But this appraisal didn't take into consideration the fierce Dream of a mother, who had another and better idea.

This is how we changed our fate and made a ladder out of a wall.

The first step, as always, was to redefine the situation so we would have the initiative and would understand clearly what we had to do. This meant that we had to study the battleground and understand the strength and weaknesses of the opposing forces. We knew—how could we help knowing? —that all the high ground and money and weapons were in the hands of our adversaries. But it was worse than useless in that day to grind our teeth and curse racism. The question, the only question, was what were we going to do with what we had in order to make things better for ourselves.

If I had to identify the most important step in a strategy of success, I would pick that question. For the basic problem for a young man or a young woman is not what other people are going to do but what *you* are going to do.

Seen from this perspective, the situation presented new and even exciting possibilities. There was no Black public high school in Arkansas City. But Arkansas City, according to the *Chicago Defender* and the letters we received from the North, was not the whole world. There were Black public high schools in Chicago and other northern cities. Millions of Blacks had migrated to the North to take advantage of these facilities. And we were "free" to join them if we could save enough money to pay for the train tickets.

There were other weapons in our small arsenal. My mother's childhood friend Mamie Johnson had married "a railroad man"—Blacks who worked on the railroad were among the elite in old Black communities. The Johnsons had bought a three-flat building on Chicago's South Side. Mrs. Johnson had written several letters to my mother, suggesting that we move to Chicago and stay with her until we could get our feet on the ground. To make things even more interesting and inviting, my half sister, Beulah, was planning to move to Chicago, too.

So there it was, wrapped up in a pretty little package. Forget, for a moment, the NAACP and the Great Depression. Forget the state of Arkansas and segregated schools. Forget Franklin Delano Roosevelt and the New Deal. The only relevant question here was what were Gertrude Johnson Williams and her son, Johnny, going to do about this situation.

When we posed that question and broke it down into

operational steps based on the direct alternatives open to us, *we* changed and the problem changed.

But it looks simpler now than it did then. For as I made my way through the eighth and final grade of the Arkansas City Colored School, and as the economic situation deteriorated, making hundreds of thousands of Black men and women, including my stepfather, migrant workers, the Dream of Gertrude Johnson Williams, the Dream of taking her boy to the city where he could get a decent education and become somebody, receded, like the fickle water of the Mississippi.

In later years a legend would grow up around this Dream, and people would say—and we deliberately misled them—that we went to Chicago to visit the World's Fair— the Century of Progress Exposition. But this was a smoke screen for our real purpose. What we wanted to see in Chicago was not a fair but a school.

We intended to leave for Chicago in 1932, immediately after my graduation from grade school. But when I graduated in June 1932, there wasn't enough money in the secret bank under the mattress to go to Little Rock, much less to Chicago.

This didn't faze my mother, who redoubled her efforts, cooking, washing, and ironing for whole camps of levee workers, and volunteering for every extra job that came up. During the whole of this summer, she was like a woman possessed. So, by proxy, was I. For I shared the feverish hours, washing and ironing clothes and cooking meals for as many as fifty men. I became, in fact, a master cook and developed a fondness for certain dishes that I prepare even today. French-fried sweet potatoes, for example, and a Johnson specialty, steak and pork chops cut into small pieces, seasoned and simmered in a gravy, and served over rice.

It quickly became apparent that we weren't going to have enough money to travel to Chicago before the beginning of the school season. And it was at this moment that my mother gave me some astonishing news: I was going to return to the Arkansas City School and repeat the eighth grade. She didn't want me running wild on the streets, she said. And she didn't want me to get used to a life of menial work. To prevent that, I was going to repeat the eighth grade two, three, four times—as many times as necessary.

"You're going to stay in the eighth grade," she said, "until we've got enough money to go to Chicago."

The wisdom of this move was plain, even then. But that didn't make it any more palatable to a sensitive young boy who had to go back to his old school and sit in the same room with younger boys and girls he had once scorned.

People laughed at us, not for the first or the last time. Neighbors told my mother that she was crazy to make sacrifices for a boy who would never amount to anything anyway. My mother said nothing. She kept on working and dreaming and saving.

She'd always believed that there was a solution to every problem, and that the solution was in God's hands, not humans' hands. But she believed also, and with equal fervor, that God helped those who helped themselves. As the catcalls and criticisms mounted, she told me to pay no attention to the doubters. "Victory," she said, "is certain if we have the courage to believe and the strength to run our own race."

The taunts came from the outside and were painful but bearable. But my mother had a different and heavier cross to bear. For my stepfather also doubted the wisdom of the planned move. There was no hostility in his opposition. He simply lacked the breadth of imagination to conceive the hidden power of the plan.

For more than a year, this argument poisoned life in the little house near the levee. It was there in the grits of breakfast. It seasoned the pork chops at dinner and the long stretches of silence in between. All that time—and this went on for more than a year—my mother never wavered, never looked back.

When, in July of 1933, the last sweat-soaked dollar was added to the pile, she turned her face to the North and freedom. In a last desperate effort to keep us in Arkansas

City, my stepfather played his trump card, saying we were traveling to disaster, and that we were going to stand in unemployment lines in the cold Chicago wind and freeze to death in the winter.

Looking back now and knowing how deeply my mother cared for my stepfather, I think this was one of the most courageous acts of her life: leaving her husband, the man she dearly loved, in Arkansas City, and embarking with me on this journey, not knowing how long we would survive in a strange city.

Her heart may have been broken, but she never looked back as we climbed into the makeshift bus—a private car operated by enterprising neighbors—for the trip to the train station in McGehee, twelve miles away. She loved my step-father, but she loved freedom and education more.

This was one of the biggest moments of my life, and I'm ashamed to admit that I remember neither the hour nor the day. But there is a wisdom in the body that is older and more reliable than clocks and calendars.

And that July day is engraved in the calendar of my nerves. I can see it now, and taste it: the fierce Arkansas sun, the rivers of sweat running down my back, the smell of fried chicken and potato salad and marble cake in the brown paper bags. And the steam and the roar of the monster train—was there ever a sweeter and more terrifying sound to a boy?—and the stirring words "All aboard!" and all the way to Little Rock, all the way to Memphis, all the way up the River to St. Louis, the beating of my heart, and the hot, cinder-filled ambience of the Jim Crow railroad car.

I was feverish with excitement, with fear, with hope.

It was July 1933.

I was fifteen years old.

Nothing would ever be the same again.

# My _____

# Kind _____

# of _____

# Town _____

# 6

# *Goin' to Chicago*

CHICAGO was to the southern Blacks of my generation what Mecca was to the Moslems and what Jerusalem was to the Jews: a place of magic and mirrors and dreams.

Millions of Black southerners migrated to Harlem, Detroit, Pittsburgh, Gary, and Philadelphia, but Chicago was a special place of special and sassy Blacks who did things they didn't do on Broadway or anywhere else.

Between 1900 and 1930 the Chicago Black population increased from 44,103 to 233,903. In this period, millions of Blacks migrated to northern cities in a movement that was as significant in its implications as the international movement that brought millions to Ellis Island.

The Ellis Island saga has been endlessly notated and hailed. Not enough attention, however, has been given to the Blacks who came up from the South with their hopes, fears, and flimsy cardboard suitcases.

These internal immigrants changed the beat of America. They brought the blues with them and jazz and gospel music. They brought the rhythms and styles that changed Broadway and American music and culture.

Day after day, week after week, and then month after month, all through the twenties, thirties, and forties, the Black migrants came in the biggest migration in American history. The first big wave (300,000) came between 1910 and 1920, followed by a second wave (1.3 million) between 1920 and 1930. The third and fourth waves, even larger, came in the thirties (1.5 million) and the forties (2.5 million).

In the ten years between 1930 and 1940, 40,000 southern Blacks came to Chicago, which had a white population of 3 million and a Black population of about 230,000 in 1934.

Gertrude Johnson Williams and her son were of the class of 1933.

Like millions of other migrants, we followed the curve of the River, going from Little Rock to Memphis to St. Louis to Chicago. For most of the journey, my face was pressed so tight against the window that I could hardly breathe. I was captivated by the tall buildings, motorcars, and bright lights. I wanted to get off in Little Rock. I wanted to get off in Memphis. I had to be physically restrained in St. Louis.

When, late at night, we finally arrived at the Illinois Central Station at Twelfth Street and Michigan Avenue, four blocks from what is now my corporate headquarters, I stood transfixed on the street. I had never seen so many Black people before. I had never seen so many tall buildings and so much traffic.

The Illinois Central Station no longer stands, which is a historical calamity. The building should have been preserved to commemorate the millions who poured through its portals in search of the same dream as the Ellis Island immigrants. Although they were native to the land and spoke the same language, the barriers the Black migrants faced were, if anything, more difficult. And their struggle, which continues even today, was and is equally courageous.

We got a taxi and went to a thin, three-story building at 422 East Forty-fourth Street. My mother's friend Mamie Johnson warmly greeted us. She'd made a bedroom out of the third-floor attic. My mother slept in the bed. I slept in a rollaway bed in the same room.

Before closing my eyes on that first night, I inspected the steam heat and the inside toilet.

I was impressed.

Chicago, as the man said, was my kind of town.

My mother quickly found a job as a domestic, making, as I remember, three or four dollars a day and carfare. And my half sister, Beulah, who'd moved to Chicago shortly before our arrival, helped us make the transition to big-city life.

Beulah was a brilliant and complex woman, a former teacher who'd mastered the dressmaking trade. There was a garment district in Chicago in those days, and she got a job in a shop on South Water Street. She was renting a room at 5610 Calumet, and we rented a room in the same apartment building.

Black Chicago, then and now, was a city within a city, called Black Metropolis by St. Clair Drake and Horace R. Cayton.* It was in many ways the best school available for a Black boy of my age and inclination. Tough, brutal, unforgiving, it lived on the edge and close to the edge. The city challenged you, provoked you, and dared you. It was said, not without foundation, that if you could make your dream come true anywhere, you could make it come true in Chicago.

Fate did me a favor by sending me to the city with the best Black politicians and businessmen. Black Chicagoans

*Black Metropolis: A Study of Negro Life in a Northern City, Harcourt, Brace and Company, New York, © 1945.

had a history of political and economic independence going back to Jean Baptiste Pointe du Sable, the Black man who founded the city. I learned later at DuSable High School that the Potawatomi Indians used to smile and say, "The first white man to settle in Checagou was a black man."

Building on that title, Black men and women made Chicago a political and economic trendsetter. In the 1870s, tailor and county commissioner John Jones operated from a building in downtown Chicago. In the following decades, Jesse Binga established the biggest Black bank in America, and Anthony Overton created a mini-empire that included a newspaper, bank, insurance company, and cosmetics corporation. Many of these businesses, the Binga bank in particular, collapsed during the Depression.

There was a fundamental difference between White Chicago and Black Chicago. For Black Metropolis was organized around rituals and institutions that were virtually unknown on Lake Shore Drive.

Not State Street but the great street of South Parkway (now Dr. Martin Luther King Jr. Drive) dominated Black Metropolis. The street ran like a concrete river through the heart of the South Side. It linked my home, which was one block west of South Parkway at Fifty-sixth Street, with Wendell Phillips High School, at Thirty-ninth Street and South Parkway, and the Thirty-fifth Street business district.

The headquarters of Supreme Liberty Life Insurance Company, the biggest Black-owned business in the North, was at Thirty-fifth and South Parkway. Nearby, at Thirty-fifth and Indiana, was the *Chicago Defender* office.

All roads of Black Chicago ran into South Parkway, a great big picture-book street with at one point five lanes of traffic in each direction. There was a tree-lined oasis in the middle of the street and two- and three-story houses and apartment buildings of every imaginable color and texture on both sides.

I would walk in later years down the Champs-Elysées

and I would ride in a chauffeur-driven limousine down Fifth Avenue. But there was never another street, in fact or in fiction, to compare with the grand boulevard that dazzled the eyes of a fifteen-year-old boy in 1933. Crossing it was an adventure. Walking it hand in hand with some old or new conquest was heaven.

From my arrival until the establishment of my first business, South Parkway was my home base and the center of my world. A few blocks to the east was the shimmering sea of Lake Michigan, which contrasted so strongly with the muddy Mississippi of my youth.

The cultural center of Black Metropolis was at Forty-seventh and South Parkway, an intersection known all over Black America. Cab Calloway, Duke Ellington, and other big-name acts played the Regal, which was on the southeast side of Forty-seventh and South Parkway. The South Center Department Store and a major office building were around the corner on the south side of Forty-seventh Street. The Morris Eat Shop, one of many elegant restaurants, was across the street. Farther to the east was another department store, the Ben Franklin Store. The store was owned by the Jones Brothers, three legendary Mississippians who came to Chicago and made a fortune in the "Policy" business.

There were other community landmarks nearby, the Overton Hygienic Company, and the Rosenwald Building, where the Black elite lived. A major South Parkway attraction was the mansion of *Chicago Defender* publisher Robert Abbott, who rode around in a chauffeur-driven Rolls-Royce, vacationed in Europe, and reportedly paid himself $2,000 a week.

In addition to "Policy" millionaires, wealthy and militant publishers, jazz players, blues singers, ball players, hustlers, surgeons, and lawyers, Chicago had political leaders who could hold their own in what was even then the most exciting political theater in America.

Of all the people I met in this early period, Oscar DePriest was easily the most outstanding. He was the first

Black congressman from the North and the first Black in Congress since the Reconstruction period. Not only did he talk like a congressman but he looked and acted like a congressman. One night at a precinct meeting organized by our landlady, Mrs. Johnson, he made a speech that compares in my mind with the speeches of Adam Clayton Powell and Harold Washington.

There was a school and a living library in all this. It was not, however, the school my mother had in mind when we left Arkansas. So, in September 1933, I was scrubbed to within an inch of my life and sent to Wendell Phillips, a virtually all-Black high school named for the White abolitionist hero.

Because of a cultural misunderstanding, I immediately gained an advantage. When I entered the school on my first day, I found students milling around the registration desks, yelling "1A!" "2A!" and "2B!" Not wanting to appear stupid, I picked a number out of the air and said "2." Nobody challenged me, and I skipped the ninth grade and started in the second year of high school. This was poetic justice since I was probably the only person in the world with two eighth-grade diplomas.

I enrolled in a general language course with a heavy emphasis in civics. Since I wanted to be a journalist, I also enrolled in a journalism course and signed up for work on the school newspaper, the *Phillipsite.* I later became editor in chief of the paper and sales manager of the school yearbook, the *Red and Black.*

This was the fulfillment of a childhood dream. I'd been in love with newspapers and newspaper people since my first encounter with the *Chicago Defender* in Arkansas City.

To this day, I'm a compulsive magazine and newspaper buyer who can't pass a newsstand without stopping. That's the first stop I make in every city I visit. I want to see what's available. I want to touch the newsprint and glossy paper and feel through them the pulse and the heartbeat of the community.

It's not surprising, therefore, that I majored in journalism with a related interest in civics. Many of my classmates believed that I would follow my second love, law. The class prophecy said "Attorney General John H. Johnson" would successfully represent the government.

Nothing in my experience had prepared me for Wendell Phillips, which had a student population larger than the total population of Arkansas City. So many students were enrolled—more than 3,000 in 1933—that there were double and triple shifts, and portable classrooms.

Chicago was up North, but it was rigidly segregated. The student body was almost totally Black, but the principal and most of the teachers were White. The assistant principal was a Black woman, Mrs. Annabel Carey Prescott.

The physical presence of Mrs. Prescott and other Black teachers and administrators was more important than the lessons they taught. I'd never seen so many well-dressed and well-educated Blacks in one place. Coming to school every day and sharing their reflected light was a learning experience that reinforced the classroom lessons.

A self-perpetuating mythology would develop later around inner-city Black schools. Many people, including many educators, would buy into the damnable idea that poor Black students can't and won't learn. Our teachers didn't believe that. They believed we could do anything we wanted to do, and they challenged us to reach for the stars.

Mary J. Herrick, our civics teacher, was one of the most unforgettable persons I've known. She was White, but she was so sincere and spoke with so much conviction that she became a legend in Black Chicago. She took us on field trips to downtown Chicago and told us what was happening in Washington and London. She also invited us into her home for tea—she was the first White person to invite me into her home on a social basis.

For the first time I learned something about Africa. The

true story was not in the books, but Mary J. Herrick taught it. She told us we were descendants of an ancient people who had created major civilizations in Africa. She challenged us to prepare ourselves for the next lap of a great race.

There's a lesson in this for people who stay up late wringing their hands over the future of public education. The lesson is simple: The letter alone killeth but the spirit transforms disadvantaged youths and giveth new life.

There's nothing wrong with public education that more resources, more love, and more C. S. Johnsons and Mary Herricks can't cure. And our most important task is to duplicate the nurturing, transforming environments that made it possible for unsung and underpaid teachers and administrators, Black and White, to perform the educational miracles of yesterday.

Mary Herrick taught as if her life—and our lives—depended on it. She was the first White person I'd met who was completely free of racial prejudice. A half century later, when she was honored by many of her former students, including Mayor Harold Washington, she mentioned my name in her speech, saying: "You know, John, you were always such a dedicated person—I always knew you were going to be a great success." And I replied, "Why didn't you tell me, Miss Herrick? It would have saved me a lot of heartache, a lot of worry, and a lot of tears."

Wendell Phillips High School later burned, and the student body was transferred to a newly constructed building, which was named later for the Black father of Chicago, Jean Baptiste Pointe du Sable. Among my classmates at both institutions were several individuals who became national heroes. Nathaniel Coles, the stick-thin son of the Reverend Edward Cole, couldn't sing but achieved local fame as the piano player at the "Spotlight" dances at the Warwick Hall on Forty-third Street. They were called "Spotlight" dances because it was the custom to turn off the lights and shine spotlights on various couples to see if they were dancing too close.

Large crowds flocked to these dances. Not, however, to listen to pianist Cole, who went on to attract larger crowds as Nat King Cole. Nobody, not even Nat, knew he could sing then. This hidden talent emerged one night on the West Coast when his singer didn't show up and the nightclub owner demanded a song.

Another and equally talented classmate was John Elrod Sanford, also known as Red Sanford and Redd Foxx. He told cleaner jokes then—well, a little cleaner—but was no less funny. There were others, including pianist Dorothy Donegan and future entrepreneurs like William Abernathy and Dempsey Travis, who made money in the taxicab industry and real estate respectively.

None of these entertainers and millionaires-to-be held a candle to the school celebrity, Charles Murray, Jr., the son of the founder of Murray Hair Pomade. I used to envy Charlie. He came to school in a chauffeur-driven limousine and spent most of his time fighting off the girls he didn't like and entertaining the ones he liked. He didn't do well in school—how could he with all those lovely distractions? —but I shared the general view that if you had to fail, Charlie's was the way to fail.

# 7

# *The Boy in the Mirror*

IF, as W. E. B. DuBois said, the worst thing in the world is to be poor in a rich country, the next worst thing is to be the poorest person in a poor country.

Most of my classmates were poor, but I was poorer than most—and I paid for it.

Since money was at a premium I walked to school, even in the bitter-cold winter months. And I wore homemade suits and pants.

As if that wasn't enough, I was shy, insecure, and inarticulate, and I spoke in a thick down-home country brogue.

How could any self-respecting student comic resist such a target?

They came from all over, from the ninth grade and the tenth grade and the twelfth grade, to poke fun at the country boy from Arkansas.

They laughed at my "mammy-made" clothes.

They laughed at my brogue.

And they thought my bowlegs were hilarious. I've heard it said that bowlegs are sexy. They weren't sexy to my classmates, who ranked them slightly below a social disease.

You know the result. If your classmates laugh every time you stand up to recite, if they follow you, shouting, "Look at that bowlegged guy in his mammy-made clothes" —if this happens every day and you have no friends or money and you're alone in a strange city, you begin to feel put upon.

I remember running home crying and telling my mother, who quickly and quietly resolved one aspect of the problem. She was working then for a woman whose husband was about my size, and she persuaded the couple to give us some old suits. Almost overnight I became one of the best-dressed students at the old and the new Wendell Phillips.

I resented the way I was treated by some students, and I decided to retaliate the only way I knew how—by beating them in class and in extracurricular activities. From the time I entered Wendell Phillips in 1933 until I graduated from DuSable in 1936, I studied harder, partly because I didn't have enough money to take girls out, and partly because I wanted to even the score. I also read self-improvement books by Dale Carnegie and others.

Faith, self-confidence, and a positive mental attitude: These three were the basic messages of the self-help books that changed my life.

Most of these books listed one-two-three practical steps for improving personal effectiveness. One step was to practice conversations and selling approaches in private before trying them out in public.

I started practicing speeches and approaches to girls before the mirror at home. Everybody was out working, and I could talk as loud and as long as I wanted to. Day in and day out, I alternately lectured and talked sweet talk to that patient mirror. Then I went to school and forced myself to stand up and speak in class. They laughed at first but they soon started applauding—because I was making sense and because I was speaking better than anyone else. This experience taught me that one of the sweetest emotions in the world is watching scorn turn into admiration and awe.

I learned something else that I've never forgotten: *There is no defense against an excellence that speaks to a real need.*

This brings us back, at a new and different level, to the advantage of the disadvantage. If I had been rich with a lot of friends, I wouldn't be where I am today. It's not satisfaction but dissatisfaction that drives people to the heights. I was goaded, I was driven to success by the whip of social disapproval.

Throughout the thirties and on into the forties, I read and reread books on self-improvement, success, and selling. One of my favorites was *Think and Grow Rich*. Another was Dale Carnegie's *How to Win Friends and Influence People*.

Perhaps the most important lesson I learned from these books was "other-focusing." We live, all of us, too close to ourselves. And all of us need to focus more on what others want rather than on what we want.

If there's one thing that life teaches us, it's that people everywhere act to preserve or advance their own interests. And if you want people to satisfy a need that is vital to *your* self-interest, you've got to study them and figure out what *they* want. You can't be indifferent to them. Nor can you challenge everything they say and do. Not if you want them to help you. If that's your goal—and half the battle in winning friends and influencing people is defining your goal and the other person's goal—you've got to study people and make it to *their* self-interest to advance *your* self-interest.

I read all the self-help books I could find. I also read the great classics of Black history and literature, including

Booker T. Washington's autobiography, *Up From Slavery*, W. E. B. DuBois's essays, and the poetry of Langston Hughes.

Vivian Harsh, the librarian at the Forty-eighth Street branch of the Chicago Public Library, had one of the major collections of books on the Black experience. I used to hang out in the branch, reading books on Frederick Douglass and other Blacks who had succeeded against the odds.

Chicago was at the center of the dominant currents of the age—Ethiopia's struggle against Italy, the "Don't Buy Where You Can't Work" movement, the Scottsboro Campaign. These issues were discussed at public forums in Washington Park and in city churches by the leading Black personalities of the day. These forums were free, and I took advantage of an urban environment that was itself a public education.

The months and years of reading and listening and practicing paid off. When the students met to organize the junior class, the sponsoring teacher asked if anyone had anything to say. No one moved. No one said a word.

After a long and uncomfortable pause, I got up and expressed appreciation to the sponsor for giving us an opportunity to organize. I said we were happy to be in this new school—this was after we moved to the building that was later named DuSable High—and that we would work hard to justify the confidence that the teachers had placed in us.

This was not, all things considered, a bad extemporaneous presentation. My fellow students were obviously pleased, for I was immediately and unanimously elected junior class president. The next year I was elected senior class president. I was also editor in chief of the *Phillipsite*, presiding officer of the student council, leader of the student forum and the French Club. When I graduated, the yearbook said Johnny Johnson had "participated in so many activities that the teachers will have to find four or five other students to fill his place."

\*　　\*　　\*

The one activity I shunned was sports. I was so involved in trying to think my way out of poverty that I didn't even take gym.

For a long time, I thought I was peculiar. Then one day I read a story in *Fortune* magazine about Stanley Burnet Resor, the head of J. Walter Thompson advertising agency. The story said "his food and drink, his unremitting daily task, and the substance of his dreams is advertising. He has no hobbies, plays no games."

I put the magazine down with a sigh of relief. At last, I said, I've found a guy like me. For I have no hobbies and play no games, and the food and drink of my life is trying to succeed.

Although I operate in a world that is made up of part-time golfers and sportsmen, success is still my hobby. One of the most amusing encounters of my life was with an industrialist who assumed that I was the token Black on the board and offered unsolicited advice on how to make it in corporate America.

"Do you play golf?" he asked. I said no. He said, "Johnson, you're never going to get anywhere in this world until you learn how to play golf."

"Gee, thanks," I said. "But I'm *already* where I want to be. If I learn how to play golf, it might mess me up."

I had no interest, then or now, in hitting little white balls, but I wasn't a monk. Like all teenagers, I had a passionate interest in the opposite sex. But that was one game that couldn't be played without adequate wherewithal. Although my approach, honed to a fine edge by practice in front of a mirror, was flawless, my social life was limited by lack of money to take young ladies to the Regal and other citadels of entertainment.

I had a crush on one young lady who lived within walking distance of the Regal—because of my poverty I could only fall in love with girls who didn't require carfare to get to the Regal. She agreed one day to go to the show with me and then decided at the last moment to go for a ride with a former classmate who'd dropped out of school to work at the post office. Many years later, she came to my office and said, "I've been wanting to say all these years, I really made a big mistake on that day."

This was far in the future, and had no influence on the young and desperate Johnny Johnson, who continued his feverish and largely unsuccessful effort to find pretty and persuadable young girls who lived within walking distance of the show.

# 8

# *My Days on Welfare*

IN late 1933, mother, Beulah, and I moved to an apartment at 5412 South Parkway, a large structure built around a courtyard. We had four rooms, a bedroom, living room, kitchen, and dining room, and we paid thirty-five dollars a month.

Beulah and my mother slept in the bedroom, and I slept on a rollaway bed in the dining room. For twenty-three years, I slept on couches and rollaway beds. In fact, I never had a bedroom of my own until I got married.

Before long, my stepfather decided to move to Chicago. As soon as he arrived, the crazy quilt of our lives came apart at the seams, and the dire predictions he'd made in Arkansas came true.

To understand the family crisis that followed, you must back up a moment and look at the limitations of the New Deal. For, a common impression to the contrary notwithstanding, the New Deal didn't end the Depression in Black

America. From 1932 to 1935, things went from bad to worse in Black communities. By the mid-thirties, almost half of the Black families in Chicago were on relief or emergency employment.

My stepfather arrived on the downside of this trend and couldn't find a job anywhere. Then, in rapid-fire order, my mother lost her job as a domestic and Beulah lost her job in the garment industry. To make things even more complicated, Beulah joined the Father Divine Movement and went through a painful conversion crisis.

This required some fast footwork, and we danced to the music of the times, renting out our only bedroom and making other economies. We rented the bedroom for five dollars a week. This provided twenty of the thirty-five dollars we needed for the monthly rent. We managed to scrounge up the additional fifteen dollars from somewhere.

My mother and stepfather slept in the dining room. I slept on a couch in the living room.

My mother tried to rent the room to men, who did not as a rule demand kitchen privileges. She tried to rent to older men, who did not as a rule have a lot of women visitors.

This was a matter of high finance and theology that revolved around the delicate issue of "privileges," the right to entertain guests in one's room. Most families in those days were renting rooms as a means of survival, and the basic question was whether the renter would have "privileges." Since my mother refused to extend privileges, she had to find a renter who was too old to be interested in younger women, or in women, period. This, as you can imagine, was a difficult task.

Despite the desperation of the period and the religious scruples of my mother, we were never hungry. We ate more neck bones than we wanted. We ate more leftovers than we wanted. But there was always something to eat.

My mother turned out to be an economic magician who always came up with money from somewhere at hole-card time. Always, when it seemed that there was no way out, she would look in a shoe box or a cookie jar or behind the canned goods and say, "Well, I was putting this aside for a rainy day...." Perhaps the most important lesson I learned from her is that life is so uncertain that you should always have something hidden under a cookie jar that you can use for survival.

But the economic crisis of the thirties was bigger than private cookie jars. And we were forced, like millions of other Americans, to apply for welfare, or relief, as it was known then. Our application was rejected on the grounds that we hadn't lived in Chicago long enough. My mother sat down, in one of the great gestures of her life, and wrote a letter to the president of the United States. She told President Roosevelt that she and her husband couldn't find work, that she had a son to support and would he please tell the local authorities to stop playing games.

One of the secrets of Franklin Delano Roosevelt's success was that he responded or, at least, hired people who were smart enough to answer letters. President Roosevelt probably didn't see my mother's letter, but it somehow found its way back to Chicago. The local bureaucrats relented and put us on relief.

My mother, who was, like almost all Blacks, a Republican, became an instant Democrat. From that day forward, she was a devoted supporter of Roosevelt and his works. She believed until her death that he had personally answered her letter.

From late 1934, then, until 1936, we were on relief. In these years, welfare came not in monthly checks but in monthly visits by government trucks. On the first days of the month, the big government trucks would roar through the South Side, like invading convoys, dropping off salt pork, beans, peas, and other commodities.

What I remember most about my days on welfare was the shame. I used to sit on a stoop with a group of young men and watch the welfare trucks cruising the neighborhood. The trucks would drive up to my house, and someone would say, "They're going to *your* house." And I would say, "That's not my house." The truck would drive up to someone else's house, and he would say, "That's not my house." We knew the trucks were going to our houses; we were just too ashamed to admit it.

There's been a lot of criticism of the welfare system from people who know little or nothing about poverty or welfare. Unlike most of the critics, I've been there, and I have no hesitancy in saying that I'm in favor of welfare for those who need it. I certainly don't condemn it. When we were on welfare, we needed it.

The problem, I think, is the purpose of welfare and the organization of the welfare system. The goal must always be to *get off* welfare, and we got off as soon as we could.

That's one of the reasons I believe the government must play a role as the employer of last resort, when all else fails. We got off the welfare rolls two years later when my stepfather got a WPA job, and I got a job with a division of the National Youth Administration headed by Mary McLeod Bethune.

We moved on from these government jobs to better times and better jobs. But the WPA-NYA ladder was a necessary first step that let us keep our dignity and hope until the private economy could provide alternatives.

As the only former welfare recipient in my tax bracket, I have earned the right to say that this experience is relevant to the economic crisis of the eighties. When you look at the armies of misdirected youths roaming urban streets, it becomes obvious that we could create taxpayers and perhaps millionaires by organizing modern equivalents of the alphabets of the thirties—the WPA and NYA projects and CCC camps—that saved the American economic system. We need to think deeply about this opportunity. For, as John F. Kennedy said, "If a free society cannot help the many who are poor, it cannot save the few who are rich."

Because we received help at a critical moment in our

lives and because we never lost the will to end dependence on welfare, we broke free and began the slow rise to that economic emancipation without which political emancipation is a mere mockery. But something of the shame and terror of those days remain with me to this day. If I don't feel like getting up in the morning, all I have to do to motivate myself is to recall the government truck stopping in front of my house—and I jump up and go to work.

# 9

## *Beauty Ray and Father Divine*

DURING the time of the welfare trucks and unemployment lines, millions turned to other gods and faiths. Things got so bad on the South Side that the only people preaching hope were the communists and the followers of Father Divine. Certain of my friends joined the Communist Party, which was, they said, the wave of the future. Some were attracted by the promise of bread, employment, and a new world. Others, I believe, attended the meetings to sample the free food and whiskey and to mingle with pretty women, Black and White.

I shunned the party because it wanted to destroy the system. I didn't want to destroy the system—I wanted to join it so I could change it and make it more responsive to poor people and Blacks.

Other Blacks, Beulah in particular, looked for salvation in other heavens. After Beulah lost her job in the garment district, she turned, out of desperation, I think, to Father

Divine. He had a headquarters or "heaven," as it was called, on South Parkway near Forty-seventh Street. His followers served free meals to anyone who came in, along with a gospel of love (the password was "Peace, it's truly wonderful") and hope.

Father Divine, who was born George Baker, attracted Blacks and Whites, poor people and rich people. Some people believed he was a prophet. Some people, including apparently Father Divine, believed he was God. In 1931 he was sentenced to prison in Sayville, New York. Four days later, the judge who'd sentenced him dropped dead, and Father Divine reportedly said from his jail cell: "I hated to do it."

Father Divine and Sweet Angel, the Canadian-born White woman he married in 1946, offered people something the government couldn't or wouldn't offer, free meals without questions or documentation. They also offered, or seemed to offer, a new way of life.

My sister, who was bright and articulate, got caught up in the movement and was transferred to Philadelphia. After several years of silence, we were told that she was living in "heaven," which was the Lorraine Hotel in Philadelphia, under her movement name of Beauty Ray.

My mother and stepfather wrote letter after letter, all of which were returned unopened. They tried to call and couldn't get through. They finally went to the Lorraine Hotel and asked for Beauty Ray. Suddenly, without warning, she appeared and walked up a flight of stairs. They jumped up and called out to her. She ignored them and disappeared.

Minutes later, they were told that Beauty Ray had renounced her worldly family and could only talk to people who accepted the teachings of Father Divine. My mother broke down in tears, and my stepfather cursed.

When they returned to Chicago, my mother indicated by word and manner that the subject was closed. She grieved almost every day after that, but she never again spoke the name of the lost daughter, who disappeared one day on the second floor of a Philadelphia hotel, never to be seen by the family again.

# 10

## *The Birth of John Harold Johnson*

I WAS too young and too busy to appreciate the full impact of the Beauty Ray family tragedy.

I was rapidly becoming a professional leader, organizing forums and even a mimeographed magazine (*Afri-American Youth*) for the National Youth Administration.

I was also involved in the planning for the DuSable High School commencement. The commencement was held on Thursday, June 11, 1936, and I was the only student speaker. On Saturday, June 6, I received my first press notice in the *Chicago Defender*, which said I would speak on the subject "Builders of a New World."

"Builders of a New World": I don't know whether I changed my mind or whether this was only a part of my title. At any rate, I spoke on the subject "The Task That Lies Before Us." The title provocatively emphasized the task, not the tasks. What precisely was this task? The task, I said, was excellence linked to service. It was a speech I could and probably will give tomorrow. And I'm pleased to find myself in agreement with the young John H. Johnson.

This commencement also marked the birth of John H. Johnson. My official name was Johnny Johnson and I fully intended to graduate that way. But Miss Herrick, the sensitive civics teacher, pulled me aside and said, "Johnny, you're about to graduate. You're a big boy now. Shouldn't you be John?"

# 206 TO FINISH DU SABLE HIGH AT JUNE FINALS

## Rev. A.J. Carey And John Johnson Speakers

A class of 206 students will be graduated from Du Sable High School at exercises to be held in the school auditorium Thursday, June 11. The class, one of the largest ever to be graduated from the institution is the first to finish the school since its name was changed from New Wendell Phillips High School to Du Sable High School.

Rev. Archibald J. Carey Jr., pastor of Woodlawn A.M.E. church, an alumnus of the school, will be the principal speaker. John H. Johnson, class president, will be the only student speaker. His subject will be "Builders of a New World." C.C. Willard, principal of the school, will award the diplomas.

I thought about it for a moment and said yes. She then said, "Perhaps you ought to have a middle name."

I picked a name out of the air, and Johnny Johnson became John Harold Johnson. Ernestine Oldham, the sponsor of my creative writing class, wrote in my yearbook: "To Johnny. Now that you are John, grown, dignified, alert, intelligent, we are very proud of you."

By whatever name, I was confused and crestfallen. I'd just graduated with a fistful of honors and a scholarship to the University of Chicago. But the scholarship only paid two hundred dollars, and I had two months to beg or borrow enough money to finance a year's study at Chicago or some other institution of higher learning.

Since this was one of those problems that seemed to be beyond my control, I did nothing. I've learned over the years that the best way to deal with an insoluble problem is to get up on the balls of your feet and keep moving, like a good boxer. While you're moving, something might hit you, or you might hit something or someone. I kept moving and walked—was it an accident or was it fate?—into the turning point of my life.

Neither trumpet calls nor drumrolls announced the moment, which occurred at a routine Urban League luncheon for outstanding high school students. The main speaker was one of my heroes, a legendary business leader named Harry H. Pace. He was president of Supreme Liberty Life Insurance Company, the biggest Black business in the North and the biggest Black business in Chicago. Pace spoke brilliantly, calling for work, service, struggle, and excellence.

When he finished, I was one of the first students to reach him. I was a long way now from the insecure and inarticulate student who'd arrived in Chicago, a bare three years before, with a cardboard suitcase and brown paper bag. Because of Dale Carnegie and all those hours in front of the mirror, I could express myself, and I had no difficulty in telling Pace how much I appreciated his remarks. He returned the compliment, saying he'd heard good reports about my high school record.

"What do you plan to do now?" he asked.

"I want to go to college," I said, "but I don't have enough money."

"Have you thought about working part-time and studying part-time?"

I said I had thought of nothing else but that I couldn't find a part-time or a full-time job. He paused for a moment— it was over, my life was sealed, in a moment—and destiny spoke and lights went on (in my heart) and bells started ringing.

"I'm going away on vacation," he said, "but I'll be back in September. See me on the first working day in September, and I'll find something for you to do."

Somebody asked me once what I would change if I could live my life over again. I replied that I wouldn't change anything. So many things happened along the way, maybe by accident, maybe by Providence, that I would be afraid to change any of the events that led to the meeting with Harry H. Pace and the big ebony road that changed and defined my life.

# 11

## Supreme Life and the Double-Duty Dollar

I WALKED into the headquarters of Supreme Liberty Life Insurance Company on Tuesday, September 1, 1936, and asked for President and CEO Harry H. Pace.

"The president," I said, "is expecting me."

This was a bold gambit for an eighteen-year-old youth, and it marked the beginning of my third life, following the first fifteen years in Arkansas City and the dramatic change after the escape to Chicago.

President Pace wasn't expecting me, but he'd told me to report on this day. And I spent an uncomfortable fifteen minutes wondering whether he would remember our conversation and his promise to give me a job.

While waiting, I looked around and noticed a strange phenomenon.

Right before my eyes, men and women, *good-looking, well-dressed* men and women, were scurrying from office to office with stacks of papers and fat files.

What was going on here?

I'd seen photographs and movies of White men and women running around like this and making deals in the offices of the Rockefellers and Morgans. But the men and women before me were Black, like me. And they were moving paper and talking big money talk just like White folk.

This was a new thing, and I sat up and paid attention.

Until that moment, the height and color of my dream had been set by the ceiling and color of the Black preachers, teachers, and lawyers I'd seen. I'd heard about Black corporations, but I'd never examined one up close. Now, suddenly, I was surrounded by Black clerks, salesmen, and money managers. And just like that—click, click, click, click, *CLICK!* —lights went on in my mind and my life.

In that light, with mounting excitement, I examined this new card that life had put into my hands.

I knew from my research—I was only eighteen years old, but I already knew that you *never* go into a man's office unless you know more about him, about his background, his interests, hobbies, loves, than he knows about you—that Supreme Liberty (now Supreme Life) was the product of the 1929 merger of three Black companies.

The three companies were Supreme Life and Casualty of Columbus, Ohio; Liberty Life of Chicago; and Northeastern Life of Newark, New Jersey. The merger combined a joint business in force of $27 million. This was one of the first major mergers in American business history, and it was at that time the biggest financial deal ever negotiated by all-Black businesses.

The merger was engineered by a group of brilliant men, notably Pace, who became president and CEO; Earl B. Dickerson, who became general counsel; and Truman K. Gibson, who became chairman and received the Harmon Award for his role in the negotiations.

The new president, Harry Herbert Pace, was one of the most interesting and enigmatic figures in the history of

Black America. He had more sides, in fact, than a geodesic dome. He was a scholar, lawyer, author, entrepreneur, entertainment impresario, and philosopher. He was also an activist who played a major role in many of the big social and economic movements of the first decades of the century.

So light-skinned that he could pass for White, he totally identified with Black causes until his controversial last years, when he moved to an all-White suburb and cut back on his activities in Black America. After his death in 1943, his heirs sold the Supreme stock and disappeared from the Black limelight.

Whatever the truth about those last years and the disappearance of the Pace name from the firmament of Black leadership, there is not the slightest question that Pace was a master of networking who carried the art of mentoring to new heights before the word *mentoring* was defined. Pace discovered and gave that first crucial helping hand to more Black artists and leaders than any other American. He was the first person to hire bandleader Fletcher Henderson and actresses Isabelle Washington and Freddie Washington. He discovered Ethel Waters and Trixie Smith and was the first person to attract national attention to the work of W. C. Handy.

A graduate of Atlanta University and the Chicago Law School, a former teacher of Latin and Greek, Pace had a genius for new trends and new talent. Walter White, the longtime leader of the NAACP, got his start as a Pace office boy, and it was Pace who recommended him to the NAACP hierarchy. Paul Robeson sold records in Pace's music shop while he was a law student at Columbia University.

Pace was only fifty-two on the day I reported for work, but he had served as president and CEO of several businesses, including the New York-based Pace & Handy Music Company and Black Swan Phonograph Company. Black Swan, a forerunner of Motown, tried to control the millions flowing from the songs and rhythms of Black America.

This was the first major Black-owned recording company, and it led to the Beatles and the Grammies. After Pace put Black artists and Black record buyers on the business map, White-owned corporations, in moves strikingly similar to the recent acts of White-owned insurance, cosmetics, and publishing companies, started issuing "race catalogs" in a generally successful effort to destroy Black entrepreneurs.

To all this finally must be added Pace's pioneering work as a magazine publisher. Long before *Time* and even long before *Reader's Digest*, he teamed up with W. E. B. DuBois in the publication of *Moon*, a weekly commercial magazine that failed in 1906.

This was the man, brilliant, bold, far-seeing, who welcomed me on September 1, 1936, and assigned me to an empty desk outside his door. I learned later that he really didn't have anything for me to do. He was just a considerate man who took great pride in recognizing youths he considered talented and promising.

After sitting at this desk for three or four months without being called on to do anything substantial, I decided one day to sneak out and get a soda at a nearby drugstore. At that precise moment, Pace did something he'd never done before: He called and asked me to come into his office.

When I got back, he said, "Young man, one thing you've got to learn. I'm paying you to sit at your desk, and you should stay there, even if I *never* call you." From then on, I stayed at the desk, whether I was called or not, and gradually the job assumed more importance.

I received twenty-five dollars a month and worked part-time at Supreme while attending the University of Chicago part-time. I intended at that time to pursue a law degree, but the Supreme Liberty curriculum was so exciting that I dropped out of the university and devoted myself full-time to my studies at Supreme. Although I later took several courses at Northwestern University night school, my real school from 1936 to 1941 was the university of Supreme Life.

I wouldn't recommend this approach today. A college degree is a basic necessity in the technocratic environment of the eighties. A student who drops out of college in this environment drops out of the race for personal fulfillment and economic security.

The situation was different when I started work at Supreme. At that point, in the depth of the Depression, the key factor was a job, not a degree. I knew several well-educated Blacks, lawyers, doctors, and dentists, who were working at the post office. Under these circumstances, it was not at all surprising that I seized the white-collar opportunity that Supreme provided.

It was at Supreme that I learned something that few Black or White business people knew (then or now).

Like almost all Blacks and Whites, I'd assumed that Black entrepreneurs had been confined to the side streets of American commerce because of a lack of experience. Imagine my surprise when I discovered that Blacks had operated in the mainstream of money from the beginning of the American drama and had sold goods and services to both Black and White consumers.

According to the information that Supreme Life historians made available to me, Blacks hit the ground running and were soon among the major entrepreneurs of the new country. By the American Revolution, there were scores of prominent Black business people, including Samuel Fraunces, the owner of New York's Fraunces' Tavern, the favorite watering hole of George Washington, and James Forten, who employed forty workers, Black and White, in his Philadelphia sail factory.

Later, in the nineteenth century, Blacks were prominent in the fashion and clothing fields, the coal and lumber industry, and retail and wholesale trade.

They operated foundries, tanneries, and factories. They

made rope, shoes, cigars, furniture, and machinery. They operated major inns and hotels in southern and northern cities and were in some cities the Hyatts and the Hiltons of their day. In addition to all this, they held virtual monopolies in the catering, barbering, and hairdressing fields.

With the overthrow of Reconstruction and the beginning of the Jim Crow age, Black entrepreneurs were confined—by Jim Crow legislation, zoning restrictions, and even violence—to the Black consumer market and the great Black streets, Auburn Avenue in Atlanta, Beale Street in Memphis, South Parkway in Chicago.

This was not, in and of itself, a fatal blow. For the road to the Fortune 500 is paved with the deeds of ethnic entrepreneurs who exploited an ethnic advantage (olive oil, pasta, clothing) and moved on to major ventures in the general market. This transition—from an ethnic Irish, Italian, or Jewish base to the general market—was closed to Black entrepreneurs, who, according to custom and, in some cases, law, could buy from Whites but couldn't sell to them.

To take one clear example, S. B. Fuller, a brilliant Chicago entrepreneur, made millions in the cosmetics industry and then moved into the general market with a line of household products, sold door-to-door. Fuller was on his way to a major market share when someone started spreading stories about his racial identity.

The story is told of the time Fuller invited his southern agents, including White men and women from every southern state, to his annual sales convention at Chicago's Palmer House. When the Whites discovered that their boss was Black, they resigned.

There were similar incidents in the sixties and seventies when some Black-owned companies started marketing beauty products for both Black and White women.

I've talked to scores of Black millionaires who say, almost to a man or woman, that they made money not because of race but in spite of race. I know what they mean, for if I hadn't operated with the handicap of racial barriers, I could have made billions instead of millions.

The Black birthrate, the challenge of foreign competition, and the $261-billion Black consumer market have forced welcome changes in this situation. The work of the next century is to accelerate these changes and create a common American market based on a free movement of money, people, and ideas across all market and racial boundaries.

This can't be done by superficial changes based on Black visibility in corporations controlled financially and otherwise by Whites. The only viable approach is to eliminate the artificial barriers that keep Black, ethnic, and female entrepreneurs from developing their own bases and moving from those foundations to parity and participation in the common market.

The road to the future, in other words, depends on ethnic entrepreneurs doing their own thing instead of depending on external banks and financiers who will, out of necessity, force them to do their thing.

That's why I've expressed reservations about recent activities of the new Black entrepreneurs. I believe Black entrepreneurs must participate at every level in all economic institutions. There is a danger, however, in undue reliance on external investors. Today, as in the heyday of great ethnic entrepreneurs, Black, Oriental, Jewish, Italian, and Irish, the commonsense approach is to build from your own base and assimilate instead of being assimilated.

This was the dream of the pioneer Black entrepreneurs. It was the dream of Madame C. J. Walker, the cosmetics manufacturer who became the first self-made woman millionaire, and the giants of the Black insurance industry, men like Alonzo Herndon of Atlanta Life, C. C. Spaulding of North Carolina Mutual, and Harry H. Pace of Supreme Liberty.

Along with thousands of other Blacks, these entrepreneurs were forced to make what author M. S. Stuart called an "economic detour." In spite of the barriers, they never gave up their demand for a free market. And they never stopped testing the barriers blocking the entry lanes to the mainstream freeway.

Supreme was on the cutting edge of that dream.

The company had succeeded in building a strong presence in a field where the high Black mortality rate had frightened off White investors. It was so successful in this effort that it survived the Depression and continued to make loans to Black property owners when White banks and realtors were routinely turning down Black applicants.

Supreme survived, in other words, not because it was inferior to White corporations but because it was superior in dealing with the challenges of an unfavorable business environment. When Supreme and other Black-owned institutions changed that environment and created a large and prosperous middle class, White corporations reevaluated the Black consumer market.

Supreme was a sound business, and it was a sound *Black* business. It emphasized the double-duty dollar, telling Blacks that a dollar invested in Supreme provided insurance protection *and* employment for Black men and women.

"Spend Your Money Where You Can Work." This was the characteristic theme of company agents.

What this meant on a practical level was that Supreme, like other Black businesses, was *more* than a business. It was a statement, a petition, a demonstration, and an argument. That's what Booker T. Washington meant when he said:

"One farm bought, one house built...one man who is the largest taxpayer or has the largest bank account, one school or church maintained, one factory running successfully...one patient cured by a Negro doctor, one sermon well preached, one office well filled—these will tell more in our favor than all the abstract eloquence that can be summoned to plead our cause."

This was the history, and the hope, of the double-duty dollar that shaped my business horizon. I had been looking for this fulcrum all my life, without knowing what I was looking for, and without even knowing that I was looking. Now that I'd found Supreme, I threw myself on it as a drowning man throws himself on a plank, not because it was better than a boat or a plane but because it was the only boat or plane I had.

My brother-in-law, the late Dr. William Walker, an eminent surgeon, told me once that he envied businessmen because they, unlike doctors and other professionals, can make money even when they're not working.

"Brother Johnny," he said, "I only make money when I'm cutting on people or diagnosing. But you make money even when you're asleep. Even while we're sitting here talking at one o'clock in the morning, people somewhere are buying your magazines and products and making money for you."

That's part of the lure of business, but it's only a part. For after the first million or two, money is only a means of measuring and keeping count. What has fascinated me, then and now, has been the electricity of making a deal, the challenge of managing the human elements, and the adrenaline-flowing gamble of keeping nine or ten balls in the air and bringing them down safely and walking away with a flair.

It was the dare, it was the gamble, it was the *deal* that captivated me. I was on the bottom rung at Supreme, but coming to work and watching Pace and his associates play with millions gave me a physical, almost a sexual, thrill.

Another element in this equation was the magic of journalism. For me, as well as for Pace, journalism was a skyscraper value precisely because it combined the ultimate business challenge with the ultimate social challenge. A magazine—and we were both interested in magazines— could not survive if it wasn't based on sound business principles. But sound business principles alone would not ensure its survival. That was the dilemma, and nobody in Black America had solved it.

Since the founding of *The Mirror of Liberty* in 1838, there had been scores of Black magazines. But they died, one after another, of terminal cash flow. Despite this history, the idea lived on and bewitched several men. Among them, Harry Pace, who was a frustrated journalist until the day he died.

It was this passion that provided my first opening. I was assigned to the company's monthly newspaper, *The Guardian*, first as assistant to the editor, who was, of course, Harry H. Pace.

After three or four months, I was named assistant editor. In 1939, I was promoted to editor.

This was a strategic post for an ambitious young man, and I made the most of it to study men, success, and power. I was guided by more than academic curiosity. I had six bosses, and my survival depended on a close understanding of the six men on the company executive committee. To give you an idea of the importance and the delicacy of this task, I used a ruler to make sure that I gave each of the six men the same amount of space in each edition of the monthly company newspaper.

In addition to Pace, the men were:

*Chairman Truman Kella Gibson*, the Harvard-educated chairman of the board, who'd served as business manager of the Atlanta University newspaper when Pace was editor.

*Secretary W. Ellis Stewart*, one of the founders of Liberty Life Insurance Company, and a graduate—he studied insurance—of the University of Illinois.

*Agency officer Jefferson G. Ish*, a Yale graduate, and a former president of Arkansas State College.

*General counsel Earl B. Dickerson*, one of the founders, and a graduate of the University of Chicago Law School.

*Medical director Midian O. Bousfield*, M.D., a graduate of Northwestern University, who later commanded the army station hospital at Fort Huachuca as a full colonel.

I learned a lot from these men. I drove President Pace

to the bank almost every day, and I used the opportunity to ask questions about business, life, success, and Black America. Not a week goes by that I don't recall and use some lesson that I learned from him and other Supreme executives.

Among other things, I learned how to ration my time and focus my activities. As a result, I'm never thrown off stride by people who barge in without an appointment. I simply tell these interlopers that I'm sorry that I can't see them or listen to their pleas, but that I had planned my day without knowing that they were going to call or come by.

I also learned how to size up a situation and determine if it advanced my interests. This was perhaps the most important lesson of all, for our destiny is, in large part, in our own hands. We are exposed daily to situations and people who can drive us up the wall *if we let them.* Most of these people and situations have little or no bearing on our life goals and can be ignored or relegated to the margins.

Even as a young man, I governed my life by this principle. If a situation was in line with what I wanted personally, I focused all my energies on that one point. While I was dealing with that one point or person or situation, I dealt with it or her or him completely, to the exclusion of everything else. If, on the other hand, it wasn't what I wanted, I simply rejected it, without wasting time, emotion, or energy.

This was before the age of computers, but the insight was based on the same principles. For you must computerize your mind and your memory. You must store up information about past failures and successes so you can call up that information and use it when you're making decisions. You must learn, in the old phrase, that the stove is hot without putting your hands on it every time.

Another lesson, often violated by managers who say they manage by delegating tasks, is that you have to constantly review and renew your commitments, to your employees, your wife, or anyone else. You can't take anything for granted. You have to check and double-check yourself and others.

I violated that rule in my first days in business. I'd assign people jobs and tell them to get back in touch with me in thirty days or so, only to discover when I called them in that nothing had been done. Being very young and inexperienced in business, I oftentimes dismissed them, only to discover that their replacements were worse. I then went back to the first principle I learned at Supreme: to delegate freely and check on the task every day.

From these early experiences at Supreme and, later, in my own business, I concluded that the two most important questions about every decision are, one, will this help me and, two, will this get me in any trouble? Of the two questions, the latter is the most important.

There was another lesson that has served me well, and that is that history, money, and all the forces of the universe are on the side of the man or woman who sets a goal and works night and day to achieve it. That person may not win today. He may not win what he wants to win—which may not be, in the long sight of history, what he or she needs to win—but if he continues to work and will, he can't be denied.

In addition to concrete lessons, I was exposed to "live" cases that forced me to draw my own conclusions. I learned, for example, that circumstances, people, and even the temperature can alter cases and that a rule that produces a stunning success on Monday will wreak havoc if applied rigidly on Tuesday.

This means that business, for all its reliance on business machines and numbers, is an art, not a science. It means also that business schools, even the Harvard Business School on whose advisory board I sit, have limits. For the most important thing an executive needs to know can't be taught.

An interesting case in point revolved around a Memphis manager who was withholding company money because of dissatisfaction with his commission. The executives threatened to fire him or to put him in jail. When the threats failed, they invited him to Chicago. The executives and the manager went into the board room looking grim and angry, and came out laughing.

I said to Pace, "How can this be? I mean, this man was withholding money from the company and showing disrespect to you and the officers."

Pace said it was simple. "The man brought the money with him and we negotiated a settlement that was not as much as the manager wanted but was slightly more than we wanted to give. We came to a meeting of the minds and there was no longer any reason to hold a grudge."

In my youth—and my ignorance—I challenged the settlement, saying that the man should have been punished. Pace smiled and said, "If you want to succeed in business, young man, you've got to learn how to work with people that you don't like. And you've got to learn how to compromise. After you compromise, you have to forget the past and go on to the future. For in business, you have no permanent enemies or permanent friends—only permanent interests."

All this was fascinating, and I drifted further and further away from my educational goals. I kept telling myself that I would go back at some point and finish my college studies. But as I moved up the ladder, I became more and more involved in company affairs.

I attended company conventions and business conferences. I even went out into the field and sold insurance to get a better understanding of the industry. Supreme by now was my whole life, and I could hardly wait to get to the Thirty-fifth and South Parkway office in the morning.

Part of Supreme's fascination was that it was a world that contained everything and reached out to everything. All roads in Black Chicago led to Supreme. All of the gossip, all of the power plays and sexual moves and social maneuvers came, sooner or later, to the crossroads at Thirty-fifth and

South Parkway. It can be said with only slight exaggeration that practically every major event in Black Chicago between 1936 and 1942 was planned, organized, or financed by people who orbited around the Supreme sun.

It was not at all unusual therefore for Supreme to play a major role in the *Lee* v. *Hansberry* suit which doomed restrictive covenants and opened up the neighborhoods around the University of Chicago for occupancy by Blacks. It was common in this period for owners to attach racially restrictive convenants to deeds, thereby barring Black occupancy or sale. Supreme and Carl Hansberry, the father of playwright Lorraine Hansberry (*A Raisin in the Sun*), challenged the covenants which covered about three-fourths of all residential property in the city. General counsel Earl B. Dickerson argued the case before the Supreme Court, which handed down a ruling that made it prohibitively expensive to enforce covenants.

Supreme and Dickerson also played major roles in the social earthquake that changed the political identity of Black America. From Emancipation to the Great Depression, Blacks were major supporters of the Republican Party, which was identified with the popular policies of Emancipation and Reconstruction.

"The Republican Party is the ship," Frederick Douglass reportedly said. "All else is the sea."

But in politics and economics, ships and seas and epigrams are relative and depend on whether you can swim, and the size and color of your life raft. Franklin D. Roosevelt and his wife, Eleanor, and the CCC, WPA, and NYA changed the ratio of forces.

If there was any doubt on this score, it was swept away by the stunning 1934 defeat of Republican hero Oscar DePriest by the relatively unknown Arthur Mitchell, the first Black Democratic congressman. Two years later, in the presidential election of 1936, tens of thousands of Black voters, including my mother, leaped from the leaking Republican ship and discovered that the Democrat water was fine. This gave satisfaction to many people, most notably Earl Dickerson, who decided that the time was ripe to challenge the country's most powerful Black political machine, which was based in Chicago's famous Second Ward.

Dickerson was one of those rare human beings who come into this world with fully developed political and business instincts. A forerunner of change and a harbinger of change, he had been a Democrat since the late twenties. He championed a political program that anticipated Harold Washington and the major Black political leaders of the seventies and eighties.

This brought him into conflict with Mayor Edward J. Kelly and William L. Dawson, the Republican alderman of the Second Ward. And it was Dawson that Dickerson challenged in the historic 1939 aldermanic campaign that changed the political orientation of Black Chicago.

Politics and economics, like love and sex, like heat and light, are closely connected. This became clear to me when Pace told me that Dickerson was going to challenge the Republican machine and that the company wanted me to write publicity and to help him in any way I could. Pace didn't say it, but I was, in effect, assigned to Dickerson as a part of my duties as an employee of Supreme.

They play for keeps in Chicago politics, which has never been a place for the timid or the faint of heart. The aldermanic campaign was short, bitter, and filled with libelous references to the inadequacies of the training, honesty, and birth of the contending parties—and I loved every minute of it.

Dickerson, like Pace, was a master of mentoring. Like Pace, he surrounded himself with talented young men and women. Among his aides in those years were labor leader Joe Jefferson and Balm Lavelle, who later became a newspaper publisher. Joe was one of the leaders of the famous Don't Buy Where You Can't Work Movement. This movement, which was started by A. C. McNeal and Joseph Bibb, organized economic boycotts that were similar to Jesse

Jackson's economic withdrawal campaigns of the seventies and eighties.

There were other talented men and women in the Dickerson camp, including two future lawyers, Elmer Henderson and Jesse Mann, and a future judge, William Sylvester White.

Working with and around Dickerson and his team stretched my mind and my vision. For three or four months, I lived and breathed politics, rising at dawn and working until the early hours of the morning, doing research for speeches, writing articles for local papers and our ward newspaper.

I learned during this campaign how to identify and exploit possibilities. I noticed, for example, that whoever saw the candidate last at night received instructions that, in effect, made him the person in charge the next morning. So I started volunteering for night duty. I told the counselor—as we called Dickerson—that I was single and had a lot of time and that I would be glad to drive him around and drop him off at home at night.

I also volunteered to pick him up in the morning, thereby putting myself in the front-running position of receiving both the night and morning instructions. As a result, I became his de facto chief of staff. Based on my recomendations, he hired several persons, notably Odas Nicholson, a bright young woman from Mississippi who went on to law school and became a Chicago judge.

When Dickerson stunned the political world by winning the race for alderman of the Second Ward, he named me—another surprise—to the key post of political secretary. I was only twenty-one, and for a moment I saw myself rising to the top of the political heap and going on to Congress and perhaps higher. But I was quickly disillusioned by one of the most stunning political reversals in Black political history. Dawson, who was defeated in the Republican primary, the defeated Republican candidate, quickly switched parties and allied himself with Democratic Mayor Ed Kelly. Kelly and the

White political machine feared Dickerson and distrusted his political independence.

The Democratic Machine then adopted the tactic of calling for unity in the Second Ward and a coalition of the Dawson and Dickerson forces. There was no need, the Machine said, for Blacks to fight. They should instead, the argument continued, unite on a common platform and fight the common enemy—racism, unemployment, and Hooverism.

This was a powerful argument, and Dickerson and Dawson held a unity meeting on March 19, 1939. In November 1939, Kelly named Dawson Second Ward committeeman with the reluctant agreement of Dickerson, who was told that Dawson would confine himself to ward problems and would only deal with the precinct captains.

This was tantamount to saying that the only thing he was going to handle was the money. For precinct workers were the currency of the old politics. They knew everything about everybody in their precincts. They knew where people worked, how much they owed, and whether they were living with their wives or their girlfriends, or both.

Precinct workers were like doctors. They were always on call. To lose your precinct workers was to lose your power. Nobody knew this better than Dawson, who used his precinct workers to destroy Dickerson's political foundations. In 1942, Dawson easily defeated Dickerson in the Democratic primary for Congress and went on to win the general election.

The situation was complicated by the political struggles in the City Council, where Dickerson denounced racism and demanded equal power and affirmative action. It was customary in those days for Black and White aldermen to clear their speeches with the mayor. Not only did Dickerson refuse to clear his speeches with the administration, he publicly denounced the administration. Not only did he denounce the local administration, but he used his position as a member of the first Fair Employment Practices Committee to attack the national administration. President

Roosevelt finally reorganized the whole committee in order to get rid of Dickerson.

Mayor Kelly and his allies counterattacked in a campaign that portrayed Dickerson as a "silk stocking" liberal with little or no interest in street affairs. Dickerson, who survived his critics and lived to the age of ninety-five, went his lonely way and was vindicated by history. He continued to live well and to dress well, but he never forgot the poor and the downtrodden. Perhaps his greatest legacy was that he demonstrated in difficult times that you don't have to stop eating to prove that you are honest.

Dawson went on to Congress and to a long career as a Democratic power broker. It was Dawson and the Black wards he controlled—not, as national media say, White politicians—who ensured the election and continued reelection of Richard J. Daley. Daley's power was the reflected power of the Black Power of the Dawson wards which repeatedly turned out 90 and even 95 percent of the vote for anyone slated by the Democratic machine.

Dawson's fatal flaw, in Dickerson's view, was that he didn't have the vision to ask for returns commensurate with his contribution. A man's reach, the poet says, should exceed his grasp. Dawson's flaw was that his grasp exceeded his reach. His eyes were focused not on the stars but on the day-to-day troubles of people who needed somebody to get them out of jail or on the welfare rolls or in county hospital.

Dawson had no peer in this arena. He used to tell me, "Dick [that's what he called Dickerson] and I are friends, and I like him. But he doesn't know how to serve the people the way I do. These people aren't going to get the things Dick's talking about for a long time. And while they're waiting, they need me to look after their needs."

Perhaps it can be said in the end that the people needed both Dickerson and Dawson. They needed Dickerson's militancy and courage, but they also needed Dawson's service. I came to respect them both for different reasons, and I remained friendly with both.

Dawson's power, like Daley's, was the power of organization and detail. Unlike Dickerson, he shunned the platform and the spotlight and concentrated on the nuts and bolts of the old politics, precinct workers. He was, like Daley, like all good politicians of the old school, a past master of the leveraged favor—the favor granted with the understanding that it would be remembered and, at some point, called in for repayment.

In a world where people had to fill out long and complicated forms to get assistance, in a world where they had to meet means tests and provide birth certificates and other documents, Dawson satisfied needs—for a price.

Every Saturday morning for almost a generation, he'd fly in from Washington and take off his wooden leg—he'd lost a leg in World War I—and prop it up on a box in his office in a storefront on Thirty-fifth Street. Anybody—drunks, prostitutes, gamblers, preachers—could walk in that office and ask for help. And Dawson would help them—if they would vote for him or the men and women he told them to vote for.

There were, of course, limits to Dawson's power and largess, particularly for middle- and upper-income Blacks with new and different problems. But Dawson always played his cards close to the vest, and he'd never tell you he couldn't solve a problem.

"Don't worry," he'd say. "I'm working on it." Then he would send you out of the door with his signature statement.

"I can't tell you who I talked to, and I can't tell you what they said, but don't worry."

During this period, a well-to-do friend of the congressman got into trouble with the government. He was, more than anything else, a victim of circumstances, and he asked the congressman to intercede on his behalf. He told me later that he was "encouraged" by his talk with Dawson.

"What did he say?" I asked.

"He said, 'I went to Washington regarding the matter

we discussed. I can't tell you who I talked to, and I can't tell you what they said, but don't worry.' "

The next thing I saw was a photograph of my friend in handcuffs on his way to jail.

That was Dawson's way. He'd never tell you he couldn't help you. He'd always say he was working on it.

I went to his office to get a former employee a job as a secretary at the Chicago Board of Education. He picked up a three-by-five card and said, "What's the person's name and what position do they want?" He wrote the information on the card and put it in his drawer, saying, "I'll see what I can do."

I returned three weeks later with the same request and Dawson said:

"Oh, yes, Johnson—I remember that. I don't know why those SOBs haven't done anything."

Out came the famous card.

"Give me that name again."

I waited another month and went back. The congressman was talking to people in the lobby and told me to go in and sit down.

The chair was next to his desk, and the drawer was open. I looked in the drawer and saw my cards in a dusty corner where they had undoubtedly rested since my last visit.

Whatever his limitations, Dawson created the foundations of a Black political machine that provided a springboard for Blacks who were more militant. One of the most sophisticated graduates of the Dawson school was Harold Washington, who smashed the machine and transformed it.

The rise to power of Dawson and other Democratic leaders coincided with the revival of the economy and the growth of war industries. After a flurry of sit-ins, demonstrations, and marches, the economic situation gradually improved, and happy days began to return to the South Sides of America.

# 12

## *Wedding in Selma*

**B**Y the end of the thirties, I was making enough money—fifty dollars a week from Supreme Liberty and another fifty dollars from my political secretary's post—to correct the blank spaces in my relations with members of the opposite sex.

In 1940, I bought my first car, a light brown 1940 Chevrolet. No purchase since—neither my first Cadillac nor my first Rolls-Royce nor the Lake Shore condominium—has given me more undiluted physical pleasure.

In the same year, I met a pretty young woman who later became my wife. Her name was Eunice Walker, and she was a Talladega College student vacationing in Chicago.

We met by accident one night at a dance at Bacon's Casino at Forty-ninth Street and Wabash. I went to the dance with another young woman, and she went to the dance with another young man. We were introduced by mutual friends, and sparks began to fly. After graduating from Talladega, she got a master's degree in social work from Chicago's Loyola University.

I found out later that she was the daughter of one of the first Black families of the South. Her father, Nathaniel D. Walker, was a physician in Selma, Alabama. Her maternal grandfather, Dr. William H. McAlpine, was one of the founders of Selma University and the National Baptist Convention.

I was not, to put it mildly, one of the great catches of 1940. People used to tell Eunice that she was wasting her time keeping company with a young man of doubtful background who was not among the young Black professionals who were most likely to succeed.

What impressed me about Eunice in comparison with the other young women I had known is that our relationship was not just a romantic fling—it was also a meeting of the minds on what was going on in the world. She was a good listener, sympathetic to my ambitions. She made me feel that maybe I would be somebody one day.

After dating for a year, we were married in Selma, Alabama, on June 21, 1941, by Dr. D. V. Jemison, president of the powerful National Baptist Convention.

Shortly before the wedding, I bought my second car, a red Studebaker. Eunice took the train to Selma, and I drove down with her best friend, Marie Daugherty, who carried the wedding gown. A trip through the South in those days for a Black man with a red car and Illinois license plates was a daring experience, but fate was with us and we made it to Selma for the fashionable wedding at the Tabernacle Baptist Church. My wife's brother, William M. Walker, who later received a medical degree, was my best man.

There was not enough money for a traditional trip. We honeymooned by driving back to Chicago, first stopping for a few days at the home of a friend, Menelick Jackson, in Atlanta.

We came back to Chicago and lived for several weeks at the Southway Hotel at Sixtieth and South Parkway. We then moved to a three-room apartment at 6526 St. Lawrence.

Forty-three years later, when our daughter, Linda, married André Rice, we gave her a wedding that was reported to be one of the most elegant—and one of the most expensive—in Chicago social history. Newspaper reporters said it cost more than $500,000, but I'm the only person who knows for sure—and I'm not saying.

Some people criticized me for spending so much money, but I remembered the poor days of 1941, and I said to myself, "What the hell, I've got the money, she's my only daughter, and Eunice and I paid our dues driving from Alabama to Illinois on the 1941 honeymoon we never had."

# *Words*_____

# 13

## Passing and Rumors of Passing

WHEN Eunice and I returned to Chicago, the stage had already been set for bombs that would explode, one after another, in Pearl Harbor, the London Blitz, and finally Nagasaki and Hiroshima.

The new world of Black and White America and the climate that prepared the ground for *Negro Digest* and *Ebony* were contained in these events. The end of European domination of the world, the rise of Afro-Asia, *Brown* v. *Board of Education*, Black mayors in Chicago and Atlanta: All these events and personalities were written in embryo in the flames and destruction and blood of World War II.

If this was not clearly seen, it was clearly felt by Black Americans, who cast disapproving eyes on preparations for yet another war to make the world safe for a democracy that was not safe on South Parkway.

I knew little or nothing about the political maneuvering that produced the first Black general and the first Black Air

Force pilots, but I saw and felt the rising expectations of Black Chicagoans, who raised big questions about the Jim Crow National Defense Program and the Jim Crow Draft.

I registered for the Jim Crow Draft at a draft board on Fifty-fifth Street, about a block from my home. The board held a lottery of the 4,000 registrants and I was 3,990 something. This meant that I wasn't going to be called right away. Some of my friends said that we'd only be called up for one year, but I didn't believe them. I believed from the beginning that it was going to be a long and bloody war, and that a lot of things and people were going to die in the process.

It was Pearl Harbor—I heard the news when I came out of Good Shepherd Church that Sunday—and the heroism of Black messman Dorie Miller that brought these vague fears and expectations together.

Nothing would ever be the same again after this Sunday, not for Blacks, not for Whites, not for Supreme or John H. Johnson, not for anyone.

And on the morning after, when there were wild rumors that Japanese bombers were approaching Chicago, there were calls for unity and a moratorium on internal conflicts over racial inequalities.

But the traditional appeal to "our Negroes" didn't work in 1941. There was a new and rising level of Black consciousness. And almost all Blacks, even more or less conservative Blacks like William Dawson, supported the Double-V campaign of the Black press, which called for victory against racism abroad and victory against racism in America. This feeling—and I have to be honest, I shared it—was fueled by the Jim Crow Draft and discrimination in defense industries.

And so in 1942—the year I was born for the fourth time—there was tumult and tension everywhere. Even at Supreme, where disgruntled employees demanded labor reforms and mounted a noisy protest campaign.

If, as they say, God and history work in mysterious ways, there is perhaps no stranger example than this event, which led to my first magazine and my first million. For to almost everybody's surprise, the employees made President Pace the scapegoat of their frustrations.

And to understand what happened next, you must have some understanding of the painful question of "passing," the acts of light-skinned Blacks who temporarily or permanently accept the social, economic, and political privileges of a White identity. Some White Blacks "pass" by going along with Whites who assume that they are White. Others actively promote the idea of identification with White America.

The whole idea of race is crazy, and the concept of passing carries that irrationality to the highest degree. There are Whites who are darker than some blond and blue-eyed Blacks, and there are Blacks who are whiter than the whitest Whites. Since slavery, armies of light-skinned Blacks have crossed over into the White race. One of the most explosive underground facts of race relations is that it's impossible to tell on inspection alone whether a particular White is a "real" White or a descendant of the millions of Whites with African ancestors.

Passing and rumors of passing were common in the thirties and forties. Most Blacks generally looked the other way, especially when Blacks used their light skin to get jobs downtown at Marshall Field's and other stores. Most of the people in my circle knew White Blacks who'd married Whites or were living on the North Side with White companions. When we met a Black who was passing, we merely winked and smiled.

What did all this have to do with Harry Pace?

Well, Pace was so light that you'd never believe he was Black unless he told you. His whole family, in fact, was light-skinned, and there were rumors, never substantiated, that his children were passing for White. Pace himself had recently opened a law office in downtown Chicago, and he'd recently moved to the White suburb of River Forest.

I told my friends that he was simply taking advantage

of new opportunities to advance the cause of his family. But the rumors spread and were broadcast by disgruntled employees, who concocted a plan to embarrass the president and the company. The plan was simple: They were going to follow Pace home and demonstrate on his lawn for the edification of his White neighbors.

I opposed the plan. I thought, then and now, that the passing story had been exaggerated or misunderstood. And I went to Pace and told him what people were saying and what they intended to do. Pace didn't deny the reports. He thanked me, got his hat, and went out the back door, leaving his car in front as a subterfuge.

From that day until his death a year later, he was a changed man, more cautious, more withdrawn, more secretive. He took taxis and buses to different commuter stations, and he stopped carrying home his usual armful of Black newspapers and periodicals.

# 14

## Negro Digest:
## *How I Made*
## *Millions With*
## *a $500 Loan*

AFTER outmaneuvering the demonstrators, Harry Pace gave me an assignment that changed my life. He said he was getting old—the rumormongers said he was scared to take Black newspapers home—and that he wanted me to read magazines and newspapers and prepare a digest of what was happening in the Black world.

We met at least once a week, usually on Monday, and I gave him a briefing so he could talk intelligently about race relations to people who came to his office.

It would have been possible in contemporary America—largely because of the Civil Rights Movement and *Negro Digest* and *Jet* and *Ebony*—for him to get some of this information in White media, but in that period there was an almost total White-out on positive Black news in White-oriented media.

There was an unwritten rule in the South in this period that a Black's picture could not appear in the press unless

in connection with a crime. There was no consistent coverage of the human dimensions of Black Americans in northern newspapers and magazines. It's hard to make people
realize this, but Blacks didn't get married on the society
pages of major American dailies until the late sixties.

The items I gathered for Pace from the Negro press and
isolated reports in the White press made me one of the most
knowledgeable persons in Black Chicago. I started telling
my friends about the amazing things I'd read. And I was
usually the center of attention at social gatherings where,
like some traveling circuit rider, I gave a digest of Negro
news or a Negro digest. The response was almost always the
same: "Where can I find that article?" Some people said
they would pay me if I would let them know where this or
that article appeared.

The next step was so obvious that I'm ashamed to say
that I didn't immediately recognize it. I'd been riding the
social circuit for several weeks, reciting my stories of Black
achievement and aspiration, before it occurred to me that I
was looking at a black gold mine. And that I could be
successful on a limited scale with a Negro digest which would
pass on to the public the material I'd been digesting for Pace.

The problem here was not my density but a general
climate of doubt surrounding Black publications. Most people had seen *Reader's Digest* and *Time*, but nobody had seen
a successful Black commercial magazine. And nobody was
willing to risk a penny on a twenty-four-year-old insurance
worker and what people told him at cocktail parties.

That's been the story of my life. At every critical turning point in my life, people, Black and White, always told
me no at first. And I almost always turned the nos into yeses.

For almost two months, week after week, I went from
office to office in Black Chicago and was told no and hell no.
I remember going to New York to get the blessings of Roy
Wilkins, the editor of the most successful Black magazine,
*The Crisis*, the noncommercial house organ of the NAACP.

Roy listened to my story and said, "Save your money,

young man. Save your energy. Save yourself a lot of disappointment." Roy went on to become NAACP executive director, and one of the sweet moments of my life was when he called me and said, "Johnny, you know, I think I gave you some bad advice." He returned to the same theme in his autobiography, *Standing Fast.*

"One day in the early forties," he wrote, "a bright and eager young man named John Johnson came to the office to talk to me about an idea he had for starting a new magazine, a pocket-sized publication that would summarize newspaper and magazine articles about Negro life. I knew the almost continuous financial difficulties *The Crisis* had, and I told him that in my opinion the time was not right to venture into the field. Fortunately, Johnson ignored me...."

I got bad advice from a lot of people who also gave themselves bad advice. There are at least two people who would be multimillionaires today if they had invested the $1,000 I was asking forty-seven years ago. I will forever be grateful to them. If they'd invested back then, I wouldn't be the sole owner of Johnson Publishing Company today.

When I had exhausted every avenue of support, I returned to Johnson Rule No. 1—What can you do by yourself with what you have to get what you want?—and I made some interesting discoveries. As the low man in the Supreme power structure, I had accumulated some small tasks that I hated. For example, I ran the Speedaumat, an addressing machine which kept the names and addresses of the twenty thousand people who paid their insurance premiums quarterly, semiannually, or annually.

I looked at the mailing list. I looked at the Speedaumat. And an idea—wild, unbelievable, but definitely possible— grew in my mind. Why not send a letter to every person on the list, asking for a two-dollar prepaid subscription to a new Black magazine? If I got a 30 percent response ($12,000) or even a 15 percent response ($6,000), I would have the money to publish the first issue of the magazine. I discussed the idea with Pace, who said I could use the names and the machine.

"Since you are running the machine anyway," he said, "there's no reason why you can't use it to mail the letters."

There's a lesson in this incident, and I always stress it in my talks to youths. There are so many twists and turns in a life that you never know where a job, however small, will lead you. It's in your best interest, then, to do every task assigned you well, for you never know when these skills can be utilized later.

It's fashionable nowadays for employees to talk about what they call the s——detail, the petty and sometimes menial tasks assigned to low-ranking employees. Well, the s——detail made me a millionaire. Although I resented some of the little things I was doing, one of them—running the Speedaumat machine—was the key to the *Negro Digest* sweepstakes.

I had the twenty thousand names, I knew how to run the machine, and I had permission to use the company's clear stationery. There was only one more hurdle: I needed $500 to buy stamps.

If you've ever been in this situation, you know how I felt. I was so close to victory that I could taste it, and yet I was so far away. Five hundred dollars. That was a lot of money in 1942. Where could I get $500?

I must have been desperate, for I did something that was unheard-of in those days. I went to the First National Bank of Chicago and asked for a $500 loan to start a business. I'm one of First National's premium customers today—I have an open line of credit and the officers call me *Mr.* Johnson—but the assistant to the assistant that I managed to see in 1942 laughed in my face.

"Boy," he said, "we don't make any loans to colored people."

I felt a flash of anger, but the self-help books I'd been reading said don't get mad, get smart. I got smart and looked the assistant to the assistant in the eye and said, "Who in this town will loan money to a colored person?"

"The only place I know," he answered, looking at me

with new interest, "is the Citizens Loan Corporation at Sixty-third and Cottage Grove."

I asked if he knew anyone at Citizens and he gave me a name.

"Can I tell him that you referred me?"

He looked at me now as if seeing me for the first time and said, "Of course."

The man at the loan company said, "Yes, we'll give you a loan but only if you have collateral."

"What do you mean by collateral?" I asked.

He said a house that you can mortgage or new furniture or some tangible asset that you can pledge as a guarantee that you'll repay the loan.

I didn't have a house to mortgage, but my mother had managed with my help to buy some new furniture. I asked her to let me use it as collateral for a $500 loan. For the first time in all the years I'd known her, she frowned and balked. It had taken her a long time to pay for the furniture. She was proud of it. And she didn't intend to lose it. I pleaded and she said, "I'll just have to consult the Lord about this. It's not a decision I can make by myself."

Every day, for almost a week, I'd come home and check with my mother to see if the Lord had said anything, and she'd say, "No, I'm still praying."

I said, "Maybe I'd better pray with you."

For three or four days, we prayed together and cried together. Finally, she said, "I think the Lord wants me to do it." She gave me the paid-up document, and I took it to the guy at the loan company and he issued a check for $500.

I had already drafted the letter—I never doubted for one moment that the Lord would say the word—which was based, like my whole selling campaign for *Negro Digest*, on the most important axiom of salesmanship: *Ask not what you want but what the customer or the potential customer wants.*

This elementary rule is violated daily by neophytes and seasoned salesmen who barge into offices and make sales pitches based on what they need and want. The world doesn't give a tinker's damn about what you need or want. What the world wants to know is what you can do for other people and the world.

Perhaps the biggest violators of this rule are job applicants who tell you how much they need a job and how much it would mean to them. That's the wrong approach. The correct approach is to tell the customer or potential employer what you can do to advance his interest. The job applicant who studies a company and its needs and tells the interviewer what he or she can do for the company is more than halfway home.

The important point is that your sales pitch—to a customer, to a potential employer, to a good-looking woman or a handsome man—should be based not on your self-interest but on their self-interest and on what they want most. Not, mind you, on what they say they want but on what they *really* want.

This rule has served me well over the years. The only way I got to where I am today was by persuading thousands of Blacks and Whites, some of whom were very prejudiced, that the only way they could get what they wanted was by helping me get what I wanted.

This, then, was the situation.

I was writing a letter to twenty thousand Black Americans in 1942. What did they want? The answer was obvious. They wanted what everybody else wanted. They wanted recognition, the good life, and, in Aretha Franklin's word, r-e-s-p-e-c-t.

*Respect.*

For more than one hundred years, that had been the cry of the Black soul. One hundred years of "boy" and "girl" and "George" and "Mary" and "nigger" had created an almost inexhaustible thirst for recognition and respect.

In 1942, Black men and women were struggling all over America for the right to be called "Mr." and "Mrs." In that year, we couldn't try on hats in department stores in Baltimore, and we couldn't try on shoes and dresses in Atlanta. We couldn't live in hotels in downtown Chicago then, and the only public place a Black could get a meal in the downtown section of the nation's capital was the railroad station.

It was in this world that *Negro Digest* was conceived. It was a world where the primary need, almost as demanding as oxygen, was recognition and respect.

I wanted the letter to say to Blacks that I intended to put out a magazine that would increase their respect and add to their knowledge and understanding. I still remember every word and comma of the letter I wrote:

> Dear Mr. Brown:
>
> A good friend of yours told me about you.
>
> He told me that you are a person who likes to keep abreast of local and national events.
>
> He said you are the kind of person who will be interested in a magazine that will help you become more knowledgeable about your own people and about what they are doing to win greater recognition for you and other members of our race. Because of your position in the community and the recommendation I received, I would like to offer you a reduced rate on the magazine *Negro Digest*, which will be published in the next thirty days. Magazine subscriptions will sell for $3.00 a year, but in view of the recommendation we are offering a subscription to you for $2.00, if you send your check or money order by September 30.

Before sending this letter, I took the precaution of securing my first office and mailing address. One of my supervisors, Earl Dickerson, had a private law office and a law library in a private section of the Supreme building. I asked if I could use a corner of the law library, which contained old books and was seldom used. He said okay, and I moved a desk into the corner of the office, which was on the second floor of the Supreme building but had another entrance and another address, 3507 South Parkway.

This was the first address of what was then called Negro Digest Publishing Company. From June to November, I worked downstairs in the insurance company in the day and climbed the stairs at night to work on the magazine. One day in the summer of 1942 a man came and painted letters on the frosty glass door—Negro Digest Publishing Company—and every letter was music to my soul.

It was from this office that I sent letters to twenty thousand persons asking for prepublication subscriptions. Three thousand persons—an unusually high percentage—responded, sending $6,000.

While all this was going on, I drafted and sent out letters asking for the right to publish certain stories and articles that had appeared in Black newspapers and White magazines and periodicals. My wife, who was a social worker by day, helped at night, stuffing envelopes and assisting in editorial and circulation tasks. So did Jay Jackson, a brilliant artist and cartoonist who worked for the *Chicago Defender*, and Ben Burns, a White free-lance writer I'd met when we both worked on the Earl Dickerson campaign.

By October, there was only one remaining hurdle: finding a printing press and persuading the owner of the press to extend credit until the magazines were printed and sold. Here, once again, Supreme came to the rescue. One of my duties at Supreme was running the multilith machine and dealing with Progress Printing Company, which printed material for the insurance company. When I went to the printer's office and told him that "we" were thinking about publishing a magazine, he assumed that I was talking about the insurance company, when I was really talking about myself. Since he assumed that the magazine was either owned or backed by the insurance company, he started working without worrying about how I was going to pay him.

By these methods and others, I maneuvered, negotiated, pleaded, begged, screamed, shouted, cursed, prayed my way to the watershed day of Sunday, November 1, 1942.

The following events occurred on that day:

• A small force of U.S. Marines crossed the Mataniko

River on the western frontier of Guadalcanal and attacked the Japanese, who were reported to be retreating slowly.

• At Stalingrad, Russian forces repulsed attacks by the Nazis.

• The U.S. government took over all short-wave broadcast stations.

• Senator Elbert D. Thomas, Democrat, Utah, spoke at a New York rally commemorating the twenty-fifth anniversary of the Balfour Declaration and called for the immediate establishment of a Jewish national home in Palestine.

• The Chicago Bears football team defeated Detroit by a score of 16 to 0.

• A new magazine, *Negro Digest,* "a magazine of Negro comment," was published officially for the first time.

All of these events, with the exception of the debut of *Negro Digest,* were noted by the White press. *Negro Digest* came into the world unheralded and unnoticed, except by the publisher, who was born again that day.

Before the week was out, there were scattered comments in the Black press. On November 7, the *Pittsburgh Courier* printed a story on the new magazine, under the heading "New Negro Digest Answering Demands."

The lead paragraph said: "Should Negroes care who wins the war? Is the Negro demand for full equality sabotaging the war effort? These questions, along with many other vital ones, are answered in the November issue of Negro Digest...published this week in Chicago." The paper said managing editor John H. Johnson was a native of Arkansas who has been "for the past several years...director of publicity for the Supreme Liberty Life Insurance Company."

When I held the first copy of the magazine in my hand, I had a feeling of relief, exhilaration, and fear. I hadn't realized the true potential of the magazine until that moment, and I was overwhelmed by the idea that the life and death of this sixty-eight-page baby was in my hands.

The two-color cover (red and blue) of the 7½" by 5" magazine carried the title and explanation, "A Magazine of Negro Comment," and a list of the articles and features.

There were contributions by Carl Sandburg, Walter White, John P. Lewis, Marquis W. Childs, Langston Hughes, Rabbi Harry Essrig, and Bishop Bernard Sheil. This was not a bad group of people to hang out with. And the typography and layout emphasized excellence and quality. There was only one name on the masthead, "Managing Editor: John H. Johnson."

Why was this magazine published? What did it intend to do and say? The opening editorial said:

## *Introducing...*

NEGRO DIGEST is published in response to a demand for a magazine to summarize and condense the leading articles and comment on the Negro now current in the press of the nation in ever increasing volume.

The impact of the war and attendant discussion of what we are fighting for has focused new attention on the status of the Negro in America. There is wide spread interest in what the Negro thinks of the war, democracy and the South.

In a single, easy-to-read issue, Negro Digest gives you a complete survey of current Negro life and thought. The editors read hundreds of magazines, newspapers, periodicals, books and reports in order to bring you a choice selection of articles and features each month.

Negro Digest is dedicated to the development of interracial understanding and the promotion of national unity. It stands unqualifiedly for the winning of the war and the integration of all citizens into the democratic process.

NEGRO DIGEST
3507 South Parkway
Chicago, Illinois.

I am enclosing $3.00 for 12 issues of Negro Digest

Name ........................................................

Address .....................................................

City and State ..............................................

Published monthly at 3507 South Parkway, Chicago, Ill., by the Negro Digest Publishing Co.
Subscription Rates: 25 cents a single copy, $3.00 a year, $5.00 two years, life subscription $25.00. In foreign countries $4.00 a year, $6.00 two years.
*Managing Editor:* John H. Johnson
Copyright, 1942, by the Negro Digest Publishing Co

It has been said by people who haven't read either magazine that *Negro Digest* was an exact copy of *Reader's Digest*. There were similarities in the name and format, but there were also striking differences. First of all, *Negro Digest* printed few digests. Most of our articles were complete reproductions of articles that appeared originally in the White and Black press and even scholarly magazines. Second, *Negro Digest* developed several original sections ("The Round Table," "Dixie Drivel") and adopted a harder tone with articles like "Should Negroes Care Who Wins the War?" "Report From Ireland," "Nehru of India," "Devils in Dixie and Naziland," and "A Bishop Looks at Race Bias."

*Reader's Digest* tended to be upbeat, but *Negro Digest* spoke to an audience that was angry, disillusioned, and disappointed. You couldn't digest that world without digesting the frustration and anger.

# 15

## *The Search for a Common American Market*

THE first issue of *Negro Digest* was impressive by almost any standard. But I couldn't enjoy it. I'd produced this miracle with smoke and mirrors. And it was time now for a miracle that couldn't be talked or negotiated into existence: money to pay the printer, who discovered on publication day that he'd made a sizable investment in a new and decidedly unpromising company.

I'd ordered five thousand copies, three thousand of which were reserved for prepaid subscribers. I needed to sell the remaining two thousand copies quickly to pay the printing bill and the cost of shipping three thousand copies.

Forty years later, I explained this dilemma to a brilliant student at the Harvard University Business School. He hung on every word and asked breathlessly, obviously expecting a profound answer, "What did you do then?" He was deflated when I told him, "I looked in the Yellow Pages."

The Yellow Pages directed me to the office of Charles Levy Circulating Company, the biggest magazine distributor in Chicago. I was greeted by Joseph Levy, the brother of the original Charles Levy and the uncle of young Charles Levy, who had inherited the company but was then in the armed services.

I'd rehearsed my appeal, and I rattled it off with perfection, varying the tone, pitch, and emotional level. Joseph Levy listened with a poker face and then said: "Johnson, we don't handle colored books."

Anger wrestled with smartness, and smartness won.

"Is that," I asked innocently, "because you're prejudiced or because colored books don't sell?"

He rose in anger and indignation.

"Johnson, I'm Jewish—I don't believe in prejudice. It's because colored books don't sell."

I told him my magazine was going to sell, and that I would leave my card just in case he changed his mind.

"You can leave it," he said, "but I'm not going to change my mind."

Here, then, was my first major management crisis. How could I change Levy's mind? I could have gone to the NAACP, but that would have taken years of litigation—and I had to sell two thousand magazines quickly or go to jail. I could have gone to Jesse Jackson, but Jesse hadn't been born. So I was on my own. It was up to me to invent an original solution.

This is what I did. I went back to Supreme and asked about thirty of my friends to stop by the Levy outlets on their way home and ask for that exciting new Negro magazine, *Negro Digest*. For almost a week, they visited newsstands, offering money and demanding copies of *Negro Digest*. This was a new and novel civil rights march, and it worked.

Joseph Levy called and said, "I've been getting calls from my dealers. Maybe, Johnson, I'll try a few of those books. About five hundred." I jumped into my car—I was publisher, editor, business manager, circulation manager, and chauffeur—and rushed to his office and persuaded him to take one thousand.

This triumph was tempered by fear. Only a handful of Blacks—my thirty friends—knew the magazines were on the stand. I dipped into my dwindling treasury and gave the thirty friends enough money to buy up all the newsstand copies. This got Levy's attention, and he ordered one thousand additional copies.

Word was circulating on the streets now. If any Black came within a hundred feet of the newsstand, the vendors would call out, "Have you seen the new magazine, *Negro Digest?*" Circulation begat circulation, and I went back to press and printed another five thousand magazines.

Money, which is perhaps the greatest of all civil rights bills, was working now. Levy, who had initially opposed my efforts, now became my biggest booster. He gave me marketing ideas, stressing the importance of distributing flyers at church meetings and social gatherings. He used my placards on his South Side trucks. He said the word that opened the doors of profitable relationships with White distributors in New York, Detroit, and other major cities.

Working together from day to day, Levy and I crossed the artificial barriers that blocked trade and created our own little common market. In the process, we became good friends, and laughed about the problems we had had in our first meeting.

What brought us together and made the Levy organization one of the key ingredients in the early success of *Negro Digest* was the realization, never spoken but clearly felt, that racism was a double-edged sword that cut both ways. It cut deeply into my profits and made it impossible for me to cross the economic equator of race. It also cut deeply into his profits and made it impossible for him and other White distributors to maximize their profits in the inner city. For racial divisions kept White distributors from penetrating into the secret nooks and crannies of the close-knit Black community.

To reach these secret places and the mom-and-pop outlets neglected by major distributors, I used Negro-owned distributors, like Chicago's National News Company, which was owned by two brothers, Carroll and Raymond Ellis. In Atlanta, I used the Yates and Milton Drug Store chain. I worked with Jesse Wright in Philadelphia and Phil Jones in Los Angeles.

I also developed my own network, relying in most places on postal workers whose unique geo-racial knowledge had never been utilized. They knew the city from throwing mail. Many worked at night and were free in the day.

We recruited agents by running ads in Negro newspapers and by distributing leaflets. Most of the men and women who answered the ads didn't have enough money to buy advance copies. So I created a system that made it possible for agents to order and put the money into the special Negro Digest Publishing Company banking accounts that I opened in several cities.

Local distributors could put money into these accounts but couldn't make withdrawals. I checked these accounts almost daily. At intervals, the money was transferred to my main account in Chicago.

Under this system, which was in place for all of the life of *Negro Digest* and much of the life of *Ebony*, we single-handedly created a new stratum of Black news dealers and salesmen, much as we would later create new strata of Black photographers, and advertising, marketing, and circulation specialists.

The South was an entirely different problem, for sheriffs and police chiefs were hostile to all Black media. My approach to this problem was simple and direct. I created a southern network which sold *Negro Digest* and later *Ebony* and *Jet* on buses, streetcars, and even in cottonfields.

Most of these agents used guerrilla tactics, boarding a bus, for example, and working the seats until the next stop. Some, like Thomas Armstrong of Jackson, Mississippi, were beaten and jailed. Nothing, however, stopped them. When we celebrated our fortieth anniversary, we paid a special tribute to the agents of the southern network who did more perhaps than any other American journalists of that era to make the First Amendment real in Dixie.

These and other methods paid off. Within three months, *Negro Digest* was selling in the lucrative New York market. Within six months, the magazine was available on news-stands on the West Coast. Within eight months, we were selling 50,000 copies a month nationally.

Circulation was growing, but I was still running scared. Not knowing from issue to issue how much money I was going to make or lose, I had a sense of budget, a sense of living within my means and of avoiding overhead. For the first year of the operation, I took nothing out and put everything back in.

I am often asked how many issues I published before I made a profit. The answer is simple: If I hadn't made a profit on the first issue, there wouldn't have been a second issue.

The reason I succeeded was that I didn't know that it was impossible to succeed. If I'd known then what MBAs know now, I would have realized that I couldn't start a business that way.

For me, then, ignorance was a blessing. Since I didn't know that it was impossible to do what I wanted to do, I did it.

When *Negro Digest* was published, I didn't have a single full-time employee. I was still employed full-time at Supreme, and I was scared to break that tie because I didn't know how long the *Negro Digest* boom would last. That was part of my insecurity. It was part of my usual practice of running scared.

I finally left Supreme in July 1943, but I didn't make a clean break. I asked for and was given a leave of absence. From 1943 until I bought controlling interest in Supreme, a period of some twenty years, I was still on leave of absence.

Shortly after I left Supreme, I hired my first full-time employee, a secretary. There was no room for her desk in my tiny office, and she had to sit at a desk in the hall. At first, as I later told the War Production Board, "the magazine was a one-man operation. My wife and I did all the work. We gathered the material and edited the magazine. I wrapped the magazines myself, and I hauled them to the post office."

The secretary and I were the only full-time employees until 1944. I disguised this fact by listing free-lancer Ben Burns and my relatives on the masthead. One of the early mastheads listed Burns as associate editor and E. M. Walker and G. J. Williams as assistants. E. M. Walker was my wife's maiden name, and G. J. Williams was my mother.

# 16

## The President's Wife Turns the Tide

WITHIN six months, we were selling more magazines than anyone had thought possible. But we
were stuck at a first-stage plateau of 50,000. And
magazine circulation, especially in the critical first stage, is
like the moon: It either increases or decreases.

What we needed at this crossroads was a major story or
gimmick to generate publicity and sales and push us over
the next barrier.

I studied the situation and decided that the most promising area of development was one of our regular features,
"If I Were a Negro." We were getting a lot of unsolicited
advice in this period from Whites, some well-meaning,
some not so well-meaning. I decided to take advantage of
this trend by asking Whites to put themselves in our shoes
and answer some difficult questions:

Would they, for example, want their children to wait
another generation for quality education? (That was forty-

seven years ago, and the question, God help us, is still relevant.)

Would they want their sons and fathers and brothers to fight Nazi racism in a segregated army?

We posed these and other questions to major figures like Pearl Buck, Orson Welles, and Edward G. Robinson. We offered a modest honorarium of fifteen dollars, thinking, of course, that most of the celebrities would refuse the money or sign it over to charity.

I remember waiting with interest to see if multimillionaire Marshall Field would cash his fifteen-dollar check. He cashed it—so did most of our rich and famous contributors. Since that time, I've noticed that rich people seldom turn down payments and honoraria. One of the reasons rich people are rich is that they accept and cash all contributions, no matter how small.

Marshall Field, Pearl Buck, and other contributors had attracted some attention, but we needed a bigger attraction. Someone, for example, like Eleanor Roosevelt, who was the wife of the president of the United States and who was denounced somewhere almost every day for talking to Blacks or meeting with Blacks or eating with Blacks.

To get the wife of the president of the United States to write an exclusive article on anything would be a major story for any magazine. But it would be a real coup for a Black magazine to get her to tell what she would do if she were Black.

The idea was pure gold—no doubt about it. But how was I going to get to the wife of the president of the United States? I sat down and thought about it and decided that Mother, as usual, was right. If you want to say something to somebody, write a letter.

I wrote Mrs. Roosevelt and received a prompt reply, saying that she would like to write the article but that she simply didn't have the time. Since she didn't say no, I wrote her again three weeks later. She said she still didn't have the time.

Soon afterward, I read that she was coming to Chicago to speak at the Stevens Hotel (which is now the Chicago Hilton). On the day of her scheduled arrival, I sent a telegram—in those days telegrams arrived on time—and asked if she would have a few minutes to dictate the article. I received almost immediately in return a manuscript "written expressly for *Negro Digest.*"

People are always telling me that I'm lucky, but luck is a word we use for an order that is not understood. I made some of my luck. I made it by working hard and trusting the logic of events, which always favor the bold and the active and the prepared.

When Eleanor Roosevelt visited our office for the first time, she told us that when my telegram arrived, she had just finished dictating her column, "My Day." She had hardly finished reading the telegram when a sudden change in her schedule made it possible for her to dictate the article. Was that luck or was it, as usual, the wages of a persistence that refuses to take no for an answer?

Whatever it was, the result—an October 1943 cover story by the wife of the president of the United States— marked a major turning point in the fortunes of *Negro Digest.* The president's wife said in the article that if she were a Negro, she would have great bitterness *and* great patience.

Southern White newspapers picked up the part about the great patience. Black newspapers and northern White newspapers picked up the part about great bitterness. And our circulation jumped, almost overnight, from 50,000 to 100,000. After that, we never looked back.

I was making so much money that I didn't know what to do with it.

The magazine sold for twenty-five cents on the newsstands. I got about fifteen cents of that, which meant that I made $15,000, give or take a few dollars, from every 100,000 copies sold.

No matter how hard I tried I could only spend $6,000 a month, and the money was piling up. And that, believe it or not, was a problem. For the stringent excise tax laws of the time said that if you started with nothing, that's what you could keep—nothing.

I hired a brilliant young Black CPA, Charles A. Beckett, who introduced me to the mysteries of high finance. The solution to my problem, he said, was to invest in properties that would lose money, thereby creating holes that would make it possible for me to keep some money. That sounds crazy, but it worked. It was also the beginning of a long and warm relationship with Beckett, who was my accountant until he retired forty-five years later.

When the company went over the $100-million-a-year mark, the officer of a major bank told me that I was too big for "a small Black CPA" and that I needed one of the "Big 8" White accounting firms. I cursed him out and told him that if Beckett was big enough for the small Johnson Publishing Company, he was big enough for the big Johnson Publishing Company.

It was at this point that I realized for the first time the power and witchery of money, which is, with the possible exception of sex, the most fascinating subject in the world. Like sex, money inhabits a realm of magic and sorcery that transcends machines and numbers. Money can be counted, measured, weighed, but it can't be commanded or predicted.

Always, everywhere, it overflows the experience, giving you more or less than you expected. There's no balance in the life of money. You either have too much or too little. When you don't have it, you run like the devil to get it. And when you have it, you run like the devil to keep it.

Based on Beckett's advice, I plowed most of the money back into the business. In late 1943, I bought my first building, paying Carroll and Raymond Ellis of the National News Company $4,000 for a building at 5619 South State Street.

\*     \*     \*

The first headquarters of Johnson Publishing Company was a typical Chicago storefront with a big plate-glass window facing the sidewalk. My desk was up front inside the plate-glass window next to the bookkeeping department. That made me happy, for I always wanted to be close to the money—and I still am.

I bought some used furniture and moved into the new office in November, which was now my lucky month. In the weeks that followed, I started assembling a permanent staff. Among the first employees were Mildred Clark, Lavada McGhee, Willie Miles Burns, and Prince Winkfield, all of whom worked for me until they died or retired. As the only male executive in a company deemed essential to the war effort, I received a deferment.

In organizing the staff, I reached out to everybody, for I knew nothing about magazine publishing and editing. How, for example, do you organize a circulation department or an advertising department? What forms do you need? What is ABC (Audit Bureau of Circulation)? And what is a rate card?

I knew nothing about these matters. But I'm a quick study, and I learned fast—by asking and listening. I've found that people, Black and White, will tell you everything you need to know if you confess your ignorance and approach them in the right spirit.

I got a lot of help from friends on the staff of the Catholic magazine *Extension*. I also received advice and assistance from a brilliant young White couple, Jim and M. J. Clement, who read about the new magazine and volunteered their services. Jim was a young lawyer and his first wife, M. J., who worked for *Esquire*, wrote many of our first direct-mail appeals.

When all else failed, I looked in the phone book and called an expert. Since I had nothing to lose, I always started at the top. I received valuable advice from Henry Luce of *Time-Life* and Gardner Cowles of *Look*.

It was hard to get through to Luce, but I finally convinced his secretary that the only thing I wanted was advice. I've found that you can get through to anybody if you're persistent enough and if you can convince secretaries that you want neither money nor employment.

I used a simple approach that almost always worked. I simply told the secretary or aide that I was the president—I stressed the word *president*—of my company.

"It is," I said, "a small company but I *am* the president, and I want to talk to your president. I'm making this request—from one president to another. If the president of the smallest country in the world comes to Washington, our president, as a matter of public policy and protocol, will see him. So it seems to me that your president, in the American tradition, will see me for a few minutes if you pass this request on and tell him that I don't want a donation or a job."

I used that on Henry Luce's secretary, and I got in to see him. He received me in a big office on one of the upper floors of the old *Time-Life* Building. He was uptight at first, not knowing what to expect and how to react. But he warmed up quickly when I told him what I was trying to do and that I just wanted exposure to *Time-Life* staffers who could tell me whether I was moving in the right direction. He pushed buttons, and editors and business experts came from everywhere. With Luce's blessing, I talked to experts in the New York office and returned to Chicago for discussions with his circulation and promotion departments.

I had a similar experience with Gardner Cowles of *Look*. After I spoke to him in New York, he arranged for me to go to Des Moines, Iowa, to meet with the managers of the magazine's circulation department.

I was secure enough by now to splurge. I made some long-overdue personal investments, buying with a $9,000 down payment my first home, a three-story apartment building at 6018 St. Lawrence.

Eunice and I moved into the first-floor apartment, and

my mother and stepfather lived on the second floor. We rented out the third floor.

This was a sound, even conservative, investment. But children, wise men, and fools know that to truly appreciate money it's necessary, from time to time, to spend it on candy or fine wine or love. So I went out and bought three cars—a Buick for my mother, a Buick for my mother-in-law, and a Cadillac for me.

My mother had taken a lot of flak from friends and neighbors. It gave her great joy to go out into the streets and say, "Look! Look what my boy has done for me."

I later did something I'd dreamed of for years: I retired my mother and told her that she'd never have to work again. From that day in 1943 until she died in 1977, a period of thirty-four years, she had a car, chauffeur, and maid, and money and leisure to travel anywhere in the world.

The day I told her that I was putting her on my personal payroll we both broke down in tears. And the feeling of release I had on that day, the feeling of accomplishment—I don't think I've ever had such a feeling, before or since. It was one of those memorable moments when words fail you. I read somewhere that nothing is quite as eloquent as silence. This was a time of silence and tears.

After we moved to the new apartment, I went to a party for Eddie ("Rochester") Anderson, who was in town with Jack Benny. This was one of the rare interracial parties of the time, and I met Robert Wachsman, the publicity agent for Jack Benny and Rochester. Wachsman was an up-front guy with a sense of humor, and we quickly moved from cocktail party chitchat to shared hopes and dreams. I told him that I'd just moved into a new apartment and that I was having a hard time finding an interior decorator.

"You won't believe this," he said, shaking his head, "but my sister-in-law, Viola Marshall Wachsman, is an interior decorator. I'll tell her to call you."

Viola Marshall called, and Eunice and I showed her the

apartment and discussed decorating ideas. There was never any doubt after this first discussion that she was the woman for the job. The end result, one of the most tastefully decorated apartments on the North or South Sides, confirmed our judgment.

Viola Marshall was a new phenomenon for us—a well-to-do White woman totally dedicated to racial equality without one iota of racial arrogance. I've only met in my lifetime five or six Whites who were so sure of themselves that they could lift themselves and everybody around them to another realm on the other side of race. Viola Marshall was one of them. I don't think she ever thought about race. And when we were with her, we didn't think about race.

After completing the apartment, she invited us to her Lake Shore Drive apartment for dinner. This was in 1944, and it was almost revolutionary for Blacks to walk into the front door of a Lake Shore Drive apartment as guests. The Black doorman was amazed. The Black maid was flabbergasted. Twenty-three years later, when I saw the scenes of Sidney Poitier and the maid in *Guess Who's Coming to Dinner*, I said out loud, "I've seen this movie before."

When we sat down to dinner in this real-life movie, the maid was very slow in serving the courses. To make sure we got the point, she slammed doors and disappeared into the kitchen for long periods of time. When Viola Marshall asked her what was the problem, she said—and this was undoubtedly the most embarrassing moment of my life—"I don't serve niggers."

"I didn't invite any niggers," Viola Marshall replied. "And if you can't serve my guests, you're fired."

Viola, Eunice, and I served and ate the dinner. She remained a close friend until her death in 1984.

# 17

## *The Secret of My Success*

ALL through 1943 and 1944, as the Allies pressed German and Japanese forces in Europe and Asia, *Negro Digest* grew, setting new records and new standards for a Black magazine. But progress doesn't run in a straight line. There are zigs and zags and ups and downs. And sometimes it's hard to tell the difference between the two.

When there were liquidity crises—I didn't know what the word meant then, but I quickly became the world's greatest expert on solving liquidity crises—I postdated checks and moved money from one bank account to another. Some of this was illegal—but I didn't know it then—and, anyway, the statute of limitations has passed.

Sadly but unavoidably, I parted company with some old friends and associates, telling them that there was no hard feeling but that I was prepared to make almost any sacrifice to ensure the survival of the company.

When we became too big for the printing press at Progress, I moved to Kallis Printing Company, leaving a $14,000 bill behind. I told the skeptical owner that I was going to pay every penny. He didn't believe me, but I did. This, incidentally, is the foundation stone of my philosophy: Never burn your bridges behind you. And leave every job and every situation so you can come back, if you want to or need to.

From time to time in this period, we ran up big bills at printing companies. But in these instances, as in others, money has changed the scale of values. In my early days, executives used to call me and say, "John, I want you to come over here and discuss your bill." A few years later, when we started spending millions of dollars a year, executives would call and say, "*Mr.* Johnson, this is *Harry*. When can I come over to discuss your account?"

We solved these and other problems and moved to the John Maher Company and finally to Hall (now Krueger-Ringier), where we've been one of the biggest magazine accounts for years and where we've created another common market based on mutual respect.

This brings us to the key question of this period.

What was the secret of my success?

Why did I succeed when so many other Black publishers failed?

The answer to that question is simple. I was lucky, the timing was right, and I worked hard.

Victor Hugo said that nothing can stop an idea whose time has come. The time for a Negro magazine, the time for a *Negro Digest* or an *Ebony* or *Jet*, had come and nothing could stop it *if*—and it's a big if—the idea could find a man or a woman who was willing to do anything, or almost anything, to make the time come.

I was the man history selected. It was through me that history proved once again that the greatest victory is always closest to the greatest danger and that the darkness, as the poet said, is light enough.

Can it be done again?

Can you start with $500 and build a $200- or $300-million empire?

I've been asked that question many times. I received a postcard several years ago from a man who said he'd acquired $500—presumably by legal means—and that he wanted to know what to do next. I told him, first, that $500 in 1942 was the equivalent of at least $5,000 today. I told him, secondly, that he'd put the cart before the Rolls-Royce and that what he needed was not money but an idea for a business that meets a need that cannot be satisfied elsewhere. If you don't have that, I told him, a million dollars won't help you. And if you have it, you have all the money you need.

Scores of Americans, Black and White, have made that discovery. I know a man who made a fortune with a chain of all-night grocery stores. I know a woman who got rich by organizing maids and house cleaners.

The chances and the opportunities are as wide as this world.

Another point is relevant here. I didn't start a business to get rich—I started a business to provide a service and to improve myself economically. I think it's a mistake to set out to get rich. You can't get rich trying to get rich. What you need to do is to dream small dreams, because very often when you try to see things in their largest form, you get discouraged, and you feel that it's impossible. But if you can somehow think and dream of success in small steps, every time you make a step, every time you accomplish a small goal, it gives you confidence to go on from there.

I never thought I would be rich. Never in my wildest dreams did I believe that *Negro Digest* would lead to the Johnson Publishing Company of today. If I'd dreamed then of the conglomerate of today, I probably would have been so intimidated, with my meager resources, that I wouldn't have had the courage to take the first step.

All of which brings us back to the question:

Can it be done again?

Yes, it can be done again.

I could do it again.

So could you.

So could any man or woman who comes up with an idea that provides a service no one else is providing and who is willing to subordinate everything to the idea and the dream.

# Words and Pictures

# 18

# The Plea That Saved the Company

I KNEW I was in trouble when I saw the envelope.

It was fat, white, with that black-black type that says Official, Warning, *We got you.*

I ripped open the flap and the first line confirmed my worst fears:

> You are in violation of Regulation L-244. You are hereby ordered to cease and desist publishing the magazine called *Negro Digest* until you reduce your paper usage to your allotted 7.43 tons per quarter.

There was more, a lot more, about certification and notices of appeal. But that was a mere formality. The bottom line was that the U.S. government had the said John H. Johnson by the private parts and had no intention of letting go.

And so it was over, almost before it began.

I had pulled myself up by my bootstraps and I saw, for the first time, some light and green paper at the end of the tunnel. And a bureaucrat who'd never met a payroll in his life was telling me that I had to return the boots—and the bootstraps.

That's what the letter meant.

For there was no way I could comply with that order. I was using in April 1945 twenty-five tons of paper a quarter to print 100,000 copies of *Negro Digest*. If I cut back to 7.43 tons per quarter, I would destroy the circulation base of the magazine and wreck my business.

It wasn't fair.

It wasn't equitable.

It wasn't American.

But it was legal.

For a war was going on, and the government controlled almost everything, including paper, which was parceled out according to a nothing-keeps-nothing formula. If, for example, you were using twenty-five tons of paper in October 1942—a month before *Negro Digest* was founded—you could use twenty-five tons of paper in 1945. If, on the other hand, you were using zero tons of paper in 1942, you could use—the government was fair—zero tons of paper in 1945.

All this was as clear as the Washington Monument. It had been written down and published in the trade papers. And ignorance of the law was no defense. There was even a Catch-22 provision. To get paper to print your magazine, you had to sign a paper saying that you'd read and understood Order L-244.

The bureaucrat who signed the letter came down hard on the Catch-22 provision. He wanted to know how I obtained additional tons of paper. He used the ugly word "collusion" and hinted at penalties or worse for willful violation of the code and—this was the stinger—impeding the war effort.

I had a sudden vision of prison bars. And I ran to the nearest lawyer, who told me that it was too heavy for him and that I needed a specialist who knew the ins and outs of the War Production Board. I talked to my printer, who said he was a member of the Graphic Arts Association, which retained a lawyer named J. Norman Goddess.

"Talk to him," the printer said. "He's supposed to help our customers."

I took the letter to Goddess and told him I wanted to hire him to go with me to the appeals hearing in Washington. Goddess, a tall, stooped White man who never rushed or hurried, read the letter and looked at me the way a doctor looks at a patient with a new and interesting—and terminal—disease. He read the letter again and looked at me again, this time with the consoling look that surgeons, ministers, and undertakers give the next of kin.

Since he wouldn't say it, I said it.

"I'm in trouble, and I need the best lawyer I can find."

He corrected me.

"You're in so much trouble that the best lawyer in the world can't help you. You've been violating an admittedly unjust law. You've signed two documents which say that you *knew* that you were violating the law. If you go to Washington with a lawyer, you compound what has been done, and the board will eat you and the lawyer alive."

"What can I do, then?

"There's only one thing you can do but uh—uh—uh . . ." He turned red and started shuffling papers on his desk.

I knew what the problem was. The problem was the live wire of race which intrudes on the most private relations of Blacks and Whites, short-circuiting communications between husbands and wives, doctors and patients, lawyers and clients. Goddess had something to say to me, man-to-man, and nothing in his past—neither Blackstone nor Holmes—had prepared him for the task of eliminating the (White) man/(Black) man barrier. I waited, knowing that there was no future in our relationship if he couldn't cross this new and dangerous road by himself.

"I hope you're not offended," he said finally, dropping his voice. "I won't go to the Washington hearing with you, and the best legal advice I can give you is that you should pretend that you've had no legal advice." He added:

"The law set up a paper quota based on what was used in the first months after you started your magazine. Since you could only use 7.43 tons in the first months, you're stuck with 7.43 tons. But the law says that in cases of extreme hardship, the board may, at its own discretion, grant relief and permit you to continue publishing."

He pulled his chair closer to me and crossed the great divide, saying:

"If I were you, I would go down to Washington alone, and I would be—please don't be offended—a poor colored man who knows nothing about these complicated laws. Your only hope now is to create confusion and sympathy for you and your plight."

I took this advice and walked into Room 5066 of the Railroad Retirement Building in Washington, D.C., on Tuesday, June 12, 1945, without a lawyer or a legal pad. Twenty-five people appeared before the Appeals Board of the War Production Board on that day. Most came with lawyers, CPAs, marketing experts, charts and graphs.

I came with fear and trembling and a cry for help. The other petitioners were fighting for an economic advantage; I was fighting for my life. If their appeal was rejected, they would go on to something else. If my appeal was rejected, I was going back to the edge. So I sat there, aware of the bump, bump, bump of my heart, and waited for the War Production Appeals Board to hear Docket No. R-375:

APPEAL BY
THE NEGRO DIGEST
CHICAGO, ILLINOIS

FROM ORDER L-244 of the
PRINTING AND PUBLISHING
DIVISION

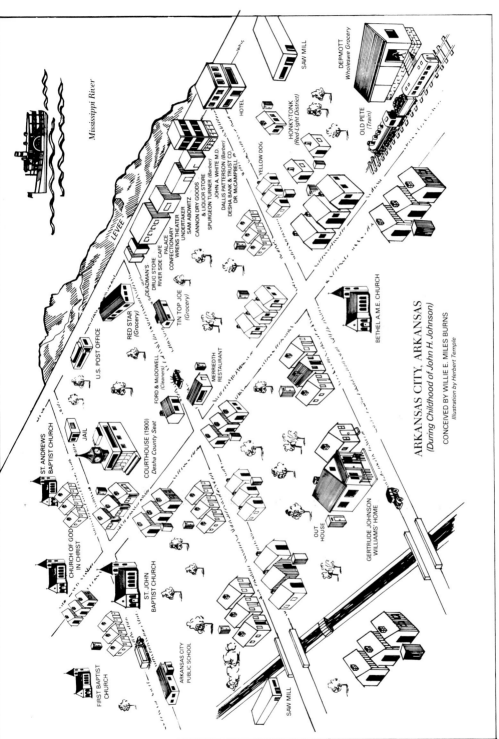

Map of my hometown, Arkansas City, Arkansas, in the 1920s.

My mother, Gertrude Johnson Williams, as a young woman.

A friend and mentor, Harry H. Pace, president of Supreme Liberty Life Insurance Company.

The future publisher as a young commencement speaker, Du Sable High School, 1936.

With another friend and mentor, Earl B. Dickerson.
(NORMAN L. HUNTER)

Wedding party, Selma, Alabama, June 21, 1941. (ART CRAFT STUDIO)

First office of Johnson Publishing Company in small law library
on second floor of Supreme Life Building, 1942.

The company's second office in a storefront at 5619 South State Street, 1943.

With Henry Luce, founder and publisher of *Time* and *Life* magazines.

My first major office building and the home office staff, 1955.

With my mother at a Chicago dinner, 1973. (NORMAN L. HUNTER)

Our first child,
John H. Johnson, Jr., 1957.
(LEROY JEFFRIES)

Celebrating the fiftieth anniversary of the
National Urban League with Governor
Nelson A. Rockefeller *(right)*, New York
Mayor Robert F. Wagner *(second from the
left)*, and League Executive Director Lester
B. Granger, 1960. (G. MARSHALL WILSON)

Addressing star-studded crowd at
*Ebony*'s 20th-anniversary celebration
at the Waldorf-Astoria, 1965.
(MONETA SLEET, JR.)

Admiring 20th-anniversary cake
with Arthur Godfrey, Lena Horne,
and Thurgood Marshall, 1965.
(MONETA SLEET, JR.)

First office building constructed in
downtown Chicago by a
Black-owned corporation, 1972.
(NORMAN L. HUNTER)

"Linda's father" with the bride, 1984. (DAVE SCHUESSLER)

Chairman and CEO with Eunice, the secretary-treasurer, and
Linda, the president and chief operating officer.
(JAMES L. MITCHELL)

I had rehearsed my appeal a thousand times, but when Docket No. R-375 was called, I spoke from the heart. I told the five members of the board present how hard I'd worked to start my magazine and how much it meant to me personally and to Black people in general. I told them I needed a production of 100,000 copies to keep my organization intact and to permit me to discharge my debts until the inevitable victory of our brave soldiers permitted the lifting of paper restrictions.

"We feel," I said, "that to limit us to the quota which has been recommended would not only work a hardship on the magazine as a corporation, but it would also work a hardship on our men, who are distributors, many of whom gave up other positions in order to get into this type of work."

Magazine content was not considered a basis for appeal. But it was unrealistic, I said, to ignore the racial tensions in America and what *Negro Digest* was doing to try to ease those tensions.

"We have attracted a number of liberal persons—Negroes and Whites—who have contributed articles which we believe have improved racial relations. We have printed articles which have told something of the history and achievement of the Negro group in particular, and these have bolstered the morale of the men in service...."

As I talked, I noticed, out of the corner of my eye, that one member of the board—his name was C. Osborn and he was, I learned later, an entrepreneur and publisher himself—was nodding his head and smiling. Recalling my debating class at DuSable High School, I talked directly to him.

"I believe," I said, "that to practically put us out of business, which this quota which has been recommended would do, would create an unusual hardship not only on our part, but it would set the Negro magazine publishing field back a good many years, because I wouldn't be able to go around and explain to each member of the group who has been reading the magazine that we were denied an appeal by the War Production Board. They would assume that perhaps for some financial reason we were discontinuing publication, and this, I believe, would make it unusually difficult for a new magazine to begin after the war because these people would say, 'I invested my money in the *Negro Digest* and it failed....'"

So far, so good. But what about the clear language of Order L-244? What about the regulations established by the War Production Board to further the war effort?

I told the board that I was not a member of "any publishers' association, and ... did not have direct access to information regarding these orders."

Why wasn't I a member of the all-White publishers' association?

Why didn't I have direct access to the conventions and luncheons and country clubs of the publishers?

I didn't raise these questions. By not raising them, I said to the members of the Appeals Board that *we* know why I didn't have *direct*—code word—access to the information.

A lawyer who read the transcript told me that Thurgood Marshall on his best day as an advocate couldn't have done much better. More to the point, my advocate on the board—C. Osborn—expressed his approval. When the chairman, Dr. A. N. Holcombe, asked for questions from members of the board, Osborn said: "I would like to first compliment the appellant on his excellent presentation, and say that if I had any sympathies at all, they would certainly be in the direction of a one-man magazine publisher because I was one myself once." He then had me read into the record Section F-8 which authorized exceptions for "unforeseen, unusual, extraordinary or emergency conditions constituting undue and excessive hardship."

William Cunningham, the consultant of the Magazine Section of the Printing and Publishing Division of the War Production Board, recommended denial of the appeal. But

Osborn and the board overruled him and granted me twenty-five tons a quarter.

Of the twenty-five persons who appeared before the board on that Tuesday in 1945, only John Johnson, who came without counsel and who had to win or go to the wall, prevailed. And it seemed to me as I walked out of that building into the suddenly bright Washington light that there was a sign or a portent in this and that somebody or something was trying to tell me that God and history had blessed this venture. At any rate, I went back to Chicago and hired J. Norman Goddess. A lawyer who knows that no lawyer is sometimes the best lawyer is a lawyer you ought to have on your payroll.

# 19

## Ebony

NOW that the future of *Negro Digest* was assured, I turned my attention to the proposal for the magazine that became *Ebony*. I wish I could say that it was my idea. But I had my hands full with *Negro Digest*. And I was in no mood to embark on a new venture.

The first suggestion for the new venture came from my two principal freelancers, Jay Jackson and Ben Burns, who had been pestering me for weeks with an idea for a new entertainment-oriented magazine. They wanted to call the magazine *Jive*, a slang word referring not only to what is now called rapping but also to the music and life-style of "hip" musicians.

I had no interest in jive, but to keep two valued contributors happy I said I would go into a three-way partnership. We decided to put up $1,000 each and split the profits three ways. But at put-up time, neither Jackson nor Burns had the money.

"Well," I said, "we've gone this far and we might as well see the hole card. But if I have to put in all the money, then I have to own the whole thing."

Both men agreed. They said they would go along with the deal if I would pay them more money for their free-lance work.

We shook hands, and the rest, as they say, is magazine history.

Ben Burns and Jay Jackson got a raise in pay, and John Johnson got a multimillion-dollar magazine.

But it wasn't—key point—the magazine that Burns and Jackson had proposed.

"Now that the magazine is mine," I said, "I'm going to put out something entirely different. I don't like the name 'Jive' and I don't like the 'Jive' audience. I've been thinking a lot about picture magazines. I've been doing some crude market research, checking newsstands in the Black community, and dealers tell me that the only magazine selling almost as much as *Negro Digest* in Black communities is *Life*. I think the time is ripe for a Black picture magazine."

There was another argument in favor of a Black picture magazine:

"The war will soon be over and Black vets will soon be coming home, looking for more glamour and more pizzazz than we're running in *Negro Digest*. They'll need a period of relaxation and relief from the day-to-day combat with racism."

This was a crucial turning of the road in my personal and corporate life, and I almost missed it. For if Ben Burns and Jay Jackson had come up with their thousand-dollar shares, *Ebony* probably would not have been published.

So I got the keys to a gold mine by default. Once I got into the thing and realized the hidden potential, I began to get more excited. The more excited I became, the more I realized that fate, which knows us better than we know ourselves, had dragged me, protesting and screaming, onto the freeway of the future.

There's something in human nature that fastens like a

leech on what worked yesterday. And the executive suites of America are filled with men and women who have been disqualified for tomorrow's success by yesterday's success. Most of the problems of American industry, including the failure to anticipate and adapt to changes in the electronic and car industries, can be traced to the fatal disease "WWY" —what worked yesterday.

The road from *Negro Digest* to *Jive* to *Ebony* cured me of that disease and taught me that you are only as good as your next success. It taught me that no matter how well you're doing and no matter how well you've done, you've got to keep your eyes open for new opportunities.

The history of American business is a history of No. 1's who were made obsolete by changing moods and fads. I've been No. 1 in my business for forty-seven years—and the reason I've been No. 1 for so long is that I've never been satisfied with the No. 1 rating I got last year.

Show me a man or woman who's satisfied with what he's got and I'll show you a man or woman who's not going to get anything else and is in danger of losing what he or she has. I speak from personal experience here. For if I had continued to rely on *Negro Digest* alone, I would be out of business today.

Change. That's the only thing that never changes.

That's what Longfellow meant when he said there are no birds—or Toyotas or Sonys—in yesterday's nest.

It's what Duke Ellington meant when he said that "things ain't what they used to be."

A good businessman knows that. He anticipates change, prepares for change, and rides the winds of change. He puts himself in the consumer's place and walks a mile or farther in his or her shoes. From that vantage point, he tries to see what the consumer sees and to want what he wants.

And let there be no misunderstanding here: It's not enough to sit in a big office and read reports and study bar graphs. You've got to get out of your office and walk the streets with customers and sell products with your salesmen.

Somebody said once that "in order to get lion's cubs, you have to go into the lion's lair." I'm no expert on lions, but I know people, and I tell you there's no other way to keep up with their changing needs.

I met a woman in a community supermarket who was shocked to find me pushing a cart down the aisles and taking canned goods off the shelves.

"You shouldn't be doing this," she said. "You should have an aide to shop for you."

"It's no problem," I told her. "I do this because I like to do it."

I could have added that I do it because I practice what I preach, and because there is no other way to keep your finger on the pulse of consumers.

People are always asking me what kind of business I'm going into next. I always say I don't know. How could I know until people tell me what product they're going to demand next? To find out what they're going to demand next, I keep a finger in the air, an ear to the ground, and both eyes on the marching throng. What I'm looking for is a target of opportunity. When it presents itself, I act.

That's the only way to run a business in the modern world. You can't be satisfied with yesterday's success, no matter how enjoyable or satisfying it might be. And you're a fool if you think that what you did yesterday is going to satisfy your customers or your board or your wife forever.

There was another marker on the road to *Ebony*, and that was a change in the world's color guard. By 1945 we had come to a great divide in world history, and this was reflected in the changing geography of media. The great Negro weekly newspapers—and the great White dailies— had by this time reached their peak and were giving way to the blitzkrieg of the photograph, first in *Life* and *Look*, and then in television.

When, twenty-seven years later, I received the Publisher of the Year award from the Magazine Publishers Association,

I said, "Some publishers were born great; some had greatness thrust upon them—and others merely survived TV."

I survived TV and the age of the photograph, and historians have been kind enough to say that I invented a new journalism that made it possible for Black media to weather the storms of change.

This is a flattering assessment, but I wasn't trying to make history—I was trying to make money. My moves were dictated not by abstract theories but by hunches that came from the deepest layers of my psyche. I can see with the benefit of 20/20 hindsight that the Black newspaper publishers were making the same mistake in neglecting pictures that I was making in holding on to the successful *Negro Digest* idea.

People wanted to see themselves in photographs. White people wanted to see themselves in photographs, and Black people wanted to see themselves in photographs. We were dressing up for society balls, and we wanted to see that. We were going places we had never been before and doing things we'd never done before, and we wanted to see that.

We wanted to *see* Dr. Charles Drew and Ralph Bunche and Jackie Robinson and the other men and women who were building the campfires of tomorrow. We wanted to know where they lived, what their families looked like, and what they did when they weren't onstage.

The picture magazines of the 1940s did for the public what television did for the audiences of the fifties: they opened new windows in the mind and brought us face to face with the multicolored possibilities of man and woman. The more I dealt with photographs, the more I understood their importance. I didn't see it in the beginning—I don't think anyone is that clairvoyant. But as I went from one small success to another, step by step, I began to understand the revolutionary importance of the new journalism.

Out of these bits and pieces evolved the *Ebony* philosophy. We wanted to emphasize the positive aspects of Black life. We wanted to highlight achievements and make Blacks proud of themselves. We wanted to create a windbreak that would let them get away from "the problem" for a few moments and say, "Here are some Blacks who are making it. And if they can make it, I can make it, too."

We started out saying, in effect, that Black newspapers were doing a good job of reporting discrimination and segregation and that we needed, in addition to all that, a medium to refuel the people, and to recharge their batteries. We needed, in addition to traditional weapons, a medium to make Blacks believe in themselves, in their skin color, in their noses, in their lips, so they could hang on and fight for another day. Last but not least, we needed a new medium— bright, sparkling, readable—that would let Black Americans know that they were part of a great heritage.

There was still another role wandering the streets of Black America, and that was to say we had White allies and that we could not win this struggle alone.

This was the idea.

We intended to highlight Black breakthroughs and pockets of progress. But we didn't intend to ignore difficulties and harsh realities. We intended to call a spade a spade and an ace an ace. And we intended to say, always and everywhere, that they are part of the same deck and can't be understood in isolation from each other.

Beyond all that, we wanted to focus on the total Black experience—something no one else was doing then and, I am tempted to say, now. For Black people, in addition to being members of the NAACP and National Urban League, were also members of sororities and fraternities and lodges. They marched and raised hell but they also raised children and gave debutante balls and watched baseball and football games.

We wanted to show Negroes—we were Negroes then— and Whites the Negroes nobody knew.

If you had relied on the White press of that day, you would have assumed that Blacks were not born, because the White press didn't deal with our births.

You would have assumed that we didn't finish school, because the White press didn't deal with our educational achievements.

You would have assumed that we didn't get married, because the White press didn't print our wedding announcements or pictures of Black brides and grooms cutting cakes.

You would have assumed that we didn't die, because it didn't deal with our funerals.

Back there, at the ending of World War II, the idea and the dream were on the defensive in the media and the streets. There were no Black mayors in major cities then, and there were no Blacks in organized baseball. Or organized football. Or organized basketball.

You won't believe this, but people said then, in all seriousness, that Blacks were biologically incapable of playing on the Brooklyn Dodgers and the Chicago Bears and the New York Knicks.

This was the situation in 1945.

This was the year the United Nations was founded with Black American participation.

This was the year the lights went on again in the hearts of Black and Brown people all over the world.

This was the year America and the world changed forever.

Jesse Jackson was four years old.

Sidney Poitier was eighteen.

Martin Luther King, Jr., was sixteen.

And I was twenty-seven.

Nat King Cole was singing "Straighten Up and Fly Right" ... Remember? ... and Charlie Parker, the apostle of the new sound, was playing "Now Is the Time."

They were jitterbugging in that year at the Apollo and the Regal and the Howard, but they were also dreaming and marching and mobilizing.

This was the world that midwifed *Ebony*. And I recall it not to cast stones but to emphasize how far the idea and the dream have traveled. For *Ebony* was founded in that faraway world to testify to the possibilities of a new and different world.

In a world of despair, we wanted to give hope.

In a world of negative Black images, we wanted to provide positive Black images.

In a world that said Blacks could do few things, we wanted to say they could do everything.

We believed in 1945 that Black Americans needed positive images to fulfill their potential. We believed then—and we believe now—that you have to change images before you can change acts and institutions.

This, in brief, was the prospectus for the new magazine.

Words and pictures, *Black* words and pictures, and a holistic presentation of the Black image, showing professionals and entertainers, athletes and doctors and preachers and women and men and children, everybody: This was the idea.

The only problem was the name.

If not "Jive," then what?

Since we could not register a name that was fully descriptive of the product, we started looking for a word that meant *black* but didn't mean magazine. I discussed the problem with Eunice, who has an arts background and keeps up with new developments in fashion and design. By coincidence, she'd been reading some material on art and color.

"What about 'ebony'?" she asked. "It means fine black African wood."

End of search.

And the beginning of a real-life adventure that has given new meaning and new color to an old name.

The name means, as Eunice said, a tree, the hard, heavy, fine black wood that the tree yields, *and* the ambience and mystique surrounding the tree and the color.

The magazine would become so successful that the

word would also mean the magazine published by and for Black Americans.

We had a name and an idea. The only thing lacking was paper, which wouldn't be available, the War Production Board said, until the Japanese were defeated.

While we were waiting, we made mock-ups and went through dry runs and watched the world turn.

On April 12, Franklin Delano Roosevelt died.

On May 7, Germany surrendered.

On August 15, Japan surrendered.

On November 1, I published Vol. 1, No. 1 of *Ebony* magazine.

The first editorial in the new magazine struck a new note in American journalism:

> We're off! Like a thoroughbred stallion, we've been straining at the starting gate for months now waiting for the gun from the almighty, omnipotent, superduper War Production Board. We've brain-trusted and blueprinted, rehearsed and dummied over and over again anxiously keeping a weather eye pealed on Washington for the 'go' signal. And sure enough when the V-J whistle did blow, we were caught with our plans down.
>
> Here's your paper and scram, the WPB boys suddenly said. And there we were with tons of slick, shiny stock, a sheaf of dummies but no magazine. But this story having a happy ending as do all good tales, we can confide that we pulled a reconversion act out of an ancient hat with slick style that would put magician Houdini to shame. And here we are.
>
> As you can gather, we're rather jolly folks, we *Ebony* editors. Sure, you can get all hot and bothered about the race question (and don't think we don't) but not enough is said about all the swell things we Negroes can do and will accomplish. *Ebony* will try to mirror the happier side of Negro life—the positive, everyday achievements from Harlem to Hollywood. But when we talk about race as the No. 1 problem of America, we'll talk turkey.

The 13¾″ by 9¾″ magazine sold for twenty-five cents.

The first cover was a black-and-white photograph of seven boys (six Whites and one Black) from New York's Henry Street Settlement. The cover story, "Children's Crusade," was a first-person piece by the Reverend A. Ritchie Low, a White pastor who was trying to eliminate bias by taking Harlem Blacks to Vermont farms for their annual vacation. Reading this story today, you realize suddenly that the world of 1945 was an innocent world, bright with a hope that is no longer available to people who have lived through Birmingham and Watts and Memphis.

There were fifteen stories in the fifty-two-page magazine. There was a profile on novelist Richard Wright and a story on a Black businessman who went from "slave to banker." We also highlighted "Catholics and Color," "The Truth About Brazil," and "Jam Session in Movieland."

People said, then and now, that we only dealt with the "happy" side. But we talked turkey, then and now. The first *Ebony* photo-editorial called for "Sixty million jobs or else...." It's ironic that Black unemployment is even more of a problem forty-four years later.

The first issue had the same flair and format as the White picture magazines. But there was one major difference. There was not a single ad in the whole issue.

I took the high road from the beginning, announcing that I wouldn't accept ads until we had a guaranteed circulation of 100,000. I had never asked for anything I was not entitled to. I had never asked for charity or handouts, and I had no intention of starting in 1945. I also discouraged the small and unsightly "charm" and "reader"-type ads that had been the staple of the Negro press.

They didn't believe me.

They laughed at my plans and pretensions.

But nobody could mistake my message. I intended to go first class. I wanted the big four-color ads that were the staple of the White magazines.

\*    \*    \*

The public response to the new magazine was immediate and spectacular. The first press run of 25,000 was sold out in hours, and we went back to press and printed another 25,000.

The first printing, as we noted in the December "Backstage," "sold like dime diamond rings, and everybody kept yelling for more.... The customers are still yelling for magazines, and we have to apologize that more are not available. The first issue has become a collector's item already."

Based on cash orders, the magazine said, *Ebony* had taken "the circulation championship among Negro magazines away from the longtime title-holder, its sister *Negro Digest*," and was now "the biggest Negro magazine in the world in both size and circulation." *Ebony* has held that title now for forty-four years. The press run has grown from the original 25,000 to more than 2 million. The magazine has grown from a readership of some 125,000 an issue to more than 9 million per issue, and it is the flagship of a miniconglomerate that grosses more than $200 million a year.

The reason for the magazine's success was plain. We were giving people something they wanted and couldn't get anywhere else—a basic formula for success in any business. From Jackson, Mississippi, from Oakland, California, from Harlem and Washington and Atlanta, from cities and hamlets all over America, came the same message: We've never seen ourselves before in large photographs presented in a positive light unrelated to crime, and we love it.

Our first four-color cover (March 1946) featured a luscious Lena Horne and sold 275,000 copies. The issue was hardly on the streets when an excited woman called and asked to speak to the editor. The editor wasn't in and she told the switchboard operator, "That picture of Lena Horne in color...is just like a drink of champagne."

A handful of people objected to the name *Ebony* and were answered in the fourth issue, which posed the question: "What's in a name?"

A name, we said, with apologies to Gertrude Stein, is a name is a name is a name. We added:

> Whether ebony is an African wood, a concerto [Stravinsky's "Ebony Concerto"], a night club or a magazine, we think it's a good name—alive, dramatic, exciting, colorful. A handful of folks think otherwise, have been writing to us to state their objections . . . 1. Ebony means black; 2. What does Ebony mean?
>
> On objection No. 1, we enter a dissent based on our contention that there's nothing wrong with black except what whites have done to blacks. As a race, Negroes have much to be proud of. Their achievements stamp black as a color to take pride in. Black is a badge of accomplishment by a people who have stood staunch and steadfast against the worst that is in the white man's soul and yet lifted their heads high through the centuries. . . . Black is and should be a color of high esteem. . . .
>
> On objection No. 2, we hope to teach through the medium of *Ebony* what the word means.

The White press had ignored the birth of *Negro Digest*, but *Ebony* was a mountain that commanded attention. *Time* welcomed the new magazine with a story entitled "The Brighter Side." *Time* said erroneously that the new magazine, "which imitates LIFE's format," was characterized by "all-around cheeriness," but conceded at least one contrasting note, a picture story on Brazil, headlined, "Starving Negroes Find They Can't Eat Equality."

*Time* added correctly: "On its editor's theory that 'most white magazines deal with Negroes as second-class citizens or freaks,' *Ebony* wants to show how normal they are."

The *Newsweek* story ("Ebony With Pictures") said the new magazine, "which follows the format of Life and Look," was a "slick-paper job . . . crammed with pictures of such Negro celebrities as Rochester (Eddie Anderson), the radio comedian; Hazel Scott, the pianist; Richard Wright, the novelist; and Maj. R. R. Wright, the banker."

*Newsweek* said there was some "lax editing" and "loose

writing" in the magazine, but it ate those words when it asked for and received permission to reprint part of an *Ebony* article.

An embarrassingly small number of people produced the first issue. There were only three names on the masthead: editor and publisher John H. Johnson, executive editor Ben Burns, and art editor Jay Jackson. Burns was a Brooklyn-born White journalist who'd spent a lifetime championing Black movements and Black causes. I'd known him since we worked together on the Earl B. Dickerson campaign, and I'd used him as a free-lancer on *Negro Digest*. He worked for the *Chicago Defender* and other publications before joining *Ebony* as a full-time employee. Burns was a hard worker, with a flair for colorful and somewhat spicy journalism, and he made a major contribution in the first phase of our development.

Within two months, I hired three additional persons. My accountant, Charles A. Beckett, came on temporarily as business manager to organize the business department. Allan Morrison and Kay Cremin were hired as associate editors.

Morrison, an elegant and eloquent writer, born in Canada, had a rich and interesting journalism background. He'd been the only Black correspondent on the European staff of *Yank* magazine and the *Stars and Stripes* daily. After the war, he and a young man named George Norford tried to start a magazine similar to *Negro Digest* called *Negro World Digest*—a magazine I'd never heard of.

When he saw the first issue of *Negro Digest*, he wrote a letter of congratulations and said he would like to work for me. This required some delicate negotiations, for Allan was a zealous New Yorker who believed civilization stopped at the Hudson River. I finally persuaded him to come to Chicago for a trial period. When we opened the New York office, he became the New York editor, a position he held until his death in 1968.

Kay Cremin was a White woman from Larchmont, New

York, who read about the magazine and applied for a job. She was qualified, we were an equal opportunity employer—and we hired her.

Later that year, I hired Robert Lucas, who'd written for radio shows and confession magazines, and Freda DeKnight, a New York City caterer who inaugurated our "Date With a Dish" feature.

In addition to the full-time staff members, we used big-name writers like Langston Hughes and world-class photographers like Stephen Deutch, Wayne Miller, and Phil Stern. One of the highlights of our first issue was a spectacular photographic essay on jazz by Gjon Mili.

There was not enough room in the State Street office for our growing staff, and we leased a two-story building. The building belonged to the famous Parkway Community Center and was directly behind its office on 5125 South Calumet. We transferred the editorial, circulation, and business departments to the Calumet Street office and used the State Street facility for warehousing and shipping.

The new central office was relatively small, ten thousand feet or so. We put the editorial department on the first floor and the library and circulation and advertising departments on the second floor. My office, which was the only private office in the building, was on the first floor near the back.

The staff was small and close-knit. We were all young, we had the same hopes and aspirations, and we were on the greatest of all highs—the high of making a new thing, of blazing a new path, of going where no Black or White had been.

There was no sharp line between departments or managers and staff people. At lunchtime, the whole staff would troop to Walgreens, put a couple of tables together, and continue animated discussions about the contents of the next issue.

We weren't editing a magazine; we were pressing a

crusade. And our excitement was contagious. It permeated our lives and spilled over into the pages of the magazine, which attracted large numbers of readers who acted like converts or fans.

It was a heady and exciting time, and almost every issue became a milestone.

In May 1946, we accepted our first ads.

In August 1946, we published our first food feature, "Barbecue Chicken." The "Date With a Dish" title was used for the first time in October 1946 ("How to Glorify the Apple").

In October 1946, we started using the facilities of Hall Printing Company, one of the world's largest printers.

In July 1947, we became the first Black magazine audited by the Audit Bureau of Circulation, which reported peak net paid sales of 309,715 in the final quarter of 1946. This was the largest circulation of any Black publication in the world.

There were only two small problems on the editorial side. A sensational story on Joe Louis ("How Joe Louis Spent $2,000,000") backfired. The story was based, to a large extent, on the charges of his estranged wife. Before the May 1946 issue hit the streets, Joe and his wife settled their differences, leaving us swinging in the cold Chicago wind.

The champ, fighting mad, sued, saying we'd attacked his manhood and his honor.

I was embarrassed, not only because of the threat to the new venture but also because I truly admired Joe. Although he'd been denied a formal education by the Old South, he was one of the most educated and thoughtful men I've ever met. He could be mesmerized by a golf ball or a pretty leg, but he was also capable of great eloquence. What athlete—or politician, for that matter—has given a better definition of the limits of evasion and retreat: "He can run but he can't hide." When, during World War II, preachers and leaders said we were going to win because God was on our side, Joe corrected them, saying: "We're going to win because we're on God's side."

A public fight was not in Joe's interest or my interest, and I called him and told him so.

"Johnny," Joe said, "I don't want to hurt you—I just don't want you attacking me. Whenever anybody attacks me, I fight back."

What did Joe want?

"If you'll apologize," he said, "and pay my attorney's fees, I'll drop the suit."

I apologized. If I've learned anything in the last fifty years, I've learned that the best way to deal with a mistake is to admit you made a mistake. Don't waffle. Don't make excuses. Don't explain. Open your mouth, say you're sorry—and move it.

People appreciate that approach. They appreciate executives and politicians who are big enough to fold a bad hand and walk away, without making excuses and without looking back.

I had an interesting discussion with Mayor Daley on this subject at a civic reception. The mayor was seated between me and real estate magnate Arthur Rubloff, with whom he was apparently feuding at the time. At any rate he turned his back on Rubloff and started an animated conversation on Lyndon B. Johnson and the Vietnam War. He said he'd tried to get Johnson to pull out of Vietnam because it was a no-win situation.

"I told him," the mayor said—and this was in the early days of the war—"the story about my dear old Irish father who told me that the only thing you can do with a bad poker hand is to turn it in."

I learned the same lesson from my stepfather, who *couldn't* walk away from a bad poker hand and always paid the price. My mother, who didn't play cards but who knew when to hold and fold the cards of life, taught me an even more important lesson.

"If you make a mistake," she said, "and you're going to

make mistakes, because you're not God, the best thing to do is to admit it publicly, put it behind you, and get on with the business of life."

It's human to make mistakes, and readers and customers know it. What they dislike is dishonesty, and attempts to defend the indefensible.

I didn't try to defend the editor who wrote the Joe Louis story. I apologized privately and publicly, and Joe and I became friends again and remained friends until his death. I heard shortly before his death that he was working as a greeter at a London gambling spa. I asked our then Paris editor, Charles Sanders, to stop by the club and get a photograph of the former champion.

Joe pulled him aside and said: "Tell Johnny that I've always cooperated with him and I want to cooperate now. But a lot of young Black kids look up to me and I don't want them to see me as a greeter in a gambling house. Tell him to give me a pass on this one."

I gave him a pass. When he died, in 1981, I ordered a five-page salute to the man who is still the undefeated champion in my memory and my mind.

The only other problem we faced on the editorial side was a national coal strike which shut down some departments at the printing press and made us miss the June 1946 issue of *Ebony*. With that one exception, I have never in forty-seven years of publishing missed an issue, or a payroll.

Despite the coal strike and the temporary setback of the Joe Louis suit, the *Ebony* plow continued to open new furrows, printing stories that can be consulted today with profit. They don't make them any better than Gordon Parks's story on the "Sugar Hill" section of Harlem or Wayne Miller's story on childbirth.

And it is fascinating to recall the information in our pioneering career series: "Negro Lawyers," 1,300 in April 1947 compared with 24,000 in 1988; "Negro Profs at White Colleges," "60-odd" in October 1947 compared with 10,000 in 1988; "Lady Lawyers," 70 in August 1947 compared with

10,000 in 1988; "Negroes on White Dailies," "15-odd" in April 1948 and 2,136 in 1988.

It's difficult to believe that there were only sixteen Black disc jockeys in December 1947, and some future historian will probably find it difficult to believe that there are an estimated five thousand today. We thought we were saying something in May 1948 when we identified "an army" of forty "Brown Hucksters" selling goods and services for American corporations. But it's impossible to count the Black salesmen and sales representatives today.

We were among the earliest and most passionate defenders of Black beauty. We were fascinated by the different hues (smoke, cinnamon, chocolate, cream, golden, pecan, coffee) in the Black rainbow, and we were astonished by the inability of White Americans to appreciate that beauty. We didn't apologize for it—it was a part of our mission, as we noted in our May 1946 issue.

"Beauty," we said, "is skin-deep—and that goes for brown as well as white skin. You'd never think it, though, to look at the billboards, magazine, and pinup posters of America. Cheesecake (photographers' jive talk for sex-appeal pictures) is all white.

"But the Petty girl notwithstanding, [Black women] are beautiful too. And despite the fact that Miss America contests hang out 'for whites only' signs, there are thousands of [Black women] lovely enough to compete with the best of white American pulchritude."

To prove that point, we asked George Karger, one of the top photographers of the forties, to capture the beauty of a Black woman. And to make the comparison even more complete, we selected a beautiful and scholastically brilliant young woman, Barbara Gonzales, the first Black to graduate from Sarah Lawrence College.

The elegant result, printed in the June 1946 issue ("Glamour Is Global, Negro pulchritude ranks high despite U.S. lily white standard"), was an eye-opener. We also printed four-color photographs of Black women in bathing suits, leading one White magazine to say that we "could lift a skirt with the best of them."

Perhaps the most interesting story in this early period was photographer Wayne Miller's dramatization of Sinclair Lewis's *Kingsblood Royal* novel about Neil Kingsblood, a Minnesota banker who discovered at the age of thirty-one that he was 1/32nd Black. In June 1947 we presented a picture-dramatization of the novel, using models to illustrate scenes from the novel. The White journalism world picked up the story and proved, once again, that imitation is the sincerest form of flattery.

*Life* picked up the story and ran a four-page spread. *Time* bought two *Kingsblood* pictures to run with its review of the book, along with a blurb on *Ebony*. The *New York Herald-Tribune* book section ran one of our *Kingsblood* pictures on its front page.

But that was not all of it. *Newsweek* reprinted four pictures and several photographs from another *Ebony* story.

*Tide*, the weekly newsmagazine of advertising and marketing, said that "today the outstanding Negro magazine is *Ebony*."

Publisher Bennett Cerf said in *Saturday Review of Literature* that "*Ebony*... is edited with taste, intelligence and a shrewd understanding of what its public wants."

In the same period, *Reader's Digest* reprinted one of our editorials, "Time to Count Our Blessings." One of the magazine's top editors, Stanley High, came to Chicago to negotiate the price.

"What about $500?" he asked.

I was shocked into silence; I had no idea that magazines paid that much for articles. High misinterpreted my silence and said, "What about $1,000? Would that be all right?" I said yes, and he went into his pocket and pulled out two checks, one for $500 and the other for $1,000. He gave me the $1,000 check and returned the $500 check to his pocket with a smile.

I learned something that day. Never accept a first offer, and don't make your move too soon.

It was clear by our sixth issue that we were more than a magazine. To our readers, some of whom apparently believed we were capable of miracles, we were a combination general store, service bureau, and post exchange. One man, for instance, sent the following request on a penny postcard (yes, postcards cost a penny then):

"I would appreciate it very much if you would send me all the information possible about the Negroes."

Another asked us to send him a wife.

When Josephine Baker found herself in Paris without addresses for Americans on her Christmas list, she sent the batch to us and asked us to address and mail them.

# 20

---

# *"Failure Is a Word I Don't Accept"*

WE were a legend after only six months of publication. And it seemed on the surface that everything was going my way.

I was turning deals left and right, I had two hot magazines, and I was selling 400,000 copies a month.

I had it made.

Right?

Wrong.

Success was killing me.

The more *Ebony*s I sold, the more money I lost.

And bills were piling up.

I owed the printer and the engraver and suppliers all over town.

They were singing my praises in Harlem and Hollywood, and I was hiding in my office to avoid my creditors.

The problem was obvious to anyone who could read a balance sheet.

I was selling too many magazines without a supporting advertising foundation, and I was confronted with three interlocking problems.

The first was the economics of slick paper. Which cost money. Big money.

The second problem was the economics of printing a magazine with quality reproduction on million-dollar presses.

Again money.

Big money.

The third problem was the economics of numbers.

Two hundred thousand magazines with slick paper and good reproduction require more trees, ink, and postage stamps than 100,000 magazines.

Three hundred thousand cost more than 200,000.

And so on.

The situation would have been funny if it hadn't been so serious. The glamorous *Ebony* was getting all the attention, and all the praise, but the steady, undramatic *Negro Digest*, 100,000 to 150,000 copies monthly with relatively small production costs, was paying the bills. But there was a limit to the debt structure *Negro Digest* could carry. The runaway success of *Ebony* was stretching the *Negro Digest* corset to its breaking point. And if *Negro Digest* collapsed, John H. Johnson and the whole structure were going down with it.

Why didn't I rein in *Ebony* and cut back on its growth?

I couldn't. It was a simple matter of arithmetic. The more *Ebony* readers, the more potential advertisers.

Why didn't I walk away from the *Ebony* sweepstakes?

You've got to be kidding.

Walk away from a potential gold mine that dwarfed anything I'd ever dreamed of?

No way.

There was no way I was going to give up a publication which had grown in a short time from 25,000 to nearly half a million. I wasn't confused. I knew what I was doing. The only question was: Could I find continuous advertising support before the new magazine wrecked me and my company?

And so, as we headed into the backstretch of 1946—the most dangerous and difficult year in my personal and corporate life—my position was roughly this: I had a tiger by the tail and I couldn't afford to hang on or let it go.

For the moment—for a *brief* moment—I considered the possibility of failure. But the mere thought of the word made my body shake and my heart pound, and I banished it once and for all from my life and vocabulary.

I remember firing a young man for using the word *failure.*

"Nothing personal," I said, "but I'm too insecure myself to have people around me who believe that failure is a possibility. Failure is a word that I don't accept."

I dismissed another associate who kept trying to tell me that I couldn't make it.

"I've got to fire you," I said. "I'm not sure I can make it myself. The last thing I need is someone telling me that I can't make it."

Failure: I was at war with the word and all its variations.

The word I wanted to hear, then and now, was *success.* The energy I sought, then and now, was the energy that comes from focusing all your powers, like a beam, on a single point. I used to lock myself up in my office and say the word *success* out loud, over and over, like a Buddhist monk chanting his mantra. I used to say to myself, "John Johnson, you can make it. John Johnson, you can make it. John Johnson, you can make it, John Johnson, *you can and must make it.*"

When things got real tough, I'd call my mother and she would say, "You can make it."

I told her one day in perhaps the worst week of my life, "Mother, it looks like I'm going to fail."

"Son," she said, "are you trying hard?"

"Yes."

"*Real* hard?"

"Yes."

"Well," she said, closing the conversation, "whenever you're trying hard, you're never failing. The only failure is failing to try."

I also called Mary McLeod Bethune, the former National Youth Administration executive who headed Bethune-Cookman College. Mrs. Bethune, who was another one of the most unforgettable characters I've known, was short and black as polished ebony. She was not what the world considers beautiful, but she had so much soul force and authority that when she walked into a room all eyes were pulled to her, as if to a magnet. I was a graduate of her NYA program, and she considered me one of her boys. It was only natural for me to turn to her when the difficulties mounted.

"Hang on," she told me. "Have faith, keep trying." She paused and added:

"The project is too good to end, the Lord wouldn't want it to end."

Years later, when I met W. Clement Stone for the first time, I told him, "I've been practicing PMA—Positive Mental Attitude—since I started my first business. I didn't know what to call it, and I didn't know how to define it, but I was doing it—and it helped me survive."

The reason I survived is that I refused to believe the signs that said I was defeated. And I dared to do things I couldn't afford to do.

And I'm convinced that the only way to get ahead in this world is to live and sell dangerously. You've got to live beyond your means. You've got to commit yourself to an act or a vision that pulls you further than you want to go and forces you to use your hidden strengths.

For you're stronger than you think you are. And what you need—what all men and women need—is an irrevocable act that forces you, on pain of disgrace, jail, or death, to be the best you that you can be.

I was driven by the fear of going back. And I was

forced, in the absence of conventional financing, to develop creative financing techniques. One technique was to put off paying bills until the last possible moment. I developed a sixth sense about the limits of delay. I told my staff that I always paid my bill just before my credit went bad.

Why didn't I go to the bank and get a loan?

Because banks didn't lend money to Blacks in those days. I was in business twenty years before I got a loan from a bank. And I was in business forty years before I got what I consider a White man's loan—a loan based on my signature alone.

For two years, from November 1945 to November 1947, I walked a tightrope without a net, pyramiding creditors, postponing bills, stalling, improvising, selling. Perhaps the strangest aspect of this strange season is that some of my warmest relationships were with the people I owed the most money. There was, for example, the paper mill executive who extended credit far beyond the known or potential resources of my company.

The bill became so large that the executive developed anxiety attacks that could only be stilled by listening to me explain how I was going to pay the bill. He called me in one day and said, "Your bill is getting bigger and bigger and I want to know what your plans are. I mean, how soon will you be able to sell some advertising and get things under control and reduce your obligations to us?"

Sincerity is perhaps the greatest selling force in the world. And I was sincere in wanting to survive and get a handle on *Ebony*, which was like a runaway horse, hurtling down the streets and pulling me behind it.

I explained all this to the executive. He was all right as long as I was talking to him, but I had to call him every day and tell him how many ads I'd sold, how great the future looked, and how I planned to pay the bill. It was almost like a fix that I had to give him every day so he could survive.

I made the mistake one day of going to New York without calling him, and all hell broke loose. My secretary finally reached me in New York, and there was this breathless voice on the phone, saying, "Johnson, tell me again, how do you plan to pay this bill?"

I developed many techniques for keeping him satisfied. If I had a $5,000 payment to make, I wouldn't pay it all at one time—I would buy myself five days of peace by sending $1,000 a day.

Looking back now, I would say that we were good for each other and that the fire we went through together strengthened us.

# 21

## *Breaking Through the Ad Barrier*

BY creative financing and PMA and JRT—Johnson Reinforcement Techniques—I bought enough time to identify and formulate the three elements necessary for a strategy of success.

The first element is identification of the problem. This is the most important point in developing a success strategy, and it's the one most frequently overlooked by business people from the mail room to the boardroom who leap into the saddle and ride off in all directions before they identify the objective and the obstacles.

That's the wrong approach. The first problem of any problem is to decide exactly what the problem is.

I didn't have a big staff and I didn't have a big bank account. The thing that saved me and Johnson Publishing Company is that I made the right diagnosis. I did what every businessman in a tight corner should do. I sat down and wrote a declarative sentence that defined the problem.

My problem was not the editorial content of the magazine—the readers were yelling for more. My problem was not circulation—I couldn't print enough copies. My problem was advertising or, to come right out with it, the lack of advertising.

How did I intend to deal with the problem?

I intended to deal with the problem by persuading corporations and advertising executives to give *Ebony* the *same* consideration they gave *Life* and *Look*.

To do that I had to convince corporations and advertising executives that there was an untapped, underdeveloped Black consumer market larger and more affluent than some of the major White foreign markets.

This was a revolutionary approach—revolutionary from a racial, marketing, and advertising standpoint—and I couldn't sell it to lower-level functionaries. I had to go to the top and sell the Black consumer market the same way you sell a foreign market.

The plan of action was implicit in the definition of the problem.

I needed, first of all, a team of advertising specialists who understood the new concept and believed in it with the passion of true believers.

The team didn't exist.

I had to invent it.

I started, as usual, small. A small step gives you the confidence to make a big step. And a big step gives you courage to run.

I started small, hiring a White advertising manager, a man named Irwin J. Stein, one of the most honorable men I've known. There were no Blacks who knew the mysteries of the White advertising world, and I hired Stein with the understanding that he would train a Black to take his place.

Stein wasn't a salesman; he was a manager. He helped design the rate cards and worked with me in determining rates. He also trained Isaac Payne, who succeeded him as advertising production manager and remained with the company until his death.

Since we didn't have a staff of salesmen, we asked a Black-owned firm of publishers' representatives to sell ads and look out for our interests on Madison Avenue. When our self-imposed advertising moratorium ended in May 1946, two of the first four ads in *Ebony* (Chesterfield, Kotex) were sold by this firm. I sold the other ads, Murray's Hair Pomade and Supreme Liberty Life Insurance Company.

The Chesterfield, Kotex, and Murray's ads were full-page color ads, and the Supreme ad was a full-page black-and-white. Murray's used a Black woman model. Chesterfield, which ran several ads in 1946 and 1947, used a White male model, and Kotex used a White couple.

When, after a few months, the Black firm did not seem to be making substantial progress, I turned reluctantly to a White firm. I was told that Whites could get in to see White advertising managers more easily and could socialize with them and promote the magazine better.

It didn't turn out that way. White salesmen were no more effective than Black salesmen, and they created other problems. The turning point came on the day I got a call from an angry man in an advertising agency.

"John Johnson," he said, "I don't know whether I'm ever going to advertise with you, but I want to give you some free advice. You sent a White man to sell me an ad for a magazine about Black people. This White man doesn't know any more about Blacks than I do. If you've got all those intelligent, affluent Blacks reading the magazine, why don't you send one to sell me an ad?"

It was a good question, and I decided, after thinking about it for a while, to send myself. What did I have to lose? I had tried everything, or almost everything, and I was floundering in a rough sea and going down for the third time.

From that day in 1946 until we turned the corner a year later, I spent almost every waking hour selling advertising.

*Ebony* readers helped. They jumped the gun and started asking manufacturers why they weren't advertising in *Ebony.* Some went further and told backsliders that they were only going to spend their money with companies that showed them the elementary respect of asking for their business.

An avalanche of postcards and handwritten petitions prepared the ground, and I planted seeds with letters and phone calls to corporate chiefs and agency heads. It was hard getting through, but I was fighting for my life and I placed as many as four hundred telephone calls to the same CEO.

There's an art in talking to secretaries, and it should be taught at MBA schools. I taught myself, and soon became a master of the art of leaping over secretarial shields. I was so persistent, and so patient, that some secretaries either put me through or gave me helpful hints.

The secretary to Fairfax M. Cone of Foote, Cone & Belding advertising agency told me that she couldn't make an appointment for anyone.

"But," she said, "I'll give you a tip. He doesn't like to fly. He goes to New York every Sunday afternoon on the *Twentieth Century Limited.* He has a couple of drinks in the bar, eats dinner, and goes to bed. If I were you, I would just happen to be on that train, and I would wander into the club car and strike up a conversation with him."

I caught the train and wandered into the club car. And I was surprised and delighted to find Fairfax Cone there. I talked to him on that Sunday and the next Sunday and the Sunday after that. I became a regular on the *Twentieth Century Limited,* and Fairfax Cone and I became good friends. He arranged for me to talk to executives at his agency, and I sold some accounts. Cone himself later made a movie for us on the importance of the Black consumer market.

I used another approach to break the barrier at Tatham and Laird, headed by Kenneth Laird. Ken and I were active in the Roundtable of Christians and Jews. We served to-

gether on a number of committees and were virtually insep-
arable during Brotherhood Week. But the brotherhood slo-
gans never led to anything concrete. We didn't get any
business from Ken's agency, and when one of our standard
accounts moved to his agency, we lost it. I pointed this out
to him one day at a committee meeting on brotherhood,
and he bristled with indignation.

"We don't believe in anything like that around here," he
said. "I'll check it out and let you talk to our key people."

I talked to his executives and discovered what I already
knew. They weren't the real stumbling block.

I went back to Ken and said, "Ken, I've finally found
the person in your agency who's keeping us from getting
business."

"Who?" he said. "Tell me who it is, and I'll fire him."

"Ken," I said, "it's you."

He denied it. But he was forced to reexamine his own
attitudes and to come to grips with the fact that a corporation or agency necessarily reflects the attitudes of the chief
executive. Before long, we started getting business from
Tatham and Laird.

In this instance, as in others, I anticipated the insights
of a book called *Selling Dangerously*, by Elmer Wheeler.
When all of the traditional selling strategies have failed,
Wheeler said, and when you've gotten a final and definite
no despite all your efforts, anything you do—shouting, cursing, standing on the table, denouncing racism—is right.
What Wheeler neglected to say is that all selling, if it's
effective selling, is dangerous selling. And that it takes a
master salesman or an artist to identify the right psychological moment for turning insult into gold.

# 22

## The Turning Point: Zenith, Matt Henson, and the North Pole Expedition Revisited

WORKING alone on unplowed ground with no guide-lines or precedents, I had to improvise and make snap decisions based on my reading of how far far I could go and what the traffic would bear.

Like an itinerant preacher with no permanent church, I went from advertising pulpit to advertising pulpit, choosing my text and my sermon according to the size, inclination, and attention span of the audience.

I won some victories, but my losses overshadowed my gains. When we celebrated our first anniversary in November 1946, the future of the company was still in doubt. We put up a brave front, announcing a new advertising guarantee of 400,000, but we weren't making enough money to pay our bills. And behind the scenes things were going from bad to worse.

It was at this crossroads, at one of the low points of the *Ebony* trajectory, that I inaugurated one of the most controversial programs in our corporate history. On a Sunday in December 1946, millions of White Americans opened their morning paper and found big ads urging them to subscribe to *Ebony* magazine. The ads in the *New York Times, Chicago Tribune,* and other papers were designed in part to pump-prime the Madison Avenue well. But they had another and larger purpose. We wanted to improve race relations. We believed the time had come to inaugurate a two-way dialogue. The announcement in the December 1946 issue was upbeat.

"Departing from the tradition of Negro publications sticking to the Negro field only, *Ebony* is venturing out into the white magazine market to sell white readers the idea that a Negro magazine is worth buying."

The campaign was a mistake. I misread the American public. I thought at first that if more Whites were exposed to more information on Blacks, they would be better informed and less uptight about race. But what happened, in many cases, is that younger and better educated Whites used their education to create more acceptable and sophisticated ways to justify racism.

Although I abandoned the campaign almost before it began, I continue to reach out to Whites with the hope that images and ideas can break down the barriers that separate us. Since 1946, the number of White readers has continued to grow. Whites now make up 9.4 percent of our readership. We're glad to have these readers, but we don't aggressively seek them.

Far more important and of far greater economic benefit in the end were the four or five mail-order businesses I started. Since advertising was uncertain at best, I decided to organize businesses that would advertise with me and produce revenue to pay for the advertising I needed and couldn't get.

The first business, Beauty Star cosmetics, marketed several hair-care products, including Satene. Long before I had a daughter, I liked the name Linda, which was used in

Linda Fashions, a mail-order business that sold dresses and clothes. I also sold vitamins, books (Negro Digest Book Shop), and Star Glow wigs.

These businesses, especially the hair-care business, gave me breathing room, and I returned to the advertising campaign with new enthusiasm. The 1946 campaign had focused primarily on advertising agencies. In 1947, the turning point of the advertising campaign, I decided to focus on companies, which tell advertising agencies what to do. And I decided to focus on companies with a big but unacknowledged stake in the Black community.

My first target was Zenith Radio Company. Almost all Blacks owned radios, and most of them were Zenith radios. My mother owned a Zenith, all the people I knew owned Zeniths. If a case could be made for anybody advertising in *Ebony*, a case could be made for Zenith.

The head of Zenith was Commander Eugene F. McDonald, a hard-driving, brilliant executive who ran the company the same way he ran navy ships. I wrote the commander and asked for an appointment to talk about Zenith's advertising stake in Black America. The commander answered immediately—I'm sure he just wanted to get rid of me—and said, "I received your letter, but I can't see you, for I don't handle advertising."

He was still my best target, and I wasn't going to let him get by with that routine reply.

All right, I said to myself, he's the head of the company and he doesn't handle advertising. What does he handle?

The answer was clear. He handled policy, including, presumably, advertising policy. I wrote another letter, asking him if I could come in and talk to him about his *policy* on advertising in the Black community.

"You're a very persistent young man," he said in his reply, adding:

"I'll see you, because I always want to sell more things to more people. But"—and he emphasized these words—"*if you try to talk to me about advertising, if you try to talk to me about placing an ad in your publication, I will end the interview."*

I'd won—and I'd lost.

I had an appointment to talk to a CEO who said I could talk to him about anything except the one thing I wanted to talk to him about.

That presented a new problem. What would we talk about?

I went to *Who's Who in America,* which told me that the commander was an arctic explorer who'd visited the North Pole several years after it was first explored by Matthew Henson and Commodore Robert E. Peary.

I knew from my own research that Henson, who reached the North Pole forty-five minutes before Peary and who was the first human to set foot on the icy hub of the world, was Black, that he was living in Harlem, and that he had written a book about his experiences.

This was the opening I needed. I asked Allan Morrison, our New York editor, to find Henson and ask him to autograph a copy of his book to the commander.

It occurred to me at that point that Henson was good copy, and I pulled a story out of our July 1947 issue and inserted a four-page story on Matt Henson.

As it turned out, Commander McDonald was thinking along the same lines. The first thing he said to me when I walked into his office was, "You see those snowshoes there? They were given to me by Matthew Henson. He was a Black man and he was as good as any two White men I know. What do you think about that?"

I told him that Henson was also my hero.

He invited me to sit down—I was awestruck by this huge office, the size of a small auditorium.

"You know," he said, "I've often wondered what happened to Matt. I liked him and considered him a friend. I heard that he was living in New York and that he has written a book. Do you know anything about that?"

"Yes," I said, "I just happen to have a copy with me, and he was kind enough to autograph it to you."

He leafed through the book, obviously pleased by the autograph. He then said, with a challenge:

"You say you put out a Black magazine. It would seem to me that any Black magazine would have done a story on a guy like Matt."

I agreed with him and said I just happened to have a copy of the magazine that contained a story on the Black explorer.

He looked through the magazine, nodding his head up and down in approval.

I told him I started the magazine to highlight the achievements of men like Matthew Henson, who'd demonstrated that excellence would break down all barriers.

"You know," he said finally, using the banned word himself, "I don't see any reason why we shouldn't advertise in this magazine."

He pushed a button and in came his advertising manager, a man named William Mackey, who'd told me no, a thousand times no.

The advertising manager bowed at the waist and said, "Yes, Commander." The commander was a real commander—he was not only president of Zenith, he was president and commander of all the tubes, radios, desks, and people in the building.

"Mackey," he said now, "why aren't we advertising in *Ebony*?"

I thought to myself, "I've got Mackey now."

But Mackey was cool.

"We're considering it, Commander," he said.

"By God," the commander said, "we ought to do it."

"Of course, Commander," Mackey said.

This was the turning point in my advertising campaign. We'd run ads before from Chesterfield and other companies, but the Zenith contract was our first major advertising schedule. And it paved the way for other schedules.

After Mackey left, the commander said, "I like your magazine and your story. I'm going to call a few of my friends and I want you to go in and tell them the same story you've told me."

While I was sitting there, he called the chairmen of Swift Packing Company, Elgin Watch Company, Armour Food Company, and Quaker Oats.

"I have a young man here," he said, "who's putting out a magazine. I think it has great potential, and I want you to see him. I can't tell you what to do about it, but will you please see him?"

All agreed to see me, and all bought ads.

McDonald died in 1958, but the company is still one of our most faithful advertisers. In a development the commander couldn't have anticipated, I was elected to the Zenith board in 1971, and I'm still a member. There are more than 150 television sets in my homes and offices around the world—and they're all Zeniths.

By coincidence in this bright summer, I found and hired a brilliant advertising specialist who made similar breakthroughs on the East Coast. His name was William P. Grayson, and the decision to persuade him to leave his job at the Baltimore *Afro-American* and go to work for me in New York City as our eastern advertising manager was one of the most important decisions I've made as CEO of Johnson Publishing Company.

Grayson, who handled all advertising for the *Afro-American* chain, suffered a stroke a few years ago and is no longer active, but he was one of the giants of the advertising field. He was creative, determined, and daring. He had an art background, which meant that he knew how to prepare and make presentations. He was a prodigious reader of different publications, which meant that he knew what was going on in the world and could relate our advertising appeals to the particular problems of advertisers.

It is rare in our field to find great salesmen who are also great managers. Bill excelled in both areas. When he started work in 1947, we rented a small office at 55 West Forty-second Street. He and his secretary, Margo Hughes, who came with him from the *Afro-American*, created the foundations of the crucial East Coast staff.

The first year Grayson came we were billing less than $25,000 a year. When he retired in 1970, we were billing more than $15 million.

Men with his skills are rare in Black or White America. To get him, I offered him more than I was making and a bigger office. I used to say jokingly that I motivated Bill by giving him a bigger salary than I was making, a bigger office, and a prettier secretary—and by threatening to take it away if he didn't perform.

It was worth it. After Bill joined the staff, advertising sales increased dramatically. In November 1947 we had to omit 4,600 agate lines of advertising because of lack of space. By that time, our second anniversary, we could announce with pride that *Ebony* had weathered the storm.

"This magazine," we said frankly, "has proved the most costly publication ever issued in the Negro field and there have been times when red ink threatened to wipe out the black on our ledgers.

"But at the end of two years of publication, *Ebony* has become an established institution in the publication world. It is here to stay."

Lena Horne, our perennial beauty queen, was on the cover of that issue, which sold 333,445 copies.

In the months that followed we went from strength to strength.

In February 1948 we increased the magazine size to sixty-eight pages to accommodate the new pages of advertising.

In June we reached a peak of forty-eight pages of advertising and noted that we had broken, in the past six months, major accounts at Pepsi-Cola, Colgate, Beech-Nut,

Old Gold, Seagram, Remington Rand, Roma Wines, and Schenley.

In December, we ran the first four-color ad ever to appear on the inside of a Negro publication. Among the new corporations advertising regularly by that time were Elgin Watch, Zenith Radio, MGM, and Capitol Records.

All through this period, while the advertising campaign was developing, *Ebony* was locked in a life-and-death struggle with another Black magazine, *Our World*. There were other competitors, but *Our World* kept me up more nights than any other publication. It was owned by a brilliant guy named John P. Davis, a Harvard Law School graduate who'd been a debater at Oxford.

The struggle between us was the old story of the tortoise and the hare. Davis was colorful and flamboyant, and I was quiet and steady. The tortoise won. Somebody had to win, for there were not enough advertisers or readers for both magazines.

Davis's problem, I think, was his brilliance. He was such a multitalented guy, and he was involved in so many different things that he didn't concentrate completely on *Our World*. While he was off making speeches and dealing with the law and other things, I was in the trenches, digging, fighting, worrying, and even crying. In the end, persistence and doggedness won out. *Ebony* was not that much better than *Our World*—I simply tried harder.

I have often said jokingly that the fundamental difference between the two magazines was dramatized by the last issue of *Our World*, which had a story on fifty-eight ways to make a fruitcake. I maintained then, and I maintain now, that people don't want to know fifty-eight ways to make a fruitcake. What they want to know is *one* good way to make a fruitcake.

When *Our World* went into bankruptcy, I bought their assets, including their files and an art piece from John Davis's office, for $14,000. I got their photo files, and they had some great photos. One of the magazine's photographers, Moneta Sleet, Jr., joined our staff and became the first Black photographer and the first Black male to win a Pulitzer Prize. He was cited for a dramatic photograph of Coretta Scott King holding her young daughter at the funeral of Martin Luther King, Jr.

# 23

## *Adventures on the Color Line*

I SPENT a lot of time in the late forties recruiting editorial talent.

One of my first discoveries was Era Bell Thompson, a native of Iowa who'd written a book called *American Daughter.* I was always on the lookout for authors and graduates of journalism school, and I went to her small apartment under the "El" at Sixty-third Street and South Parkway and persuaded her to join our staff. She told me that she knew nothing about Negroes.

"That's all right," I replied, "we'll teach you."

When she retired twenty-eight years later, she said, "I think I'm beginning to understand Negroes."

For thirteen years, Era Bell was co-managing editor of *Ebony* with Herbert Nipson, a writer-photographer who'd earned a master of fine arts degree from the Writers Work Shop at the University of Iowa. Nipson, the second *Ebony* executive editor, retired in 1987 after thirty-eight years of service.

In the next two years, we added several major writers, artists, and photographers. Among the best known were Edward T. Clayton, who came from the *Louisville Defender* and was the first executive editor of *Jet;* photographer Griffith Davis, who was recommended by Langston Hughes; authors Roi Ottley (*New World A-Coming*) and Dan Burley (*Original Handbook of Harlem Jive*); art director Leroy Winbush and artist Herbert Temple; and librarian Doris Saunders. In March 1948, the company had close to one hundred full-time employees and more than four thousand independent distributors.

Here again we were forced to create something that hadn't existed before: a new stratum of Black magazine editors and photographers. We sought out authors and major writers, and we stole the best talent from Black newspapers. One of the nicest tributes I've received came from Era Bell Thompson, who said, "The greatest compliment I can pay you is that you took a group of inexperienced and undisciplined writers and artists and molded them into an organization that puts out a professional magazine."

Another interesting staff member was circulation manager J. Unis Pressley. Pressley was so light-skinned that he could pass for White, and we quickly made him our official White. When we traveled it was his duty to register for a suite in the best hotels and to order a meal for four or five. We would then go up the freight elevator, pretending that we worked at the hotel, eat a good meal, take a hot bath, sleep in a soft bed, and sneak down the freight elevator the next morning. When we traveled in the South, Pressley would go into White cafés and buy food for the whole group.

Traveling in this period was a nightmare for Blacks. No matter how much money you had or how many degrees you'd earned, you could never be certain that your hotel reservation would be accepted. I'll never forget the night

Bill Grayson and I showed up at the Washington Shoreham to claim our reservations. Without even looking, the clerk said, "Sorry, we can't find your reservations."

Grayson and I were exhausted, and we didn't know anybody in Washington. We decided to sit in the lobby until they "found" our reservations or until we were arrested and taken to a cell where we could get a good night's sleep.

As it happened, the Daughters of the American Revolution were meeting at the hotel. When these little old ladies, many of them from the South, came out and saw two Black men sitting in the lobby, they started screaming and hollering, "Eek! Eek!" and running for cover.

"All right, fellows," the manager said. "You win. I found your reservations, but I want you to know, I will never, *never* find them again."

That experience is still alive within me, like an open wound. And I will sleep anywhere in Washington today, even on the ground—but not at the Shoreham.

Black frequent travelers knew one another. Almost all northern hotels had special floors or special sections on special floors—generally the fourth, fifth, or sixth floors where they had the catering offices and the banquet offices— that were reserved for Blacks.

There were similar problems in fancy nightclubs. Sammy Davis, Jr., and other Black headliners went to bat for us and forced clubs to seat us in special sections. At Chicago's famous Chez Paree, the Black side was always on the right side of the stage.

While we were fighting these battles, the world continued to turn. Jackie Robinson integrated baseball, Charles ("Chuck") Cooper integrated basketball, Kenny Washington integrated football, Ralph Bunche got a Nobel Prize for negotiating a settlement in Palestine, Harry Truman integrated the armed forces, and a federal court struck down segregation in D.C., prompting an *Afro-American* headline that I wish I had run: "Eat Anywhere."

Most of this progress was a product of impersonal forces, like the Cold War, but some of it was pressured by men like Adam Clayton Powell, the new congressman from Harlem; Walter White, the blond and blue-eyed Black who headed the NAACP; and Asa Philip Randolph, who launched the March on Washington Movement.

Walter White, who was perhaps our first celebrity leader, was the de facto president of Black America. Whenever anything happened to a Black anywhere, even in Europe, Walter fired off a telegram and demanded action.

He was a charming man, probably the most charming man we've had in public life, and he called everybody by his or her first name. I remember that we waited with anticipation to see how Walter would address President Roosevelt's wife. We should have known. He treated her the same way he treated all Americans, Black and White. He called her Eleanor.

Adam Clayton Powell, Jr., the flamboyant congressman from Harlem, was another *Ebony* favorite. Powell, like White, was a newspaperman's dream. Audacious. Outrageous. Colorful. Willing to talk about anything and to admit anything. He was the exact opposite of Congressman Dawson, who worked quietly behind the scenes. Powell, unlike Dawson, would call a racist a racist, and he would say it on the radio, in newspapers, anywhere. Although he was so light-skinned he could have passed for White, he gave a new meaning to the word *Black*. He was perhaps the first Black to talk about "audacious Black power."

Powell was attracted to women and attracted women. He and his wife, pianist Hazel Scott, had a life-style that fascinated the press. Adam was seen in public with women of all races, and Hazel lived her own life. I asked her about it once and she said in a quote that was picked up by the White press, "Nobody understands Adam and me, but we understand each other."

There was also a lot of discussion about Paul Robeson, who set a new record for Shakespearean drama on Broadway with his 296 performances in *Othello*. We don't know, we will probably never know the truth about Robeson's political activities, but he was a persuasive symbol to Black men and women of all stations and situations.

I met him for the first time at a party given by Earl and Kathryn Dickerson. He was tall, the tallest man in the room, handsome, with a deep booming voice and a dazzling smile. I don't think I've ever seen a more impressive man.

I thought to myself, Here's a man who's made it. A world figure. Phi Beta Kappa. All-American. Singer. Actor. Scholar. Why doesn't he just enjoy his success and live a quiet life?

As if in answer to my unspoken question, he told us that night that no Black would ever be truly free until all Blacks were free. He said that although he was a celebrated figure, he made it a practice never to go anywhere as Paul Robeson that he couldn't go as a Black man.

"None of us," he concluded, "can be satisfied with our little personal successes. Having made it ourselves, we must find our own particular way, depending on our education and profession, to give something back to the community and to those who are less fortunate than we are."

It was the first time I'd heard that kind of talk from a man as successful as Robeson.

It was at this party, incidentally, that I met Freda DeKnight, who was a personal friend of the Dickersons. She flew in to help Kathryn prepare the meal, which was so delicious that she was brought out and introduced to the guests. She told me that she liked *Ebony* but that we needed a feature on cooking. One thing led to another, and I hired her to do free-lance work from New York. She later joined the staff and moved to Chicago.

# 24

# *Going First Class Is the Best Revenge*

OR as long as I can remember, I've been fascinated by the idea of going first class. That idea, which has nothing at all to do with money, is part of my management style. It's part of my operating philosophy. It informs my view of men, women, events, and the world.

From my standpoint, going first class is only a rough approximation of a meaning that transcends meaning. For, as Fats Waller told the woman who asked for a definition of jazz, "If you've got to ask, you'll never know."

Going first class means, among other things, going with class *and* style. There are people who have class but who don't have style. There are people who have style but who don't have class. Going first class is going with class, style, grace, elegance, and excellence.

It's impossible to define the concept with mathematical precision. But most people know it when they see it.

There's first-class wine, and second-class wine.

There's first-class work, and second-class work.

There's first-class love, and second-class love.

For as long as I can remember I've been fascinated by the concept, and for almost as long I've believed that going first class is the best revenge.

This goes back, I think, to my childhood in the second-class section of Arkansas City and my days on welfare in Chicago and the years of being turned away from first-class hotels and restaurants.

I decided in those years that if I ever, *ever* had a chance to go first class I was never going second class again. I've held to that view. It's my personal policy, a policy born of experience, that Johnson Publishing Company goes first class or we don't go at all.

That policy came to the fore in 1949 when I tried to renegotiate my lease at our corporate headquarters at 5125 Calumet. I'd made extensive improvements in the building, and I thought this entitled me to a lower leasing rate. To my surprise and disgust, the owners prorated the improvements over the lifetime of the lease and said that I would have to pay a higher leasing rate.

This infuriated me, and I stormed out of the meeting in search of other accommodations. What I really wanted was to move downtown. I was tired of working on back streets. South/South State Street was a back street. Calumet Avenue was a back street. I wanted to work on a front street. I wanted to go first class.

This was a tall order for a Black in 1949, and Eunice and I looked all over the South Loop for a two- or three-story building. One day she rushed into my office and told me that the old Hursen Funeral Home at 1820 South Michigan Avenue was for sale. I was delighted. Michigan Avenue was one of Chicago's great streets and 1820 was only eighteen blocks from the center of the Loop.

I called and asked Hursen the price of the building. He said $52,000. I asked if I could come by and see it. He said, "Of course, what's the name of your company?"

"Negro Digest Publishing Company."

Silence.

A long silence.

Then Hursen said he had a previous commitment and couldn't show the building to me then or later. There was a problem, in fact, and the building was no longer for sale.

I knew what the problem was. But it was useless to argue over the phone. Eunice and I found a White lawyer, Louis Wilson, who told Hursen that he represented a publishing house in the East and that he was sorry to hear that the building was no longer for sale. Hursen told Wilson that he had been misinformed. The building was still for sale. And the price of $52,000 was negotiable.

Wilson told Hursen that the eastern publisher was not interested in haggling, that he wanted to move in right away.

"There is, however, one stipulation. The people out East will have a Black man living on the place, as a kind of custodian, janitor, and bodyguard. Since they can't come out here, they want him to see the place and tell them what he thinks."

The arrangements were made, and I put on work clothes and followed Hursen around the building. He gave special attention to the boiler room that I would have to fire, he said, and the quarters on the top floor, where I would probably be living.

I told him, at the end of the tour, that I was impressed and that I was going to report favorably to my boss. Which I did, since I was the boss. The building was bought in trust so no one could identify the purchaser.

We paid $52,000 cash for the building—the money came from the sale of Beauty Star hair products—and spent $200,000 renovating it. When our friend, interior decorator Viola Marshall, got through with the old funeral home, it was one of the most elegant office buildings in Black America.

The showplace of the building was the editorial department operations room. It was decorated with blowup panels of some of the best photos from *Ebony*. The building included an employees' dining room, where employees paid forty-eight cents for a full-course meal.

"The publisher's mammoth private office," *Newsweek* said, "where he sits behind an oversized desk, is trimmed in blond mahogany. Decor in the roomy, three-floor building is sleekly modern."

On Wednesday, June 1, 1949, we opened the new building with a champagne party that marked the real beginning of the *Ebony* success story. There were Black and White media executives, Black and White businessmen, and so many authors, artists and politicians that it was difficult to keep count. Among the celebrities on hand were Lena Horne, Pulitzer Prize-winner Gwendolyn Brooks, and former track star and politician Ralph Metcalfe.

I was thirty-one on the night of my coming-out party, and I was a millionaire—seven years after I started *Negro Digest* with a $500 loan and a bootstrap.

There were stories on the *Ebony* miracle in media all over America. But few people knew my name. And nobody or almost nobody knew the man behind the name.

I was, in fact, a mystery man.

Some said I was White.

Others said I was a nonentity fronting for Whites.

Still others said I didn't exist.

Some people, betraying their ignorance and their bias, said the magazine was so slick and professional and our offices were so elegant and functional that the owner couldn't possibly be a Black man.

There were others who pointed to our White employees and said that if Whites didn't own it they soon would. It was widely said that Ben Burns, the highly visible White executive editor, was going to take the magazine away from me.

I was flabbergasted by this talk, which indicated, at the least, a lack of confidence in Black entrepreneurial skill and a lack of information on the steel inside John H. Johnson. For how could any White person "take" the company from me if I owned all the stock and if he or she didn't work with or near the money?

I tried to explain this, but rumors—which are impervious to facts—continued. They became so widespread that we took the extraordinary step of printing my photograph over a story which said, in effect, that this is John H. Johnson and he is a Negro.

The story in the "Backstage" section of the January 1947 *Ebony* said that I owned 100 percent of the stock along with my wife and mother.

"Johnson," it added, "is a Negro, as anyone with eyes can see....He is the brains and money behind this enterprise...."

This didn't end the rumors, which continued until *Life* folded and *Ebony* survived.

I ignored the rumors and dug in for the next phase of the *Ebony* journey. I was a success, by the world's reckoning, but I was a long way from home. I felt a sense of achievement, of exhilaration even, but I was still running scared. I was only sixteen years from the Mississippi mud, only thirteen years from welfare, and it was impossible for me to feel secure. Even today, I don't feel secure. A person who comes up from poverty, up from segregation, up from outhouses, up from welfare and humiliation and nos, can never feel secure, no matter how high he rises. He can never forget where he came from, for he knows, if he's intelligent, that he can go back to that place or to a lower and hotter place.

The magazine had changed, my bank account had changed, but I hadn't changed. There was, however, a critical and disorienting change in the way the world organized itself around me. People who'd never noticed me before noticed me. Society people who'd never sent me invitations before sent me invitations. And women, pretty women, who had never spoken to me before went out of their way to say hello.

I seemed to have grown larger in the world. I seemed to occupy a new space.

I'd been down and now I was up. Up was better.

# The _____
# Color _____
# of _____
# Success _____

# 25

## Jet

**E**BONY.
Tan.
Copper.
Hue.
Jet.

These were the colors of my personal rainbow, along with the white contributed by advertisers and the green, gold, and silver of money.

In the wild and fruitful years following the opening of my new building, I used four of these words to christen new magazines that were designed to corner the color market.

The runaway success of *Ebony* had made me king of the mountain in the undiscovered Negro consumer market. But the kingdoms of the media world are fragile things, and I lived in constant fear that someone or some thing might overrun my position and push me back down the mountain.

To forestall this possibility, I tried to anticipate every

change in the market. Whenever I found a White magazine with strong Black readership, I brought out a Black counterpart, using names which tried to capture the color black, which, in Black America, includes all colors—cream, chocolate, anthracite, plum, café au lait, and burning brown.

During the true-confessions period, I brought out two magazines, *Tan Confessions* (November 1950) and *Copper Romance*. When, in 1951, the market shifted to pocket-sized magazines like *Look* magazine's *Quick*, I responded with *Hue*, a pocket-sized feature magazine, and *Jet*, a pocket-sized newsmagazine.

*Tan*, *Copper*, and *Hue* made money and passed away, having satisfied the transient needs that called them into existence. But *Jet* was a magazine of a different color. Like *Ebony*, which survived the *Look* and *Life* models, *Jet* survived *Quick* and added a permanent dash of blackness to the American media rainbow.

The word *jet* was tailor-made for my purposes. A talking word that sounds its message, jet means on one level a very dark velvet-black. And it means on another level fast, as in the airplane. From these dictionary definitions, it is but one step, and not a long one at that, to the Black American definition of "a fast Black magazine."

The name came to me in a roundabout way. Walter Winchell kept running items saying that this person or that person was going to put out a Negro magazine called "Jet." This went on for several months when I had no interest in starting a small magazine. When the winds changed and I decided to put out a compact, easy-to-read magazine, *jet* was clearly the best word for what I wanted to say and do.

I investigated and discovered that the name had been registered by a company that put out magazines for airplane mechanics. While other people were talking to Walter Winchell, I acted, buying the name and publishing on Thursday, November 1, 1951, the first issue of *Jet* magazine.

The pocket-sized magazine (5¾" by 4") sold for fifteen cents. Edna Robinson, who was the wife of former middleweight champion Sugar Ray Robinson, and who was pound for pound one of the most beautiful women in the world, was on the cover of the first magazine.

"In the world today," I said in the first issue, "everything is moving along at a faster clip. There is more news and far less time to read it. That's why we are introducing our new magazine, JET, to give Blacks everywhere a *weekly news magazine* in handy, pocket-sized form. Each week we will bring you complete news coverage on happenings among Negroes all over the U.S.—in entertainment, politics, sports, social events as well as features on unusual personalities, places and events...."

The lead story in the sixty-eight-page magazine was on the quashing of the remaining indictments against two Negroes and two Whites accused of conspiracy in the anti-Negro riots in the White Chicago suburb of Cicero. There were two other major stories. One was on the snubbing of Josephine Baker by Manhattan's Stork Club. The other was on the U.S. Senate confirmation of Dr. Channing Tobias as a delegate to the United Nations.

The first issue of the new magazine sold out everywhere and became a collector's item. Within six months, we were selling 300,000 copies a week and the magazine was the largest Black newsmagazine in the world, a position it has held now for thirty-eight years. Even at that early date, it was the focus of whole-souled attention in Negro America, where it was affectionately known as "the Negro's Bible." When a character in one of Maya Angelou's plays was asked if she'd read about a certain event in the *New York Times* or *Time*, she said, "If it wasn't in *Jet*, it didn't happen."

The phenomenal growth of the magazine continued after we increased the size (to 7⅜″ by 5¼″) and the price ($1.25 in 1989). Thirty-eight years after it was founded, *Jet* sells 900,000 copies a week and usually has a full complement of ads from major advertisers.

\*      \*      \*

When I did it the first time with *Negro Digest*, they said it was a fluke.

When I did it the second time with *Ebony*, they said I was lucky.

When I struck black gold the third straight time with *Jet*, there was a barrage of media stories, and people started talking about "the Johnson magic."

Two months after the first issue of *Jet* was published, I received my first major national award, selection as one of the Ten Outstanding Young Men of 1951 by the U.S. Junior Chamber of Commerce (Jaycees). In previous years, the organization had honored, among others, Walt Disney (1936), Orson Welles and Nelson Rockefeller (1941), John F. Kennedy and Joe Louis (1946), Richard Nixon (1947), and Gerald Ford (1949).

As the second Black selected, and the first Black businessman, I was the center of attention at the awards ceremony in Dayton, Ohio, on Friday, January 19, 1952, my thirty-fourth birthday.

Among the other honorees, all of whom were between twenty-one and thirty-five, were physician-educator Arthur C. Guyton; Stanley Hiller, Jr., the twenty-seven-year-old president of the world's largest manufacturer of helicopters; Gordon B. McLendon, head of the Liberty Broadcasting System; Congressman Charles E. Potter; and American Legion commander Donald R. Wilson. Thirty-seven years later, two of the ten—Dr. Guyton of the University of Mississippi and John H. Johnson—are still listed in *Who's Who in America*.

There was a flip side to this shining coin. It was unusual in that era for a Black to break bread at this level. Dayton friends told me that no Black had been admitted to the exclusive Horseshoe Club and that I would almost certainly be turned away at the door. I wasn't turned away at the Horseshoe Club luncheon or at the awards dinner at the Hotel Biltmore. But I still felt a chill. Most of the guests, with the delightful exceptions of McLendon and Hiller, were cool and distant.

Despite these tensions, the Jaycees citation was a turning point in national recognition and acceptance by the business leaders of America. Even to this day I recall the personal citation, which said, in part: "He developed publications that record and describe the progress of the Negro in America and serve as inspiration to all Negroes. Through these publications, he has made available for the first time a current history of the Negro people in America."

# 26

## Building the Foundations of the Dream

SOMEBODY said once that you have to cut off old branches for new buds to blossom.

That's good advice in dealing with trees and bushes, but pruning institutions linked to you by the umbilical cords of your first hopes is like cutting off your own arms and legs.

*Negro Digest*, the major Johnson Publishing Company casualty of this era, was a classic case of the conflict between the heart and the balance sheet. It was my first magazine love, and it will always have a special place in my heart. But it became clear early in the fifties that my new magazines, *Ebony* in particular, had destroyed the circulation foundation of *Negro Digest*.

The old magazine still had a fanatically loyal group of subscribers, but the parade of pictures had passed it by. I discontinued it in November 1951, the same month that *Jet* was born. I'd learned by that time something James Bond didn't learn until later, that spies and businessmen and survivors should never say never. I made that clear when we discontinued the magazine, saying that we were stopping it for the moment but that we might revive it in the future.

In discontinuing *Negro Digest*, I acted from strength, not weakness. I was discarding from a strong hand because I needed the time and space to focus on the major managerial tasks of the decade: refining the formula and building a strong foundation for the surviving magazines.

The immediate problems before me at that juncture were almost overwhelming. I had to recruit, train, and equip a business staff to count and manage the money. I had to invent and motivate a new staff of editors and advertising specialists. I had to move from this foundation and expand the shallow advertising beachheads of the forties. This work had to be done under tremendous pressures in the face of mounting cash flow problems and the repeated recessions of the postwar years.

What made this so challenging was that I couldn't slice up the problems, salami-like, and deal with them one by one. Everything had to be done at the same time, and everything had to be done at once.

I solved the administrative problem by recruiting bright men and women and training them on the job. I found some of my first employees in White-owned publishing houses and corporations where they'd been confined to minor and even menial positions. My cousin, Willie Miles Burns, who'd shared some of my Arkansas City experiences, was a whiz at mathematics. I put her in charge of counting and managing the subscription numbers. Mildred Clark, who started as a clerk in the finance department, worked her way up to the position of vice president and comptroller. Lincoln T. Hudson, a war hero and a former fighter pilot, became an advertising specialist and broke some of our biggest accounts.

Sylvestre Watkins was an author and an editor at Follett Book Publishing Company. I made him circulation manager. Watkins was succeeded by Robert H. Fentress, who sold magazines on southern buses and on Harlem street corners before moving to headquarters and mastering the intricacies of circulation.

James E. Beifuss was a computer expert who came in to help us iron out some glitches in our system. He was so competent that I persuaded him to leave St. Jude Publishing Company to manage our computer operation, with the assistance of Claudia Hunter. It didn't matter to me that Beifuss was White. And it didn't matter to Beifuss that I was Black. What we wanted to do together was to create the best magazine computer operations in the world. We are not there yet, but we are on the way.

We were selling success, and we practiced what we preached, turning out more certified individual success stories than any corporation of comparable size. June Acie Rhinehart was a high school graduate who joined our organization as a secretary and worked her way up to the position of executive secretary to the publisher. She worked days and studied nights, earning a bachelor's degree and a law degree. She is now vice president and general counsel of the corporation. Another vice president, LaDoris J. Foster, learned modern personnel practices the old-fashioned way: on the job. Few personnel managers are as knowledgeable and efficient.

There were other managers and executives who came on board in the early years and stood the test of time, assistant circulation manager Virginia Tibbs, for example, photo editor Basil O. Phillips, and art directors Norman L. Hunter and Herbert Temple.

Under the system I set up in the fifties, these individuals were expected to master several skills. We prided ourselves on being supermanagers and super-Negroes. We had neither the time nor the resources to afford the luxury of overtrained specialists who could only do one thing. This spilled over into the editorial department where editors were expected to be generalists who could write sports today, politics tomorrow, and entertainment the day after that.

To make the jobs of staff members easier, I made major capital investments in computers and other office machines of the future.

While supervising this process with one hand, I used the other to corner the market on Black journalists and photojournalists. Some came from journalism schools, but most came from the staffs of Negro newspapers, whose pay scales were notoriously low.

Audrey Weaver, Bill Gibson, Vincent Tubbs, Louie Robinson, and Ken Carter came from the *Afro-American*. Robert E. Johnson, Lerone Bennett, Jr., and Ariel Strong came from the *Atlanta Daily World*. A. S. ("Doc") Young came from the *Chicago Defender*, and Francis Mitchell came from the *Norfolk Journal and Guide*.

I got Clotye Murdock from the *Michigan Chronicle* and Charles L. Sanders from the *Cleveland Call and Post*. Alexander Poinsett and Hans J. Massaquoi were recruited from the University of Illinois and Northwestern University, and Simeon Booker, a Nieman Fellow, came from the *Washington Post*.

It took months and, in some cases, years to persuade these men and women to move to Chicago. No one gave me a harder time than Gerri Major, the New York *Amsterdam News* society editor. I was trying to establish *Jet* as a magazine for all people from the lowest levels to the highest, and I needed Gerri, a descendant of a distinguished family who'd married a prominent doctor and who knew every important Black.

I explained all this to her and offered twice what she was making at the *Amsterdam News*. We agreed on the salary, and she went to the office of Dr. C. B. Powell, the publisher, to tell him that she was resigning. Powell, who was a friend as well as an employer, started crying and told her, "You can't leave me!" Whereupon Gerri started crying.

She called me and said she couldn't accept the position, and then I cried.

I didn't get where I am today by accepting the first no as a final no. I sent Gerri a Christmas present in 1951. I dropped her little notes of congratulations on stories she'd written. Then history dealt me an ace—the coronation of Queen Elizabeth II. No self-respecting socialite could turn down a chance to see that event up close. So I arranged for accreditation and called Gerri again.

"Gerri," I said, "we just got accreditation to send a reporter to cover the coronation of the queen. I don't know anyone who belongs there more than you. Before I give the assignment to someone else I just wanted to run it by you one more time."

There was a squeal on the telephone. "Oh! Mr. Johnson," she said. "You know I can't turn that down. All my life I've wanted to be present at something like that. Of course I'll take it."

I asked how she was going to handle Dr. Powell.

"This time," she said, "I'm going to write him a letter."

She wrote the letter, covered the queen, and worked as society editor and senior staff editor of *Jet* until she died in 1984.

The raids on the staffs of Negro newspapers didn't endear me to Negro newspaper publishers, who called me many names, none of which can be published in a book of this kind. There were other conflicts, conflicts of personality, style, perception, and background, to add to this feud. Most Negro publishers, with the notable exception of John Sengstacke of the *Chicago Defender,* considered me an upstart and went out of their way to emphasize their disdain.

This conflict didn't serve the interests of Johnson Publishing Company or Negro newspapers, and we decided in the fifties to end the wrangling. On the recommendation of John Sengstacke, I was elected a member of the National Negro Newspaper Publishers at its Atlanta convention.

This angered publisher Carl Murphy of the *Afro-American*, who had missed the Atlanta meeting. Citing constitutional provisions on proper notice to the members, Murphy called for another vote. The venerable Mr. Carl, as almost everybody called him, was the dean of Negro publishers and what Mr. Carl wanted, Mr. Carl got. So I was voted in in Atlanta and voted out in Pittsburgh. About the same time I became the first Black member of the prestigious Magazine Publishers Association.

The Negro publishers later reversed themselves and accepted my application, but I was pretty bitter by then and never attended meetings. The high-level struggle continued until 1966, when the publishers association gave me its highest award, the Russwurm Award. Just before I was introduced to receive the award, E. Washington Rhodes, publisher of the *Philadelphia Tribune*, leaned over and said, "Johnson, you deserve this award, you've earned it, and we're happy to give it to you. But I don't want you to misunderstand. We didn't like you before, and we don't like you now."

I told him that I understood and stood up and accepted the award.

Staffing the advertising department presented a different problem.

There were no Black advertising specialists to borrow or steal, and I had to roll my own. From 1949 to 1960 I crisscrossed the country, looking for ambitious Blacks with a complicated and somewhat contradictory profile. I wanted men and women who were comfortable with Whites but who were not afraid of Whites.

The first trait was desirable; the second was necessary. For you can't sell people if you're afraid of them. Sooner or later, you've got to disagree, especially when they say no. If you don't have the courage to confront them at that point and persuade them to change their minds, then the romance of selling in the big leagues is beyond you.

I fired one young man who didn't have the courage to sell. No matter what the client said, he always said yes, sir.

"How in the hell can you change anybody's mind," I asked, "if you agree with them all the time?"

I finally developed a profile of an aggressive, well-dressed individual who'd had contact with Whites and experience in persuading them to act in the interest of Black Americans. A profile, in other words, of an Urban League executive. I didn't plan it that way, but the skills we needed were the skills of National Urban League industrial secretaries, who dealt primarily with corporate America. It is no wonder, then, that we had at least five former Urban League executives working for us at one time.

The most talented of the Urban League recruits was LeRoy Jeffries, who served as assistant industrial director of the Nation Urban League before joining us as Midwest advertising manager. Smooth, charming, and aggressive, Jeffries broke several major accounts before retiring to the West Coast where he opened his own marketing and consulting firm, LeRoy W. Jeffries and Associates.

Another talented Urban Leaguer was Kenneth Wilson, who left us to take a senior advertising position with the *Afro-American*, thereby evening the score. I took a senior advertising executive from the *Afro*, and the *Afro* took one from me.

# 27

# *Looking for Front Streets*

AFTER assembling the best advertising and editorial staff in Black America, I started looking in the midfifties for branch office space in major cities.

The search was complicated by racial barriers and my personal requirements. I didn't want *any* office space. I wanted the best space available. And it had to be on a front street. For I believed then, and I believe now, that an address says something about an individual or a company. It's a way of saying that you represent quality.

This was, in part, an extension of the lessons I learned at Supreme Life from senior executives like Harry Pace and Earl B. Dickerson. They were men of quality. They wore the best clothes, lived in the best neighborhoods, drove the best cars. They taught me a lesson I've never forgotten, that quality is the guarantor and hallmark of success.

I was also influenced by my early experiences on the other side of Front Street in Arkansas City. The name was accurate. Arkansas City's Front Street was the foremost street. It occupied the best real estate, and it was at the center of the commercial and social life of the city.

The first office we rented in New York City was a compromise. The only downtown office space I could find was at 55 West Forty-second Street, which was a kind of back street. Since I couldn't do any better at that time, I took the minimum and started planning for the maximum.

When our lease expired, I went to the landlord and asked for space in one of his properties on Fifth Avenue.

He looked at me as if seeing me for the first time, and said: "Johnson, you're not ready for Fifth Avenue yet. When you're ready, I'll let you know."

Livid with anger, I went to see William Zeckendorf, a wheeler and dealer of the day, who seemed to be buying every available piece of property in Manhattan. He apparently was not paying much money down on his acquisitions, for one of the jokes of the day revolved around his problems in buying a $25-million building in California. According to the joke, one of his associates said, "It's a good price, the only problem is that they want $5,000 down."

Regardless of what might be said of Zeckendorf, he was, at least in my view, a genuinely decent human being. A little eccentric perhaps, but decent. He had this thing about time. No matter who you were and what you wanted, he'd give you a few minutes and ask you to leave.

The day I saw him he was sitting behind this little glass desk with nothing on it except five telephones, a pencil, and a pad. The phones were ringing and Zeckendorf was sitting there, serene, unflappable, buying and selling.

When I walked in, he put down one of the telephones and said, "What do you want, Johnson?"

I told him I was having a hard time finding office space in New York City. "Every time they discover that I'm Black, they remember a previous commitment or a prior negotiation, and they won't let me have it."

"We don't believe in anything like that here," he said.

"I only have one good building now, that's the Chrysler Building. You can have anything in it you can afford."

He pushed a button and an aide came in.

"This is John Johnson," he said. "He's a friend of mine. Give him anything he wants that he can afford."

I was impressed and wanted to sit down and talk to him. But he looked up, surprised apparently to find me still there, and said: "That's all, Johnson."

As I left, a man who'd come all the way from Kansas City filed in and asked one question. Zeckendorf said yes. The man then tried to explain his proposition. Zeckendorf held up his hand and told him, "I said yes. Do you want me to say no?"

I had a yes for the Chrysler Building, but I was aiming higher. A sales representative had told my New York manager, William P. Grayson, that space was available at Rockefeller Center, 1270 Avenue of the Americas, directly across from the new *Time-Life* Building. Grayson and I talked to the sales representative, who told us that he'd checked our credit references and that we didn't qualify.

"What do you mean by references?" I asked.

He said the traditional credit sources for real estate.

"Well, sir," I said, "what you really mean is that you want to be sure people will be able to pay the rent for the period of time that they lease the space. Is that correct?"

He said yes.

"Well," I said, "we want a two-year lease. What if we give you all the cash in advance? Would that meet your requirement?"

He had the decency to blush in shame.

"Look, fellows," he said, dropping his head. "It's really not me. It's somebody higher up."

I knew a man who was as high as you could get in Rockefeller circles. I'd met Winthrop Rockefeller at an Urban League affair, and I got his number in Arkansas and called him.

I was afraid that he'd forgotten me, but he said, "Yes,

Johnny, Johnny—yes, I remember you, you're Johnny Johnson. You have those magazines. What can I do for you?"

I told him that I was trying to find office space in New York and I understood that space was available in Rockefeller Center.

Winthrop sometimes stuttered when he talked because he thought faster than he could enunciate the words.

"John-John-John-Johnny," he asked, "is there space there?"

"Yes."

"Du-du-du-du-do you have the money?"

"Yes."

"You got it!" he said.

"What do I do now?" I asked.

He said, "Do nothing, somebody will call you."

In less than an hour, I got a call from the president of Rockefeller Center. Mr. Rockefeller had told him that I was interested in space in Rockefeller Center. He said he would be glad to show it to me personally at my convenience.

I leased the space, hired an interior decorator, and ended up with one of the best-looking office suites on the island of Manhattan.

I called Winthrop Rockefeller and told him it was a pleasure doing business with people at the top. He was pleased that the Rockefeller Center staff had been able to work something out. He didn't ask for a quid pro quo but he said, in passing, that his brother Nelson was thinking about running for governor of New York and that the family would appreciate it if I would make sure that he got fair treatment in my magazines. I said I would, and I did.

The problems I faced in New York City were not unique; I was confronted with higher barriers in Washington D.C., where Blacks couldn't even get office space in the downtown section on a back street, to say nothing of a front street. I went from real estate office to real estate office until I found an honest White southerner, who said: "Now look, Johnson, I have space but I'm not renting to you. I'm going to be honest with you. Washington is a southern town, inhabited and controlled by southerners. And nobody is going to rent you any space."

He dropped his voice and added, "There's only one place in this town that will rent office space to a Black, and that's a building owned by Standard Oil Company [which was a Rockefeller interest]. There's a man at that building who will rent you an office. He's the only one in this town who'll rent space to you. So quit wearing out your shoes and running up your blood pressure."

I went to 266 Constitution Avenue Northwest, at the foot of Capitol Hill. And, sure enough, the agent rented space that made us the first Black-owned company with a downtown office in the nation's capital.

We later moved to a better location, still not front street, on the corner of K Street. We stayed there until the building was torn down. In the meantime, Simeon Booker, our Washington Bureau Chief, had made friends with Walter Trohan, the chief of the Washington Bureau of the *Chicago Tribune*. Booker mentioned to Trohan one day that the old management of our present building had rejected our application.

"That's ridiculous," Trohan said. "Give me the name of the agent. I know there's space in that building."

He called the agent and said, according to the information we received, "These people from Johnson Publishing Company are as fine a people as you'll find in any race or religion. I've worked with them side by side for several years. They have the money, they conduct themselves the way other people conduct themselves, and they deserve to be in that building just as much as I or any other White person. And if you don't give them space, I'm going public with the story. I'm going to run it in the *Tribune* and I'm going to urge all my colleagues in the National Press Club to boycott the building."

Because of Trohan's intervention, we were given space on the thirteenth floor at 1750 Pennsylvania Avenue, a half block from the White House. It quickly became apparent that superstition is a universal trait. Superstitious Whites shunned the thirteenth floor. We were, in fact, the only tenants on the thirteenth floor for many months. Which didn't bother us at all. We rented a suite and got a whole floor and a long sweep of windows overlooking Pennsylvania Avenue.

When John F. Kennedy was inaugurated, we threw a big party for seven hundred people, all of whom had a front seat overlooking the parade. After the management changed, the number of tenants on our floor increased, and our situation improved markedly.

Roughly the same thing happened in Los Angeles, where I tried for years to get office space on Wilshire Boulevard. While waiting for the winds to change, we rented office space in the Black community. It was on a main street, Adams Avenue, but I never stopped testing the Wilshire Boulevard line. We finally found space at 1125 Wilshire Boulevard, which is a very desirable location today but was an industrial area then.

I followed the Johnson rule and took what I could get while continuing my campaign for something better. During this campaign, I met a White real estate agent who told me that he had space but didn't have the authority to rent to Blacks. "But if I ever get authority," he said, "I'm going to call you." Fate favored the White agent and Johnson Publishing Company. He made it to the top and recommended us to the agent at our present location, the Travelers Insurance Building at 3600 Wilshire Boulevard.

Thus, by a roundabout route, with many strange turnings, we completed the circuit of front streets. Was it worth it? Of course it was worth it. Quality, like virtue, is its own reward.

The Avenue of the Americas, Pennsylvania Avenue, Wilshire Boulevard—we were on front streets from sea to shining sea. The only remaining real estate task—a task of the seventies—was to find the road to downtown Chicago.

# 28

# *Persistence Pays Off*

BUILDING on new and secure foundations, we moved in the fifties to implement Phase II of our advertising plan.

In Phase I, we had broken several individual accounts. The major objective of Phase II was to make *Ebony* and the Negro consumer market integral parts of the marketing and advertising agendas of corporate America.

To accomplish this, we had to make four points: (1) that Black consumers existed; (2) that they had disposable income; (3) that they bought brand-name products; (4) that they could and would buy additional products if they were appealed to directly and personally.

Simple points. Obvious points. Why did it take so long to make them? One reason was the invisibility of the obvious. Nothing, in fact, is harder than to see than what stares us in the face. The Negro consumer market was so big, so obvious, and so critically important to the balance sheets of American industries that advertising and marketing experts couldn't see the forest for the trees.

Another reason, of course, was race and the myths that made foreign markets more visible and appealing than the invisible and more profitable Negro markets in the undiscovered countries of Negro communities a few blocks away.

We broke through the plate glass of invisibility by proving that Black consumers not only existed but that they bought proportionately more brand-name products than White consumers. We proved, for example, that Blacks were buying, proportionately, more premium Scotch and more big cars than their White counterparts.

How did agencies and corporations respond to all this?

They refused to believe it, even when Black researchers proved it, even when White researchers proved it, even when the U.S. Census Bureau proved it.

We were forced therefore to go back into the trenches and wage an agency-by-agency struggle that was so hard that it hurts me to think about it, even today.

By far the hardest industry to sell was the automobile industry. We sent an advertising salesman to Detroit every week for ten years before we broke our first major account at Chrysler, followed a few years later by General Motors. And this was in the days before routine air travel. The salesman made the round trip on the train every week.

Another major advertiser, Campbell Soup, didn't advertise with us or any other Black medium. Eastern advertising director William P. Grayson said he spent seventeen years, six months, five days, two hours, and thirty minutes on that account. It was, he said, like the labor of Sisyphus, pushing large stones up hills only to see them roll down again. He'd spend years persuading an advertising manager and then, just as he was making progress, the manager would be transferred and he would have to start over.

I had a similar experience in Chicago trying to sell Sears Roebuck. I spent years cultivating George Struthers, the ad manager. I wrote letters, sent birthday, holiday, and anniversary cards. I tried in every way I could to sell him. Then, on a day I'll never forget, he said, "John, I think we're going to do it." Would you believe it?—he died a day or so later of a heart attack. I said to myself, Even the Lord doesn't want us to have this account.

I kept on working on the theory that the Lord or somebody would have a change of heart. Fortunately for me, Struthers was replaced by James Button, who'd been working for Sears in Canada and who was not familiar with American racial barriers. I told him the same story I'd been telling Struthers and he gave us our first Sears ad.

The basic point of these cases is persistence. I refused to give up. I refused to take no for an answer, and I refused to let others take no for an answer.

# 29

## *How to Sell Anybody Anything in Five Minutes or Less*

IF I know enough about people, and if I have enough time, I can sell anybody anything.

Even if I don't have enough time, I can open the door to a future sale.

In my early days as a salesman, I usually asked clients and prospects for only five minutes. I've been known, in fact, to ask for only two minutes.

Sometimes you can't tell your story in five minutes, but if you ask for five minutes, people are more inclined to give you an appointment. If you get your foot in the door and tell a good story, they'll probably let you finish, even if it takes thirty minutes or an hour. If, on the other hand, there's no interest in what you're saying, a minute is enough.

It was my custom in the early days to ask for five minutes and to take fifteen or twenty minutes by creative ad-libbing. I would make my presentation in about five minutes, then stand up as if I intended to go. This usually relaxed the client, and I would say, "There's one more point I want to make."

Then, two or three minutes later, I would say, "I'm really going now, but I want to make sure you understand this point."

As I was going through the door with my briefcase, just before I pulled the door shut, I would pause, like TV detective Peter Falk, and say, "I just want to leave this final thought with you."

What made this five-minute drill effective was not the five minutes the client could see but the weeks and months of preparation that he couldn't see. For when the five-minute clock started ticking, I knew more about him—more about his interests, passions, hobbies, desires—than most members of his family.

Whether I had five or thirty-five minutes, I always based my presentation on three tried-and-tested rules:

1. Grab the client's attention in the first two or three seconds with a fact or an emotional statement that hits him where he lives or does business.

2. Find the vulnerable spot. Everybody has something that will make him or her move or say yes. It may have nothing in the world to do with his or her business life. It may be a dream or a hope or a commitment to a person or a thing. Selling is finding the vulnerable point and pushing the yes button.

A remarkable example of this was reported by William Grayson, who discovered that a powerful advertising executive was a fan of Roy Campanella, the great Brooklyn Dodgers catcher. The executive and his son virtually lived in the old Ebbets Field and virtually worshipped the home-plate ground Campanella walked on.

Grayson, who lived down the street from Campanella, asked the baseball star to autograph one of his home-run balls to the boy. The ball carried not only Campanella's name but the date he hit the home run. By coincidence, the advertising executive and his son had been in Ebbets

Field on the day Campanella hit the home run. That sold the account. Nothing—neither statistics nor pretty graphs nor hundreds of telephone calls—was as powerful as an unexpectedly powerful gift to a loved one.

3. Find and emphasize common ground. You and the client may disagree on many things. You may like Jesse Jackson and he or she may dislike Jesse Jackson. You're not there to talk about what divides you. You're there to emphasize the values, hopes, and aspirations that bind you together. Successful selling is a matter of finding common ground, no matter how narrow it might be, on which you and your client can stand together.

That's true in selling and life, especially in the area of race relations, where both Blacks and Whites must make a special effort to emphasize the things that unite them.

Does this mean that you have to sacrifice your integrity? Certainly not. I've been selling on the edge for forty-seven years, and I don't think I've had to compromise my integrity. I've stooped in some cases to conquer, but I don't apologize for that—the conquering, I mean.

You don't have to compromise your integrity to sell. You simply have to find and emphasize the things that unite you instead of the things that divide you.

By these different methods, by persistence and ingenuity and gall, I established narrow but solid common ground that gave me room to maneuver. Although I found and pushed a lot of yes buttons, the struggle for a fair share of the advertising dollar continued, and continues.

In advertising, as in politics, you're no better than your last schedule or your last election. No matter how many accounts you've broken, no matter how many elections you've won, you always start a new campaign at ground zero. And you're always faced with the task of going on cold and proving to a new audience how good you are.

# 30

## *Inventing the Black Consumer Market*

I T was impossible.
 Trying to reach and sell ten thousand ad managers
and CEOs individually was like trying to touch the
rainbow: The goal receded as I advanced.

I therefore changed directions and developed—some say I
invented—the Black consumer market.

I'd sown the seeds of this idea in the forties in a series
of presentations that stressed the untapped potential of
Black American consumers. As early as May 1947, I pointed
out in an *Ebony* "Backstage" that "big advertisers of consumer items fail to recognize the immensity of the Negro
market, which far exceeds Canada's total imports from the
U.S."

I returned to this theme in the early fifties, telling
advertisers that there was a gold mine in their backyards.
One of the basic documents of the Negro market campaign

was the article I wrote for *Advertising Age* (March 17, 1952) on the "do's and don'ts" of selling Negro consumers.

"The Negro market," I wrote, "is a fifteen billion dollar market. It is ripe and ready. In the seventeen largest cities the Negro population is virtually a 'city within a city.' In these seventeen cities the Negro community is from 15 percent to 42 percent of the total population. The Negro market is twice as big as the total population of Belgium, Greece or Australia—and it's right here at home."

In this article and in two *Ebony*-produced movies—*There's Gold in Your Backyard* and *The Secret of Selling the Negro*—I pointed out that Blacks were brand-conscious consumers who wanted to be treated like everyone else—not better, not worse. Based on my experiences and the reports of our advertising representatives, I offered a set of "do's and don'ts" that can be consulted with profit today.

1. Instruct salesmen to be friendly. Don't use first names unless the Negro customer or retailer indicates a willingness to "trade" first names.

2. Treat every Black as an individual.

3. Talk to Blacks on the same level that you use in talking to other customers.

4. In conversation, don't use the term "nigger," "Negress," "darky," or "boy."

5. Avoid perpetuating the stereotype of the happy-go-lucky menial, the stupid, ghost-frightened, or "Uncle Tom" servant, or the fat, overjovial "mammy."

This was not sociology; this was hard-boiled marketing. To increase the profits of corporate America and, incidentally, the profits of Johnson Publishing Company, we had to change the perceptions of corporate America.

One of our salesmen had problems selling an executive of a major flour company, who'd been told that Negroes didn't like chocolate cake or chocolate frosting on cake. To convince him that this was merely a myth, we proved by market research that Negroes not only consumed impressive quantities of chocolate cake and frosting but also bought a lot of chocolate ice cream.

By spotlighting the Negro market, we helped create new jobs for Blacks in advertising and related fields. We're accustomed today to Black advertising agencies, Black advertising specialists, and Black models. But back then, a mere forty years ago, there were no Black ad agencies or Black models. There wasn't even a single Black, not even a secretary, working for White ad agencies.

We helped change all that. After breaking an account, we stressed the importance of using Black models. Most companies resisted this idea. Wild as it may seem now, many companies were opposed to showing Black models washing clothes, although advertising managers knew full well that Black women had been washing clothes in America for centuries.

We broke the back of this prejudice by proving that Black people, like other people, respond more positively to ads featuring men and women they can identify with. It was relatively easy to make this point, for some companies ran the same ads in *Ebony* and *Life*, using Black models in *Ebony* and White models in *Life*. Invariably, without exception, ads with Black models got a more favorable response in Black America. Little by little, ad inch by ad inch, there dawned a realization that it was more believable and more effective to appeal to Black consumers in advertisements featuring models that looked like Black Americans.

There was a tendency at first to use light-skinned models who looked like White Americans. But the sixties brought the full spectrum of Blackness. Unfortunately and sadly, we're moving back to the old days, and the models are getting lighter and lighter.

Largely because of our efforts, the fashion business was opened to gorgeous Black models who posed at first for *Ebony* ads and then moved, in the sixties and seventies, to their present positions of eminence in New York, Hollywood, and Paris. Among the celebrated beauties who made their debut in our pages was Diahann Carroll, who modeled for *Ebony* when she was fourteen years old. We can also list Jayne Kennedy, Pam Grier, Lola Falana, Marilyn McCoo, and Judy Pace, all of whom appeared as *Jet* beauties before achieving fame as actresses and entertainers.

Having pulled advertising agencies across that hurdle, we next went to bat for Black advertising and marketing specialists. Our argument here, as elsewhere, was enlightened self-interest. It was simply good business and common sense to use Black sales representatives to visit stores in Black America and to represent corporate America on Black college campuses and at Black conventions.

We paid the price all pioneers pay. Since we had the only game in our town, advertising agencies and corporations got into the habit of stealing our experts instead of training their own. Other specialists left our launching pad and created or helped to create America's first Black advertising and modeling agencies. Raymond League, one of the talented young men we discovered and developed, organized Zebra, one of the first major Black ad agencies.

This was a new challenge which I met by sitting down one day and asking myself, Who are the key people I must have in order to continue the growth of the company? I made a list of about thirty key executives, and I put the list on an easel in my office. Every day when I came to work, I looked at that list and asked myself, What can I do today to make these thirty people so happy and satisfied to work here that they will not be tempted to leave?

As I grappled with this question, I got to know the individuals better. I got to know their families, their hopes and ambitions. And I discovered, not surprisingly, that they wanted different things. Some wanted more money. Some wanted more recognition. Some wanted college scholarships for their children.

There were other considerations. Some wanted to travel with their wives. Some wanted to travel with their girlfriends. Some wanted to travel with their boyfriends.

I gave them what they wanted, and the brain drain crisis disappeared. In all these years, I've never lost a single one of the key thirty. Except for the persons who have died or retired, all are still working for me.

# 31

## Fine-Tuning the Formula

S UCCESS is like a merry-go-round.

When the wheel starts turning, you can't stop it and you can't get off without endangering your limbs or your psyche.

From 1950 to 1954, the merry-go-round of success went around and around, faster and faster. Then, suddenly, unexpectedly, inexplicably, the big contraption with the flashing lights and ringing bells ground to a halt, shaking the company to its foundations.

For almost all of this period, I'd worked on the flank facing the advertisers, confident that my rear was protected. But the blow that almost destroyed the company came from the unprotected rear and was a product of two allied problems.

The first was a series of economic recessions that got progressively worse as the fifties wore on. The second was a shift in the magazine business. For as long as anyone could remember, the magazine business had been based on healthy newsstand sales. Then, in the fifties, for reasons that have never been explained to me, this situation changed and newsstand sales plummeted, catching major publishers napping, like the foolish virgins of the Bible. *Life* and *Look* began the roller-coaster ride that ended with their disappearance from newsstands. But these media had more resources than *Ebony*, 90 percent of whose circulation came from newsstand sales.

During the 1954 recession, *Ebony* newsstand sales dropped in a single issue from 500,000 to 400,000. We failed to meet our advertising guarantee, and I was forced to return $50,000 to advertisers—$50,000 I'd already spent.

This was a dangerous situation that threatened the future of Johnson Publishing Company. They used to say that when America caught a cold, the whole world got pneumonia. The same thing was true of *Ebony* and Johnson Publishing Company. If *Ebony* collapsed or was severely threatened, the whole company was at risk.

With the recession deepening and the steel industry and car industry laying off thousands of workers, I moved quickly and decisively, changing the circulation process and putting greater emphasis on subscriptions. I developed a church program, which made it possible for churches to earn money by selling *Ebony* subscriptions. I organized a school program and a direct-mail campaign.

At the same time, I shifted gears editorially and ordered the staff to play down sensationalism and sex. The world was changing, and people wanted *Ebony* to be more serious. They wanted us to move away from the sensationalism that characterized some of our early articles.

I had problems with executive editor Ben Burns, who'd been with me since the beginning, and who believed that the new policy was a mistake. I wrestled with competing visions of the future and decided that *Ebony* had to change with the changing times.

I called a meeting of the *Jet* and *Ebony* editorial staffs and banned the use of stories based on sex alone or interracial love alone.

"We won't run stories," I said, "where sex is the only redeeming feature. We won't deal with interracial marriage if the only significant part of the story is that two people of different colors got married. There must be more to the story than that. There must be achievement, something that one of the persons has done beyond the fact that they're married to each other."

Ben Burns continued to oppose the policy, and we had a kind of running battle. In fact, he literally defied me. We would agree on an approach to a story, and he'd go to the plant and insert a sensational story and claim afterward that the story came in at the last minute and that he couldn't reach me or change it. After warning him several times, I dismissed him at the printing plant, sending a letter over by Robert Winkfield, who worked as a driver and shipping clerk.

Before very much time passed, I reversed the circulation ratio, establishing a fifty-fifty balance between subscriptions and newsstand sales. Today we're like most major magazines, with 15 to 20 percent of our circulation in newsstand sales and 80 to 85 percent in subscriptions.

# 32

# *The Golden Decade*

W ITH the foundation securely laid, we celebrated the first major company landmark, the tenth anniversary of *Ebony*. I had 145 employees in November 1955, and I was publishing four magazines with a total monthly circulation of 2.6 million. The bellwether was *Ebony*, with a 500,000 circulation, followed by *Jet*, with a circulation of 425,000 a week. *Tan* and *Hue* were each selling about 200,000 a month.

We'd survived with profit and honor, and we celebrated with a special issue on "Ten Years That Rocked the World."

Looking back and forward, we said that in "The Golden Decade" that spanned publication of the first and 120th issues of *Ebony*, Black Americans had moved farther and faster than in any preceding period since the Emancipation Proclamation.

The three most momentous events of the decade were the Supreme Court decision banning segregation in the public schools, the abolition of segregation in the armed forces, and a series of federal court decisions that opened the ballot box to southern Blacks.

I was encouraged by these developments, which put Blacks within grabbing distance of full equality. I was also pleased by "a quiet turn-about among advertisers" that amounted to "a gradual revolution." We were carrying an average of sixty pages of advertising an issue, and we'd attracted more than half of the one hundred top advertisers.

For me personally, the first ten years were the hardest and perhaps the most interesting. Like the Black Americans we saluted in our special issue, I'd come up from segregation and nobodyness, and I believed that the Promised Land was around the next turning.

This turning point in my personal and corporate life coincided with a fork in American and world history. It's impossible to make young people understand the electric hope that seized us after *Brown* v. *Board of Education* ended the Jim Crow age. I remember thinking at the time, and I was not alone, that we were free at last and that the struggle would soon be over.

Like NAACP legal counsel Thurgood Marshall and Chief Justice Warren, I believed that if people could only go to school together and live together they would realize that people are people and that the things that unite us are bigger and more important than the things that separate us.

It didn't turn out that way, primarily because many people believed that "all deliberate speed" was a mandate to keep on doing what they'd been doing. That phrase was a mistake. Although the slow implementation of the Supreme Court decision has created a new Black and White America, we would be living in a different world if the court had abandoned "deliberate speed" and ordered immediate compliance.

I'm always reminded in this connection of a trip Eunice and I made to Europe on the English ship *Caronia*. Among the passengers were Barbara Brown de Passe and her three-year-old daughter, Suzanne, who grew up and became the Suzanne de Passe of Motown. Suzanne was very excited during the trip. She wanted to speak French, and she believed that she would be magically transformed as soon as she landed in France. She was sorely disappointed when she discovered that landing in France didn't teach her how to speak French.

In the post–*Brown* v. *Board of Education* period, we were a lot like the young Suzanne. The Supreme Court decision had transported us to the land of integration, and we thought we'd be able to speak the new language as soon as we read the court order. But our trip to the new land was unwisely delayed, and when we got there we still had to learn a new language. And we're still learning.

There was an editorial postscript to all this. Certain people, who apparently believed that the Supreme Court had abolished Negroes as well as segregation, called for immediate dissolution of all Black institutions—not, it should be noted, all White institutions. Everywhere I went, people told me there was no need now for both *Ebony* and *Life*.

"When," they asked, "is *Ebony* going out of business?"

I was shocked that so many people, Black and White, could not conceive of the opposite possibility—*Life* going out of business. I usually replied, "Why should *Ebony* go out of business? Real integration, not to mention the increasing Black and Hispanic populations in the major cities, will produce a society that looks more like *Ebony* than *Life*."

The questions continued until both *Life* and *Look* went out of business. (After several years *Life* returned as a monthly.)

As might have been expected, the "all deliberate speed" period was punctuated by attacks on individual Blacks and massive resistance by southern White leaders. The most traumatic incident occurred in August 1955 in Money, Mississippi, where Emmett Till, a fourteen-year-old Chicago schoolboy, was lynched for allegedly whistling at a White woman. When the horribly mangled body was returned to Chicago for burial, his mother, Mamie Bradley Mobley, asked photographers to shoot pictures, saying: "I want the world to see what they did to my boy."

There were people on the staff who were squeamish about the photographs. I had reservations, too, but I decided finally that if it happened it was our responsibility to print it and let the world experience man's inhumanity to man. The issue, which went on sale on September 15, 1955, sold out immediately and did as much as any other event to traumatize Black America and prepare the way for the Freedom Movement of the sixties.

Almost a quarter of a million people lined up for blocks outside a Chicago funeral home to see the body and pay homage to the slain teenager. A national uproar forced Mississippi officials to hold a mock trial which led to the acquittal of the two murder suspects. I sent an interracial team, which included Simeon Booker, Clotye Murdock, David Jackson, and White photographer Mike Shay, to Money, Mississippi, to cover the trial, and carried major stories in both *Jet* and *Ebony*.

In the meantime, a young minister named Martin Luther King, Jr., had arrived on the scene.

Nobody or almost nobody knew his name then, but he was not without resources and energy.

The national White press was ignoring a major event that was unfolding in Montgomery, Alabama.

This distressed young King, who placed a call to a Morehouse College classmate, Robert E. Johnson.

"Bob," he said, "you ought to send somebody down here. The Negroes of Montgomery are making history—we boycotted the buses yesterday, and you ought to hurry because I don't know how long we can keep this up."

Johnson, who is now associate publisher of *Jet*, called me and I told him to take the next plane.

In the weeks and months that followed, *Ebony* and *Jet* became integral parts of the King crusade, and we did more than any other publications to tell the story of the Dream and the Dreamer. I hadn't met King at the time, but I could recognize quality, even at a distance. I was particularly impressed by a statement attributed to E. D. Nixon, one of the boycott spark plugs. "We were looking for a leader and got Moses."

I received several calls from King, who asked me to send teams to various trouble spots in Mississippi, Alabama, and Georgia. "We're going to be in this place or that place," he'd say, "and we want people to know what's going on. The White press doesn't always cover us. When they do, they don't always tell it the way we want it told."

Not only did we report the struggle but we also became a part of the struggle. I marched and gave tens of thousands of dollars to different arms of the movement. With and without my approval, my editors marched and volunteered for difficult and dangerous assignments. We didn't stand on our credentials. We sat in with the sit-inners, rode the buses with the Freedom Riders, braved the mob in Little Rock with Daisy Bates and the nine Black students who walked up the steps of Central High School.

As an Arkansan, I had a personal interest in the Little Rock struggle, which unfolded thirty-nine years after I was born in Arkansas City. Like millions of other Americans, I watched with elation and fear in 1957 as the soldiers of the 101st Airborne Division escorted the Black children into Central High. This was the first time in eighty-one years that the U.S. government had sent troops into the South to protect the constitutional rights of Black people, and I believe future historians will say that it marked the beginning of the end of the Jim Crow system.

We were there.

We told the story. More to the point, we were a part of a story that cannot be recalled or told without referring to the pages of *Ebony* and *Jet* and the 2 million photographs in our archives.

# 33

## Upstairs at the White House

THE first time I met a U.S. president he was talking about how hard it is to stop smoking.

We were upstairs at the White House, and Dwight David Eisenhower was presiding over a stag dinner of ten or twelve business leaders.

I was the only Black and the only publisher. Val Washington, a prominent Black Republican leader, had put me on the invitation list.

I've been to the White House many times since then, but this was my first and last dinner upstairs in the private quarters of the president.

After dinner we sat around and chatted over coffee and after-dinner liqueurs. The setting, small, private, personal, was made to order for Eisenhower, a genuinely likable person, ingratiating and gracious. He'd recently stopped smoking, and somebody asked if he would ever smoke again.

"I don't know whether I'll start again," he said, "but I know damn well that I'll never quit again—quitting is too damn hard."

The president complained, like most citizens, about high taxes. He was living then in New York State, and he said he was going to move to Pennsylvania, where taxes were lower. True to his word, he later bought a farm near Gettysburg.

Toward the end of the evening, he let it be known that he would not oppose a draft for a second term. I understood then why I had been invited. The Republicans didn't have much Black support, and *Ebony* was, by then, the most powerful communicator in Black America. From Ike on, every U.S. president communicated with me because *Ebony* communicated so well with Black Americans.

Eisenhower said little or nothing that night about the problems of government. There was a feeling in Black America that he was a decent man who never really understood civil rights and the plight of Black Americans. I came away from the dinner with the feeling that he was a generous man and a great soldier whose career had distanced him from the day-to-day problems of urban America.

The White House dinner was, in part, a national coming-out party for the real John H. Johnson, who'd deliberately remained in the background until the company was organized on a sound basis.

Now, as the gathering Civil Rights Movement gained steam and force, I emerged from the corporate shadows and accepted positions on the boards of Tuskegee Institute and the National Urban League.

The Tuskegee experience was disappointing, and I attended few board meetings. Most Black college boards were dominated by a handful of White lawyers and financiers— the sixties changed that—who kept a tight rein on the budget and finance committees.

I told Basil O'Connor, the patriarchal White lawyer who

virtually ran the board, that I wanted to serve on the finance committee. He said there were no openings on this committee and that I would be more comfortable on the building and grounds committee.

I was more comfortable serving on the National Urban League board with some of America's biggest industrialists. For the first time, I found myself in the "area of gossip," that informal, social-business climate where, at a club, a wedding, a dinner, or a golf outing, business deals and projections are traded by White men—sorry about that, but it's still a White male world—who assume, as a matter of course, that there's nobody here but us chickens, and that everybody in the inner circle has a right to know and does.

One of the reasons Black Americans have made limited progress in corporate America is that they are excluded from the area of gossip, where impending deals and personnel changes are discussed freely.

The National Urban League board put me on the fringes of that world and reminded me of the words of my friend and mentor, Earl B. Dickerson, who told me once, "If you want to succeed in White America, you must let your mind roam beyond the ghetto, even if your body is forced to remain in the ghetto. You must reach out into the world and tap into the minds of the people who are running the country, so you will know how far you can go and what path to travel in order to get there."

I asked him once why he belonged to so many White organizations.

"I need the contact," he said. "I need the exposure. I need to know what they're thinking in order to plot and plan my own success."

Dickerson was right. The Urban League experience taught me that I needed exposure to the best minds in corporate America. I needed to know how they thought and how they operated to maximize my own potential. One of the curious by-products of this experience was that I learned once again how human we all are. For the corporate executives I met were just like the corporate executives I knew in Black America. Some were brilliant. Most were average. Some were dumb.

On the boards of the Urban League and other organizations, corporate executives discussed board business within the context of national and international affairs. They emphasized the latest techniques in management. They talked about the latest technology. They discussed the need for fallback positions and projections and long-term budgeting.

I learned a lot from them. More to the point, I learned how to deal with them. And, wonder of wonders, I sold ads without really trying to sell ads. Simply by being there, simply by being in the area of gossip and power, I gained entrée into a realm where answers are given before the questions are asked. Some CEOs asked their ad managers to call me. Others wrote their names on the backs of cards that opened all doors and guaranteed orders.

Dean Rusk, secretary of state in the Kennedy administration, was the first person to make me aware of the strategic importance of the area of gossip. I was a member of an advisory group on equal opportunity in the State Department. The secretary told us that he had concluded after studying the data that the problem was not so much bad people as the impersonal will of a system that penalized people who were outside the area of gossip.

"When a vacancy occurs in an all-White department," he said, "people in the department tell their friends and recommend their friends. And we're not going to make any headway here until we increase the number of Blacks who operate in that informal environment."

As an example of the power of this realm, I can cite the IBM ad I got without even trying. I was sitting at the head table at a National Urban League dinner honoring Thomas Watson, Jr., of IBM. I'd never met him before, but he had been featured in a story we did on the training school at IBM headquarters in Armonk, New York. Whitney Young, Jr., the National Urban League president, introduced me to

Watson and told him that I was the publisher of *Ebony*. Whitney started to explain what *Ebony* was and Watson interrupted.

"I know what *Ebony* is," he said. "I was in it once, and I was proud to be there."

"I'm happy to hear that, Mr. Watson," I said. "I just wish your advertising department had the same respect for *Ebony* that you've just expressed."

Whitney said, "You mean you don't advertise in *Ebony*, Tom? I can't imagine that an Urban League director wouldn't advertise in the largest and most prestigious magazine we have."

Watson didn't answer. He took out a little notebook and made a small and cryptic notation. Within a month, we had a schedule from IBM, and the company has advertised ever since.

All of this—the expanding advertising beachhead, the golden decade, and access to the area of gossip—made small but significant changes in my private life. I was still driven by the fear of failure. I still believed a day out of the office was a day wasted. But I was moving in wider circles and responding to new experiences and stimuli.

I moved our family in 1954 to a new and more luxurious building on Drexel Square, near the University of Chicago, and I bought another building nearby for my mother. The new home, like the old one, was gutted and redecorated in the style to which I had become accustomed. One of its distinguishing features was a thick, curved-glass window, made especially for the Drexel Square home by the Pittsburgh Plate Glass Company.

I'd never been a big party man, but I went through the motions of participating in the rituals of Black society, which was changing with the changing world. Because of my relationship with Earl Dickerson, who gave me the same respect when I was an office boy that he gave me when I had literally become his boss by buying control of

Supreme Life, I'd always had access to the parties and get-togethers of the Chicago elite. Like the Black elite of other cities, it had been based on old families, most of whom were fair-skinned.

The Great Migration and the rise of a new breed of Black professionals and entrepreneurs changed all that. By the midfifties, old-family background and skin color were no longer the major criteria. You could get in by achievement, and you could get in by making money.

I had achieved a little and made a little money, and Eunice and I made the social round. But as I grew older, I found more and more reasons for avoiding the social whirl in both Black and White America.

# 34

## *Ebony Fashion Fair: The World's Largest Traveling Fashion Show*

NO matter where I am or what I'm doing, I'm always looking for opportunities to make money.

I can be socializing at a party or a wedding, I can be listening to a presentation at a meeting or walking through a department store or driving through a city, and all the while, microsecond after microsecond, the radar of my mind is revolving, tracking people and the environment, looking for openings in the wall of success.

In the course of a year, people come to me with hundreds of ideas for making money. Most of the ideas are worthless, but now and then a word or suggestion breaks the beam of my sentinel system and bells start ringing everywhere.

Before the decade of the fifties ended, the crap-proof Johnson radar locked in on two opportunities that extended my reach and potential.

The first opportunity was an investment that led to

majority control of Supreme Life Insurance Company, where I'd started my career as an office boy. Although I was technically still on leave of absence from Supreme, I had little or no relationship with the company or its officers from 1943 to 1957, a period of some fourteen years. As a matter of fact, I don't believe I set foot in company head-quarters for ten or more years. There was no particular reason for this estrangement. But after the death of Harry Pace, I got the feeling that some of the company officers were not comfortable with me and my success.

Earl B. Dickerson changed that. After he was elected president, he called and said, "You ought to return to the company in some way. You're a young man, you got your start here. Supreme is a part of your business heritage—and there's no reason why you shouldn't be involved in some way."

It was a generous offer, and I accepted it with no particular agenda. At Dickerson's invitation, I bought one thousand shares of his stock for $30,000 and was elected to the board of directors. I gradually bought more and more stock from individuals and from the company. When the company ran into financial difficulties and needed a new infusion of capital, I invested about a million dollars. All told, I put approximately $2.5 million in the company and became the largest stockholder and finally the controlling stockholder.

When, in 1974, I was elected chairman and CEO, I felt a great sense of personal and corporate satisfaction. For I've only had two jobs in my whole life—and I still have both of them. In the first company, I started as an office boy and became chairman. In the second company, I started as chairman and remain chairman.

Not everyone was pleased. One veteran employee, who'd been at Supreme when I was an office boy and who had not treated me kindly, quoted Fats Waller at the end of my first board meeting, "One never knows, do one."

\*      \*      \*

The second opportunity of the late fifties was the Ebony Fashion Show, which came to me, like so many of my ventures, as a gift wrapped in a problem.

The problem was the scarcity of Black models. They were hard to find, as Ernestine Dent, the wife of President Albert Dent of Dillard University, discovered when she decided to organize a charity fashion show for Flint-Goodridge Hospital. After exhausting her resources, she called me in late June 1958 and asked if I could help her locate some Black models.

The only Black models I knew were the Chicago and New York models we used in our enterprises, and I was not about to send them to New Orleans. But—and bells started ringing—what would happen, I asked myself, if I organized and controlled a fashion show that would meet the needs outlined by Mrs. Dent while contributing to the different needs—the need for models, fashion statements, circulation dollars—of Johnson Publishing Company?

I had no idea then how I was going to do it or even if I could do it, but I said quickly, "Mrs. Dent, I can't recommend any models, but what would you think if I put on the fashion show for you?"

"Oh!" she said, "that would be wonderful. But what would you want out of it?"

Before she completed the question, I'd figured out in my mind the financing scheme that we're still using thirty-one years later. I couldn't in good conscience charge a charitable organization a fee, but each ticket could be priced to include the cost of a subscription to *Ebony*.

"There'll be no expense to your organization," I said. "I'll furnish the models and the clothes. All I want is the three-dollar *Ebony* subscription, which will go to the person buying the ticket. Everything you charge above that will be yours free and clear."

So ran the plan, and so went the execution.

Two thousand people paid six dollars a ticket to attend the first Ebony Fashion Show, which was directed by Freda

DeKnight and was held in September 1958 at Booker T. Washington High School. Mrs. Dent and her organization cleared $6,000. My share was $6,000, but I'd spent at least $25,000 for clothes, models, and production expenses. This, however, was a small price for an idea that grew into the world's largest traveling fashion show.

Almost before the first show ended, I started planning the second show. With the help of Mrs. Dent, who called friends in other cities who wanted to sponsor events for charity, we produced a total of ten shows in 1958. In succeeding years, we added new sponsors—local Urban Leagues, sororities, community centers, the NAACP and UNCF.

In the sixties, the Fashion Show, under the direction of Eunice Walker Johnson, became a national institution, carrying the latest fashions by French, Italian, and American designers to localities and people who'd never been exposed to high-fashion environments. Today's show is a year-round business that travels to 190 cities in America, England, Jamaica, Bermuda, the Bahamas, and Canada and produces more than 300,000 subscribers for *Ebony* and *Jet*. Since the first show, we have raised more than $25 million for charity.

The Ebony Fashion Show has also given Black America and the world a new concept of the kind of clothes Black women can wear. Before the Ebony Fashion Show, people said Black women couldn't wear red or yellow or purple. The fashion show proved that Black women could wear any color they wanted to wear. One of our earliest and best models, Terri Springer—tall, beautiful, shapely, and jet black—used to sashay across stages in spectacular colors that defined "Black is beautiful" before the phrase was invented. Many well-known Blacks, notably Richard Roundtree of *Shaft*, actress Judy Pace, and model Pat Cleveland, started as Fashion Fair models.

Like *Ebony*, like *Jet*, the fashion show was a quality project from the beginning. Every year we went to the fashion capitals of the world—New York, Paris, Rome—and bought two or three of the best garments of the premier designers. We also highlighted the contributions of Black designers. The current show features not only the big names of New York, London, and Paris but also promising young Black designers in Los Angeles, Chicago, Dallas, Houston, and Atlanta.

It was necessary, of course, to overcome the fears and phobias of racism. When Eunice and I went to Europe with Freda for the first time to buy clothes, we had to beg, persuade, and threaten to get the right to buy clothes. Certain designers assumed that White women wouldn't value their designs if they were worn by Black women. We finally got through to one or two of the leading designers, and the others followed. We now spend more than $500,000 a year buying clothes at wholesale prices.

# 35

## Days of Pain and Glory

EUNICE and I were so busy in the beginning building a business that we didn't have time to build a family. Then, when we wanted children, we couldn't have any.

We went from doctor to doctor, from specialist to specialist. There was nothing wrong with us physically. Maybe the timing was wrong.

We checked into Mayo Clinic, where I went through the painful and embarrassing procedure of sperm testing, and where Eunice went through the embarrassing procedure of additional examination by gynecologists.

Same result.

Same answer.

There was nothing wrong with us physically.

I know now that this happens to many couples. Sometimes a couple adopt a child and then, through the natural birth process, produce three or four natural children. Sometimes the man and woman divorce, marry other partners, and both have housefuls of children.

This was not an option in our case. We were bound together by ties that were perhaps greater than the desire to have children, and we discussed the alternative of adopting children. This was an agonizing decision, primarily because of the myths surrounding parenthood. Men sometimes feel diminished if they don't have children, and some women feel alienated if they don't give birth to children. We discussed these and other attitudes and decided that a conscious and deliberate decision to adopt a child can be as fulfilling and transforming—for the child and the parents— as natural childbirth.

Having made this decision, we went to an Illinois adoption agency which investigated us for almost a year. I was a little surprised by this scrutiny, for I thought, in my innocence, that it was obvious that I was qualified for parenthood. But agency officials seemed to know what they were doing. They were interested in compatibility. They wanted to match the child to the parents and the parents to the child.

After an interminable wait, the big day came, and we took our two-week-old son home in June 1956. There was not a moment's doubt or hesitation about the name. Even before we saw him, we knew that he was—what else?—John Harold Johnson, Jr.

You can climb Mount Everest or make a million dollars or dine at the White House, but there's nothing like the joy and terror of parenthood. I shall always be grateful to John Harold for that lesson. He hadn't been in our home for a week when I realized that being a parent is not so much giving birth as giving love and attention and sleepless nights.

From the beginning, John was a night person, who cried all night and slept all day. Eunice and I took turns walking the floor, but we were so proud to have him that we never complained. We could have hired nurses or babysitters, but Eunice wanted to do it herself. We had a house-keeper then, but the housekeeper was responsible for the house, not the children.

Two years later, we went back to the same agency and adopted a two-week-old girl and named her Linda Eunice.

Talking about happy.

We were as happy as a family can be.

Until the trouble started.

We noticed in the second year that John developed colds he couldn't shake and fevers that lasted longer than they should have. We took him to Dr. Edward Beasley, a dear friend, who hesitated and finally said he had sickle-cell anemia.

I'd been around the world, I'd read most of the material on Black Americans, but until that moment I'd never heard of sickle-cell anemia.

"What's that?" I asked.

It was, he said, a chronic hereditary blood disease that occurs primarily among Africans or persons of African descent. He went on to say a lot of big words I didn't understand about abnormal hemoglobin causing red blood cells to sickle. But I understood the end product: enlarged spleen, anemia, lethargy, joint pain, blood clot formation, death.

"All right," I said, "what's the cure?"

"There is no cure," he said. "Most of the victims die before they reach the age of thirty. I know this is sad news for you, but it's the best I can tell you. The adoption agency should have tested for sickle cell before they gave the child to you."

I left Dr. Beasley's office in a daze, not knowing what to do or where to go. I finally called the adoption agency and said, "Miss, why didn't you give my son a test?"

"Well, you know," she said, "we really overlooked that. It's our fault, and we'd be happy to take him back and give you another child."

I exploded, and it's hard, even today, for me to talk about it without breaking down.

"Lady," I told her, "you got to be crazy! He's my son, he's been in my home for two years. I don't care what he has—I'm not giving him up. I'm just saying that you ought to do these tests for other people."

And so it began, periods of calm and happiness punctuated by periods of crisis and pain, when it seemed that John was going to die. As the months and then the years slipped by, the crisis periods got progressively worse and the periods between the crises became shorter.

We lived, fortunately, on Drexel Square, which was only five minutes from the University of Chicago, and my wife's brother, a doctor, lived nearby. We were very fortunate in this respect, for John had a severe case and probably wouldn't have lived ten years if he hadn't come into our home, which was blessed with good medical service, and other resources.

He lived twenty-five years. I've said many times that I believe the Lord sent him to our home so we could prolong his life. We suffered most of those twenty-five years and we were blessed in terms of what Gladys Knight called in her song, "the pain and glory"—because there was always pain, and yet there was always happiness and glory.

Family life and the problems surrounding John's illness changed my life and my perspective. I cut back on my traveling and tried to get home every night for dinner. Although I still went to the office on Saturday, I made a point of spending all day Sunday with Linda and John. We went to the zoo or we went riding, whatever they wanted to do. Sunday was their day. And Monday and Tuesday, too. For they were always in and out of the office, and they were always begging employees for nickels and dimes for the pop machine.

Linda, who was elegant and outgoing from the beginning, developed a passionate interest in horseback riding and fashions. When she was only seven, she toured the fashion capitals of Europe with her mother. Since then she has been back to Europe at least fifty times.

John developed an early interest in photography, and shot several stories for *Ebony* and *Jet*, including one on skydiving that required so much daring that nobody else wanted to do it.

Looking back now, I think he knew his time span was limited and that he had a rendezvous with death. So he had no fear of death. He liked to race cars and to sky-dive and to ski. He liked to do dangerous things. That worried me a lot, but I never tried to stop him. I knew that he didn't have a lot of time and that he wanted to use the time he had to the fullest.

He was only eighteen when he got married. Nobody in the family was happy about the marriage, but nobody could tell him to wait, because we knew he didn't have time. We gritted our teeth, smiled over our concerns, and gave the bride and bridegroom our best wishes. And that's the way it should have been, really.

Because of my experiences with John and Linda, I grew as a person and as a publisher. I had a greater awareness of the need for strong family units, and my interest in adoption was reflected in the number of stories *Ebony* did on families and adoptions.

# 36

## *Nkrumah, Haile Selassie, and the Kitchen Confrontation*

FIVE, maybe six centuries after my ancestors were dragged in chains across the Atlantic, I went back to Africa with a vice president of the United States of America.

There was history and irony in this.

For Vice President Richard M. Nixon was the head of the integrated United States delegation to the Ghana Independence Ceremony that marked the beginning of the end of the colonial domination of Africa.

To record the event for posterity, and to gain international exposure for his predicted presidential race, Nixon asked a group of Black and White press people to accompany him.

Eunice and I were in the group that left Andrews Air Force Base in Washington and reversed the Atlantic crossing routes that brought millions of Africans to the New World.

I came away from the trip with new respect for Nixon,

who went out of his way to make sure we received equal treatment. We started out with two airplanes, one for the press and one for the vice president. The press plane was an ancient affair which sputtered and smoked and made frequent stops for maintenance. The maintenance personnel told us that it was perfectly safe, but we didn't believe it until the vice president decided to ride on our plane to prove that it was.

Whether because of his intervention or the intervention of higher authority, the plane made it to Accra, Ghana, where on midnight, March 6, 1957, the Union Jack was lowered and the Ghana flag was raised. This set off a paroxysm of cheering and weeping. It was not entirely clear where all this was heading, but one thing was obvious: The old world of colonialism and natives was dead and gone forever. Strangers, Black and White, hugged, kissed, and cried. The people of Ghana danced in the streets all night long.

This was my first visit to the land of my fathers and mothers. For the first time, I saw Black men in charge, running a whole country. I saw a Black supreme court justice, a Black attorney general, and a Black head of state. I saw Black people in authority with their heads held high in confidence and strength.

This gave the large African-American contingent a lift. It gave us a new spirit and new energy to come back home and deal with the remaining obstacles to the Dream. "We Africans," a Ghanaian told me, "have our freedom. When are you Negroes going to get yours?" We got the message and returned to America, determined to get ours.

I was particularly impressed by Kwame Nkrumah, who was a dreamer and a realist. He spoke repeatedly that week of his dream of a United States of Africa. He was, I think, right in stressing the political and economic potential of a union of the Balkanized African states, but he tried to move too far too soon and destroyed himself.

Despite all that, his place in history is secure. He gave

us pride in our being and confidence in our destiny. He was the first fruit, to paraphrase W. E. B. DuBois's eulogy to Marcus Garvey, of a mighty coming thing in Africa, in the Caribbean, and the little Africas of North and South America.

I had a long conversation with Nkrumah, who was not called Showboy for nothing, at one of the special events. He'd been trained in America at Lincoln University (Pa.) and he said, "I owe a debt of gratitude to the Black people of America. When I was a student there, I went to NAACP meetings. I read about your struggles in Black newspapers. And all this inspired me. I was tempted to stay there and live an easier life, but the struggle of American Negroes inspired me to come back and fight harder for my people."

During this event I met Martin Luther King, Jr., for the first time. I'd talked to him several times on the telephone, but we'd never met. I saw him across a crowded room at the Government House ceremony. I recognized him immediately, and he recognized me. Before I could reach him, he pushed through the crowd and pumped my hand, thanking me for the coverage and support. "Brother Johnson," he said in that rich and unforgettable baritone, "I'll always be grateful."

I left Ghana with mixed emotions. For it was clear even then that the British had given the Africans political power and had kept the economic power. They kept the banks, they kept the insurance companies and the factories and the money. It was like giving someone a Rolls-Royce without a motor.

As a result, the Ghanaians found themselves on the morning after in a no-win situation. I've thought many times since then of the similarities between the transfer of power in Africa and the transfer of power in the big cities of America. For political emancipation is provisional and ultimately meaningless if it is not followed by economic emancipation. The best of the big-city Black mayors, Harold Washington and Maynard Jackson in particular, understood that. They moved immediately to buttress political ballots with the economic ballots of set-asides. They also created concrete guidelines that gave Blacks, Hispanics, and women a piece of the economic as well as the political action.

We could see this imperative clearly as we followed the vice president on a tour that included seven additional African countries, including Liberia, which had been founded by descendants of American slaves but was still mired in economic difficulties.

The highlight of our tour was a visit to Ethiopia, one of the world's oldest countries. The country was ruled by the legendary Haile Selassie, the Conquering Lion of Judah. When we arrived at his palace, White reporters and officials pushed their way to the front, obscuring our view of the emperor, who sat on a throne, flanked by two lions. The lions, I noted with concern, were held securely by two huge men. The emperor was a small man, but he held himself erect and seemed to be six feet tall.

When the audience began, the emperor rose, looked out over the crowd, and said, "Where is the man from *Ebony*?"

There was a stir among his aides and he said again, "Where is the man from *Ebony*?" I held up my hand in the back, and Security ushered me up to the throne. The emperor congratulated me on the job *Ebony* was doing in letting the people of the world know about the progress of American Blacks. He said he was an avid reader of *Ebony* but that he was having trouble with his subscription. I told him that I would take care of it. We'd been sending his magazines directly to Ethiopia, and they were oftentimes delayed, lost, or even stolen. An aide told me to send the magazine directly to the Washington embassy so it could go by diplomatic pouch to the emperor.

In 1959, Eunice and I were among the media representatives who went with Vice President Nixon to Poland and Russia. It was on this trip that Nixon had his celebrated confrontation with Nikita Khrushchev in a kitchen at the American Pavilion of the World's Fair.

Eunice and I were standing in the dining room when the confrontation began. And we were astonished when Nixon and Khrushchev started pointing fingers at each other and talking excitedly. The story has been told many times, but I've never read an account that conveyed the sense of menace we felt. They were going at it hot and heavy and I thought, "We'll never get out of here alive." But they were both politicians, and they realized that this was a great stage, a world stage, on which to continue the Cold War struggle.

Despite the tensions of the time, I was treated courteously by the Russian people. It was a little disconcerting, however, to deal with the hundreds of Russian children who followed me around and tried to feel my hand to see if the black would rub off.

One of the fascinating sidelights of the trip was related later by Ralph McGill, the publisher and editor of the *Atlanta Constitution*. McGill noted that Eunice and I were members of the press party and added:

> We had become friends and had many talks. At Sverdlovsk (where Francis Gary Powers and the U-2 plane not long thereafter were to meet disaster) the Soviet journalists invited the visiting press corps to dinner—with dancing. The day had been long, hot and exhausting, and we sat gratefully down to a good dinner....
>
> One of the Russian-speaking U.S. staff members sought me out and said, "I thought you might like to know that I have heard the Soviet newsmen talking. They are waiting to see if you, from that South about which they have heard so much and know so little, will ask Mrs. Johnson to dance. If you do, they won't mention it in their dispatches. If you don't, it may well be a featured part of the news from here."
>
> So I sought out Mrs. Johnson. "Mrs. Johnson," I said, "I haven't danced in perhaps twenty years. I was never any good at it and, with general approval, gave it up. But I think we must dance for the honor of our country." I then told her the story. "I am exhausted," she said, "and my feet are, as the saying goes, killing me. But we mustn't disappoint them."
>
> So, later, when the music began, I went to Mrs. Johnson and

asked if she would dance. She would. Indeed, we were the first on the floor. There was no feature story from Sverdlovsk that night.

We spent a lot of time with Nixon in press conferences and briefings. When we returned to America, Nixon, who was running hard for president, invited us to his home. I noticed with delight that both *Ebony* and *Jet* were prominently displayed on his magazine shelf, along with other major magazines. One of the reporters said, "You know he did it just for this occasion." I replied, "I don't care why he did it, he did it." Nixon later sent a scroll which made us members of his Kitchen Cabinet.

# The _____
# Color _____
# of _____
# Change _____

# 37

## *On the New Frontier With the Kennedys*

T HE sixties were the most exciting years of my life.

During these magical ten years, Black Americans made their greatest gains and millions of Whites, especially White women, White students, and the White elderly, profited from a struggle that changed everything—politics, education, religion, sex.

I was forty-two when the decade began. When it ended ten years and ten revolutions later, I was fifty-two and a new and different person.

In the intervening years, *Ebony* made its greatest circulation gains, moving from 623,000 in 1960 to 1,217,000 in 1970. This was a gain of 594,000 in one decade alone. During the same decade, I received unprecedented national recognition and became for the first time a personality in my own right.

As the editor and publisher of America's biggest Black magazine, and as a businessman with access to the leaders of corporate America, I had a unique, bifocal appreciation of the events and people who made these years unforgettable.

Even before the decade began, I was drawn into the presidential campaign that foreshadowed the coming struggles. Belford Lawson, one of my Alpha Phi Alpha fraternity brothers, was close to one of the rising Democratic stars, a relatively unknown senator from Massachusetts named John Fitzgerald Kennedy. Belford called several times in 1958 to say that Senator Kennedy wanted me to come to Washington for a meeting in his office.

I declined, citing the pressure of business. But that wasn't the real reason. I'd just returned to America after a trip to Africa with the press contingent accompanying Nixon. Although I was not a Republican or a supporter of Nixon, I at least knew him.

Senator Kennedy, on the other hand, was an unknown quantity. He had a way with words, and he had dash and style. But some people thought he was a rich playboy with little or no understanding of Black America. Few believed then that he had a chance to win the presidency. I saw no reason why I should be seen going in and out of his Capitol Hill offices as if I were seeking a favor.

I explained all this to Belford, who reported to the senator and came back with a new proposal. "What," he asked, "if the Kennedys extend a social invitation—will you come to Washington then?"

"Well," I said, "the Kennedys are not a bad group to hang out with socially. If I get an invitation, I'll consider it."

We have on our wall to this day a little note we got from Jackie Kennedy:

Dear Mr. and Mrs. Johnson:

My husband and I are delighted to learn through our
mutual friends, the Belford Lawsons, that you will be in
town the week after next and available for an informal dinner at our home.  I know that Belford has mentioned the
evening of May twelfth to you, and we would certainly be
pleased to see you then.

Unfortunately, my husband is addressing a luncheon
meeting followed by a reception in Rochester, New York,
that afternoon; and we would be most distressed if poor
weather or adverse plane schedules made it impossible for
him to return that evening.  Consequently, it might be better to try to get together for an early supper on Sunday
evening -- about six o'clock -- if you will be in Washington
at that time.  If not, we will look forward to seeing you at
eight o clock Monday evening, and hope all goes well.

I am looking forward to hearing from you as to your
availability on Sunday, and to getting to know you in the
near future.

Sincerely,

Jacqueline Kennedy

Mr. and Mrs. John H. Johnson
Johnson Publishing Company
1820 South Michigan Avenue
Chicago, Illinois

Eunice and I went to Washington and stopped by the Georgetown home of Senator and Mrs. Kennedy for a relaxed and delightful supper. The Kennedys' daughter, Caroline, sat in a baby chair by the table as we ate.

The main reason Senator Kennedy wanted to see me was to express concern about coverage in *Jet*. He mentioned specifically stories which said he didn't have a Black secretary in his Washington office. The stories neglected to mention that he did have a Black secretary in his Boston office and that Nixon didn't have a Black secretary anywhere.

"I don't think that's fair," he said, drawing out the vowels in *fair* in the unique Boston accent that would soon become world-famous.

I agreed with him and told him I would see that he got fair coverage in *Jet*.

"I'm glad you're fair-minded," he said, pulling his chair closer. "Now that you're going to do this for me, what can I do for you? You know, I'm going to be president. Would you like to be an ambassador? Would you like a high government post? What do you want? I believe in paying my political debts."

"Gee, Senator," I replied. "I really don't want any of those things. I'm trying to succeed as a publisher, and I have no other ambition. I understand your father is active in the liquor business. Maybe you could speak to him and he could pass the word around so I could get some advertisers, which I need at this time."

He said he didn't know if he could do that. "But let me see what I can do."

Less than a month later, my secretary told me Henry Ford II was on the line. I told her it couldn't be Henry Ford.

"I don't know Henry Ford and there's no reason for him to call me."

She said it sounded like Henry Ford.

"How do you know how Henry Ford sounds?"

"If I were you," she said, "I'd get on the phone."

I got on the phone and, sure enough, it was Henry Ford II.

"Mr. Johnson," he said, "I was up at Hyannis Port with Senator Kennedy last week. He told me you're a fine young man who puts out a good magazine. He asked if I would consider giving you some advertising. I'm calling to tell you that we're going to consider it—ah, hell, we're going to do it. And I want you to know that I'm doing it because of Senator Kennedy."

So, after an advertising campaign of at least ten years, we got our first Ford ad. Which only goes to show that if you get up early and knock on doors for ten years—and get in the area of gossip—the doors will finally open.

That was the first lesson I learned. The second was the higher mathematics of the new politics. Long before it became common knowledge, I knew that Henry Ford II, a nominal Republican, was supporting the Democratic candidate. And I was not surprised when Robert McNamara left Ford to become secretary of defense in the Kennedy Administration.

After the 1960 election, Kennedy broke new ground, carrying Blacks and Whites across many frontiers. For the first time, large numbers of Blacks attended the inauguration of a president and danced and sipped champagne at the social events.

I'm glad I had the foresight to take my mother and stepfather and my wife's mother and father to the 1961 inauguration. For Eunice and me, it was the opening of a new door in history. For our parents and for members of their generation, it was a social and political miracle.

There was on all sides a sense of high expectations and widening horizons. Blacks of all ages felt for the first time that they were integral parts of a new administration. To support this view, there were Blacks in new places—

Andrew Hatcher as associate press secretary at the White House, Robert C. Weaver as head of the Housing and Home Finance Agency. And although President Kennedy tried at first to finesse the race issue, events made him take an active role in the opening acts of the Freedom Movement.

This was a new and heady experience for Blacks and Whites, who began the still uncompleted task of dealing with each other openly and frankly as Americans. Our offices were only half a block from the White House and the young Kennedy staffers, Black and White, used to stop by for a drink and down-home discussions.

The Kennedys never missed a trick. On Tuesday, July 25, 1961, I went to a stag luncheon at the White House for Nigerian Prime Minister Abubakar Tafawa Balewa. There was no way for us to know it then, but John Kennedy and Balewa were both on their way to assassinations.

The president introduced me to the prime minister, saying, "This is John Johnson, a distinguished publisher who sometimes *leans* towards the Democrats."

"Mr. President," I said, "I'm leaning more and more."

After the luncheon, I flew back to Chicago. When I landed at O'Hare, there was an urgent message from the White House. Flustered airport officials rushed me to a phone and a secretary told me that the president wanted me to represent the United States at the Independence Ceremony of the Ivory Coast. The four-man delegation was to be headed by the president's brother, Attorney General Robert F. Kennedy, and I was to hold the rank of special ambassador.

Within days, I was en route to the Ivory Coast on a presidential plane with Robert and Ethel Kennedy and G. Mennen Williams, the assistant secretary of state for African affairs. The fourth member of the delegation was Ivory Coast Ambassador R. Borden Reams.

Just before one of the major events of the Independence Ceremony, Ambassador Reams came to me with a surprising story.

"John," he said, "I was only able to get four tickets to this affair. It occurred to me that we could give the tickets to Mr. and Mrs. Kennedy and Mr. and Mrs. Williams, and I would find something for you and me to do."

This seemed strange to me. I was the only Black on an official delegation to the Independence Ceremony of a Black country, and the ambassador was saying he didn't think I should attend a major event. When he asked what I thought, I told him I was not the head of the delegation, and it was a matter for Mr. Kennedy to decide.

He hiked down the steps, and I hiked down behind him to eavesdrop on what was being said. He told the same story to Robert Kennedy, who thought for a while and said: "First of all, Ethel and I need two tickets. And John Johnson, of course, will need one—I don't care what you do with the other one."

The ambassador, who had only one ticket for his immediate boss and his wife, turned two or three colors, ran all the way to the palace, and came back with the proper number of tickets. We never had that problem again, and Bobby Kennedy never mentioned it to me.

From that moment on, he was one of my favorite people. I was struck then and later by the big difference between the private and public man. Probably because of his youth, he put on a serious, almost abrasive, personality in public. In private, he was a warm human being, full of fun, always cracking jokes.

When we returned to America, he sent a cordial handwritten note:

Dear John:

Thank you very much for your nice letter. As I told the President on our return, and as your other travelling companions all agree, the United States could not have had a better representative than you. I was proud to be in your company and hope that perhaps we can make another trip together for the country. As well as being a tremendous experience, it was great fun.

I hope that if your plans bring you to Washington, you will let me know so that we can get together. Ethel will be back in another two weeks and we would like you to come for dinner one evening if it is convenient.

Sincerely,
Bob

The attorney general later visited our offices, bringing with him fifteen FBI agents. One of our editors asked, "If you bring fifteen FBI agents with you when you visit your friend John Johnson, how many agents would you take with you to visit an enemy?" Without cracking a smile and without missing a beat, he said: "One hundred."

When the Ivory Coast president, Felix Houphouet-Boigny, came to America, Eunice and I attended the White House dinner, hosted by the president, and the Blair House dinner, hosted by the African president. The stars of the two nights were the wives of the two presidents. The elegant First Lady of the Ivory Coast was called by some White newspapers "the African Jackie Kennedy," and Mrs. Kennedy was called by some African newspapers the "African Marie Thérèse Houphouet-Boigny."

I was surprised by the size of the Ivory Coast delegation, which was one of the largest to accompany a visiting president. Some columnists, noting that several presidents had been overthrown while they were out of the country, said the Ivory Coast president brought everybody in the country who was qualified to be president.

I also noted that all the cabinet members were Black except the finance minister. I asked the chief of protocol about that and he said: "We are still heavily dependent on France for funds and the French are more comfortable with a Frenchman as a finance minister."

Tragedy and struggle changed both President Kennedy and his brother. Both were, in the beginning, a little aloof and, not to mince words, a little arrogant. The explosions of the sixties changed all that.

The changes were clear to me as early as February 1963 when I went to the White House with other Blacks to celebrate the one hundredth anniversary of the Emancipation Proclamation. The president I saw on that night wasn't the same man I'd met five years before in Georgetown.

The White House reception was on February 12. Five months later, after forcing the registration of two Black students at the University of Alabama, Kennedy made a fourteen-and-a-half-minute speech that was one of the defining events of his presidency. For in that speech, a U.S. president said for the first time that segregation was morally wrong.

"One hundred years of delay," he said, "have passed since President Lincoln freed the slaves, yet their heirs, their grandsons, are not fully free. They are not free from the bonds of injustice; they are not yet free from social and economic oppression. And this nation, for all its hopes and all its boast, will not be fully free until all its citizens are free."

The next day, Wednesday, June 12, a segregationist added an exclamation point to this speech by assassinating Medgar Evers in front of his Jackson, Mississippi, home.

Like almost all Americans, Black and White, I was alternately elated and enraged by these events. And I was one of the 250,000 Americans, Black and White, who climbed the heights with Martin Luther King, Jr., in the March on Washington.

I'd never witnessed a day like that before, and I'm sure I'll never see one like it again. Black and White together, celebrity, labor unionist, and entrepreneur together. And people from everywhere—Josephine Baker from Paris, Marlon Brando and Sammy Davis, Jr., from Hollywood, priests, nuns, sinners, all united in one of the greatest demonstrations for freedom in our history.

I mobilized a small army to cover the event. One of our teams flew east with the Hollywood contingent. Another team came down on the buses with the East Coast group. Still another team rode the train with the Midwest contingent.

We converged on the Lincoln Mall, more than fifty strong, the largest press group from a print medium. We have more photographs from that event in our files today than any other medium or organization.

In September, I had a private meeting with the president, who talked about race relations with a new sense of urgency and maturity. He congratulated me on our Emancipation Proclamation Centennial edition, and we posed, holding a copy of the famous cover of Frederick Douglass.

The next month, in October, Kennedy named me to the official delegation for the Independence Ceremony of Kenya, with the rank of special ambassador.

A month later, he was dead, gunned down in Dallas.

Horrified like almost all Americans, I tried to make some sense out of the whirlwind of events. After my appointment was reconfirmed by President Johnson, I went to the Kenya celebration in December 1963, convinced that freedom was on trial not only in Africa but also in America.

I was by now an old hand at independence celebrations, but neither books nor past experiences prepared you for the centuries-long explosions that always greeted the raising of the new African flag. There were, moreover, special ingredients in the Kenya celebration, notably the presence of Jomo Kenyatta, the legendary leader of the resistance, who at the age of sixty-nine dashed from ceremony to ceremony accompanied by his young wife. According to a funny story told by diplomats, Prince Philip, representing the Crown, leaned over and whispered to Kenyatta just before the British flag came down: "Are you sure you don't want to change your mind?"

Eunice and me with President and Mrs. Kennedy, Vice President and Mrs. Lyndon
B. Johnson, Ethel Kennedy and Black leaders attending Centennial celebration of
the Emancipation Proclamation, 1963.

President Johnson and I pose
with a copy of *Jet*, 1964.
(MAURICE SORRELL)

With President Nixon, 1969.
(OFFICIAL WHITE
HOUSE PHOTOGRAPH)

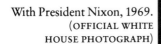

With President Gerald Ford, 1971.
(MAURICE SORRELL)

With President Jimmy Carter, 1983.

In receiving line at President Reagan's White House dinner for
General Secretary Gorbachev, 1987. (OFFICIAL WHITE HOUSE PHOTOGRAPH)

Eunice and me with Prime Minister Margaret Thatcher at President Reagan's last formal White House dinner, 1988.
(OFFICIAL WHITE HOUSE PHOTOGRAPH)

With President and Mrs. George Bush.
(OFFICIAL WHITE HOUSE PHOTOGRAPH)

At National Advisory Board meeting of First Commercial Bank Little Rock, Arkansas — 1987.

Mayor Harold Washington visits our table at celebration of Chicago's 150th anniversary. (D. MICHAEL CHEERS)

At Ghana Independence Celebration with Prime Minister Kwame Nkrumah, 1957. (MONETA SLEET, JR.)

Special Ambassador Johnson with Robert Kennedy and other members of the U.S. delegation at Ivory Coast Independence Celebration, 1961. (G. MARSHALL WILSON)

Special Ambassador with President
Jomo Kenyatta at Kenya Independence
Celebration, 1963.
(MONETA SLEET, JR.)

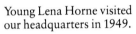

Young Lena Horne visited
our headquarters in 1949.

With Golda Meir in Nairobi, Kenya, 1963.
(MONETA SLEET, JR.)

With Elizabeth Taylor and then husband,
Senator John Warner, at JPC Washington
Office Inaugural reception — 1981.

With Henry Ford II, who provided a major advertising contract. (MONETA SLEET, JR.)

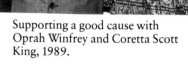

Supporting a good cause with Oprah Winfrey and Coretta Scott King, 1989.

Sharing a joke with Bill Cosby, 1983.

With popular presidential candidate Jesse L. Jackson, 1987. (VANDELL COBB)

Receiving NAACP's coveted Spingarn Award, 1966.

Named "Magazine Publisher of the Year" by the Magazine Publishers Association, 1972.
(CAMERA 1)

Inducted into the Black Press Hall of Fame, 1987.
(BOB JOHNSON)

Honored for distinguished contributions to journalism with *USA Today* Editor John C. Quinn and Executive Producer Don Hewitt of "60 Minutes," 1986.
(MAURICE SORRELL)

At Arkansas
sesquicentennial
celebration with Governor
Bill Clinton and Daisy
Bates, 1986.
(JAMES L. MITCHELL)

Returning to Arkansas
City birthplace for
first time in
53 years, 1986.
(JAMES L. MITCHELL)

Dreaming the dreams of the past on the bank of Mississippi River,
near Arkansas City birthplace, 1986. (JAMES L. MITCHELL)

# 38

## *Special Ambassador to White America*

IN the decade of the long hot summers, I held the unofficial position of special ambassador to American Whites.

As city after city erupted in riots, I was forced by circumstances and my unique vantage points on the Black and White watchtower to assume the role of interpreting Black America to corporate America and corporate America to Black America.

I made at least two hundred speeches during this period to business leaders stunned by the revolution of rising expectations. Many, in fact, called me and asked, "What should I do? Should I advertise more, should I hire more Black trainees and executives?"

I'd talked in the fifties to the president of a large company who told me he wasn't interested in sociology. The same man called in the sixties and said he had changed his mind. "I'm still not interested in sociology," he said, "but

I'm interested in my balance sheet. And sociology is showing up in my balance sheet."

I tried not to be self-serving in my response to White corporate leaders, who were astonished and dismayed by the depth of Black feeling. I seldom mentioned advertising, assuming correctly that if corporate leaders dealt responsibly with Black America, advertising would follow as a matter of course.

Whether in speeches or in one-to-one encounters, I emphasized fair employment and equal opportunity, pointing out that it was the responsibility of the CEO to ensure that his managers carried out his policies. If the CEO isn't committed, I said, and if he doesn't create goals and check periodically to see if the goals are being met, nothing is going to happen. Why not, I asked, audit equal opportunity the same way we audit everything else?

I called for larger contributions to Black educational institutions and asked corporate leaders to assume personal responsibility by becoming committees of one to ensure that the Dream was alive and well in their communities and corporations.

Enlightened self-interest: that was my theme. I asked corporate leaders to act not for Blacks, not for civil rights, but for their corporations and themselves. For it was true then and it's true now that if you increase the income of Blacks and Hispanics and poor Whites, you increase the profits of corporate America. And if you decrease the income of the disadvantaged, you decrease the income and the potential income of American corporations.

In a typical speech of the decade, "The Impact of the Negro Revolt on Print Media," I told the annual meeting of the Audit Bureau of Circulation that the winds of change were blowing but that it was an ill wind that "bloweth no man to good."

"What we have to deal with today," I said, "is a major shift in the mood of Negro people. The New Negro Consumer is demanding full participation in the American marketplace and insists that businessmen deal with him as an American and as a human being.

"The shift in the Negro's mood is directly related to the crisis in the city. The flight to the suburbs has sharply reduced the number of white readers and consumers in the inner city. As a result, an increasingly large percentage of the central city population is made up of Negro consumers and readers. Any executive who honestly seeks to do a good job for his company must come to terms with the habits, manners and desires of these new customers and consumers."

The Black population in the central cities, I added, is rising, and "if present trends continue at least a dozen major cities will be 50 percent Black within the next fifteen years. We already know that in seventy-nine of our largest cities where nine-tenths of the nation's wholesale sales and two-thirds of all retail sales are made, the Negro is now 25 percent of the population."

Summing up, I stressed the opportunities of the moment:

"The Negro revolt is an opportunity for you and your companies; it is an opportunity for America and the free enterprise system. The Negro public has an annual spendable income of $23.5 billion. If the current revolt succeeds ...the increased purchasing power of the Negro will add substantially to the growth of the entire American market. Our major financial problem is not the European common market, but the American common market, which is divided now by artificial barriers and anxieties. Integration of the Negro into the American Common Market would be the equivalent of adding a whole new nation of producers and consumers."

My message was essentially the same when I talked about "The New Negro Consumer: A Challenge, Responsibility and Opportunity" at a meeting of the New York chapter of the Public Relations Society of America.

"Negro Americans," I said, "are in the streets demonstrating and protesting. You can't service your clients adequately if you don't know why they are in the streets.... No one who watched the acres of people in the March on Washington—as I did—can say that he doesn't understand the depth of the Negro's discontent. This is a crucial turning point in the relations between Negro and white Americans. If PR people are not telling their clients the truth about this movement, their clients are going to end up with a net loss of sales."

What it all boiled down to was that equal opportunity was good business. It was clear, even by the early sixties, that the things businessmen feared most seldom happened. According to a *Wall Street Journal* survey, business was better than ever in the desegregated South. Fred Harvey, president of Harvey's Department Store in Nashville, told the *Journal* that "the greatest surprise I ever had was the apparent 'so-what' attitude of white customers." Ray Bennison, convention manager of the Dallas Chamber of Commerce, said that integration had "opened up an entirely new area of convention prospects." He added: "This year we've probably added $8 million to $10 million of future bookings because we're integrated."

Since that time, desegregated dollars have transformed the desegregated South, where Blacks and Whites are overcoming together in the convention business and the airport business and the money business.

And from this standpoint, we can say that Martin Luther King, Jr., and the Movement freed more White people than Black people.

# 39

# "From One President and One Johnson to Another"

LYNDON Baines Johnson, the first southern-based president since Andrew Johnson, hadn't been in office for a month when I started getting indirect messages from the White House. Whitney Young told me the president called him in the middle of the night and asked, "Whitney, why don't they like me at *Jet*?" Other leaders received similar calls.

One day about five o'clock in the afternoon, Carl Rowan called and said the president wanted to see me right away. I told him I would come the next morning.

When I arrived, I was ushered into the Oval Office for one of the happenings of the sixties, a one-on-one with Johnson. As soon as I crossed the threshold, the president started talking, telling me what he had done and was doing for Black people and that he didn't see why *Jet* was always criticizing his administration and picking at this and that. It was tragic, he said. It was getting in the way of the progress he was trying to create for Blacks and playing into the hands of those no-good bleep bleep bleep sonofabitches who hated Lyndon Johnson and Negroes. He went on like this for about thirty minutes without giving me a chance to say one word, and most of the words he used about his critics couldn't be printed.

When he paused for a breath, I said, "Well, Mr. President, what do you want me to do about it?"

He said, "I want it stopped."

I said, "It's stopped."

He paused, stunned. "Just like that?"

I said, "Just like that." I told him I'd reviewed the stories and that some of them were obviously unfair. The problem was that our people were Kennedy people who resented the fact that Kennedy was dead and that somebody was trying to take his place. So I told him I would make sure that he got fair coverage in our magazines.

"Well," he said, "now that that's over, why don't you and I pose with a copy of *Jet*."

I said, "Gee, Mr. President, I don't have a copy of *Jet*."

He pulled a copy out of his pocket and said, "I just happen to have one."

And the photographer was called in to record two southerners, one Black, one White, holding up a copy of *Jet*.

What impressed me about President Johnson was his persuasiveness. If he hadn't committed himself to politics, he would have made a master salesman. He'd always pull his chair up close to you and talk to you in a soft voice, looking you straight in the eyes. I mean, it was almost like he was making love to a woman. He made love to the people he was trying to convince, and it was hard to say no to anything he asked.

After our first meeting, we became friends, and I was invited to the White House so many times I was embarrassed to tell my friends. At most dinners, I was seated next to the president. When Thurgood Marshall was appointed solicitor general of the United States, I was sitting next to him, and he said, "Now, Mr. Johnson, I've just appointed Thurgood Marshall solicitor general.... You're a bright young man, I'm sure I don't have to tell you why I did that, do I?"

"Of course not, Mr. President," I replied. "I hope he succeeds and that you do what I think you're going to do." Which, of course, was to give Marshall experience at that level before appointing him to the Supreme Court.

Shortly afterward, I was seated at the president's table at a stag dinner. It was customary at these dinners to put names in a hat and pull out one name for each table. That person was supposed to get up and give the president some advice on how to run the country.

Whether by design or accident, my name was picked at my table. I sat there in a quandary because I knew that the last thing Johnson wanted was advice on how to run the country. When my turn came, I stood up and said, "My mother's name was Johnson, my wife's name is Johnson. I've never had any luck giving advice to Johnsons—and I'm not going to start tonight."

The room exploded in laughter and applause. Nathan Pusey, the president of Harvard, sent me a little note, "You are ahead." When the last speaker finished, he sent me another note, "You are still ahead."

The other speakers had tried to give Johnson advice. Pusey and I knew that this was the wrong forum and the wrong time to give Lyndon Johnson advice.

I remember another dinner President Johnson gave for Golda Meir, the foreign minister of Israel. Responding to the president's toast, she said that Israel was in the Middle East. The only problem, she said, was that Moses wandered through the desert for forty years and then settled in the only place in the Middle East that had no oil.

In 1966 I got a call from Joseph Califano, who said President Johnson wanted to put me on the National Selective Service Commission. I told Califano that I would be honored to serve but that the president should know that I had received a deferment and was not drafted during World

War II. Califano said he thought the president knew but that he would check and get back to me. He called back a few hours later and said, "The president told me to tell you that he knows that you received a deferment and that *he knows a lot of other things about you*—and that he still wants you to serve." I wondered what else the president knew about me as I quickly accepted the appointment.

To the surprise of many people President Johnson continued and extended the social practices of the Kennedy administration. During the Johnson years, everybody was invited to drink and dance in the foyer after dinner.

Johnson was a good dancer, who could apparently dance all night long. He danced with Black women. In fact, he was photographed at his inauguration dancing with the wife of Hobart Taylor, one of his Black aides.

I concluded from all this that Johnson believed in equal rights with no "ifs" or "buts." I don't know when he was converted, or whether he had to be converted. But during his tenure, he showed no prejudice I could discern. And he was willing to say in public what he said in private.

Like Kennedy, like Lincoln, like all U.S. presidents, he had to be prodded and pushed on civil rights. But after he gave his famous "We shall overcome" speech, he did more than any other president for civil rights, appointing the first Black cabinet member and the first Black Supreme Court justice.

One of my prized possessions is a letter from President Johnson, which was sent "from one president and one Johnson to another."

Many people have asked me how I rate the Kennedys and Johnson. I think the Kennedys, John F. Kennedy in particular, had class and style. He was a man of the world who knew how to put you at ease, and he could pull the best out of you. And I think his heart was in the right place— after his inauguration.

At one of the many confrontations of the sixties, Jackie

Robinson, who was a Rockefeller Republican, attacked Bobby Kennedy, asking where he and his brother were before the 1960 election and what the Kennedys knew about Blacks.

"Well," Bobby said, "if you're asking me whether my brother and I stayed up all night worrying about Black people before the election, the answer is no—we didn't stay up all night worrying about them. We think we treated the ones we knew with dignity and respect, but we didn't know that many. But once my brother became president and I became attorney general, we did stay up nights worrying about Black people. We did get to know them, and we are worried and concerned about their problems."

For the Kennedys, then, it was a learning process. I think Johnson had always known. What happened is that Black people and their allies created a situation that made it possible for him to be what he was.

I would say, then, in summary, that John Kennedy was the most charming and the most eloquent, Bobby Kennedy was the toughest, and Lyndon Baines Johnson got the most done.

# 40

# *Black Is Beautiful (and White, Too)*

B ETWEEN 1960 and 1970, Black America reinvented itself, changing both its color and its name.

The name *Black* replaced *Negro* and *colored*.

The color black replaced brown and even white in the center of the black spectrum.

Black consciousness.

Black love.

Black fire.

Black power.

*Black World*.

This was perhaps the most significant and dangerous hairpin turn in Black history, and it created havoc in the offices of institutions and people who couldn't cope with sudden change.

Suddenly and dramatically, the walls came tumblin' down almost everywhere. The number of Negroes in college doubled and tripled, and the Black middle class multiplied.

There was, at the same time, a quantum jump in Black consciousness.

For the first time Blacks came into their own. They respected themselves as Black people whether they were very dark or very light or in between. Color, in fact, lost its importance. If there was an edge it was with the darker colors. But, after a period of friction, it finally settled down to the point where we were just Blacks without regard to shades or tints.

Johnson Publishing Company played a leadership role in this process on three levels. First, and perhaps above all, we helped create the foundations of this struggle in the forties and fifties when the ground was hard and there were few laborers. Secondly, we anticipated the changes and gave focus and form to them. In 1959, for example, I detected a growing interest in Black history and authorized a pathfinding Black history series. The response was so enthusiastic that we published a book, Lerone Bennett's *Before the Mayflower*, which became one of the most widely read Black history books ever. This marked the beginning of the Johnson Publishing Company Book Division which published a best-selling cookbook, Freda DeKnight's *Date With a Dish*, and several major titles on Black history and culture.

We didn't follow the parade; we were out front, beating the drums and pointing the way. Our series on "Black Power" preceded the first call for "Black Power." We were the first major magazine to say that the race problem is a White problem ("The White Problem in America"). We were the first major magazine to say what almost all historians say today, that Abraham Lincoln had the racial limitations of most of his contemporaries ("Was Abraham Lincoln a White Supremacist?").

We also spoke frankly to Black America, denouncing "Black on Black Crime" in a prize-winning special issue and calling for community action to deal with teenage pregnancy and drugs.

I'd be lying if I said that I published these stories

without reservations. There was no way to know then how advertisers or readers would react. Before the issue on "The White Problem" went to press, one of my editors, Era Bell Thompson, asked, "Boss, do you know what you're doing?" I didn't know what I was doing, but I was preaching the virtues of "responsible daring" in the White community, and there was no alternative to "responsible daring" in the Black community.

On a third and equally important level, we changed with the changing times. In the early days we followed the consciousness of the times by defining success narrowly in terms of material things. There was perhaps a need for that then. We needed to know then that some Blacks were living as well as some Whites. But as the magazine matured and as Blacks changed, we broadened the formula for success, defining it as the achievement of a positive goal or the attainment of whatever a person set out to do.

Winning a civil rights battle was success.

Raising a family was success.

Sending children to college was success.

Earning an MBA or making an oustanding professional contribution was success.

This changed the weight of the magazine. Before the sixties we were perhaps 50 percent orange juice and 50 percent castor oil. For most of the sixties we were practically all castor oil. Our readers embraced the new formula. They hungered for it. They were more interested in being men and women than in being entertained.

To meet this rising tide of interest, and to promote the works of Black writers and artists, we revived *Negro Digest*, renamed, in response to the currents of the age, *Black World*. The magazine made a major contribution to the cultural transformation of that period, discovering and developing scores of new poets and short-story writers.

I must have been doing something right, for my leading magazines reached all-time highs in the sixties, and we received unprecedented acclaim in the Black and White communities. When we celebrated the twentieth anniversary of *Ebony* in November 1965, *Ebony* was selling 900,000 copies a month, and its three sister magazines, *Jet, Tan,* and *Negro Digest,* were selling a total of 2.3 million copies a month.

There were, of course, some casualties. I started a new magazine, *Ebony Africa,* for African readers. The initial response was good, but the magazine foundered on the hard realities of national and linguistic barriers. Later, when the Freedom Movement ebbed, the circulation of *Black World* dropped from 100,000 to 15,000, and I discontinued the renamed *Negro Digest* for the second time.

White advertisers made the hairpin turn with us. During this period, we made our most consistent advertising gains, winning new credibility and acceptability in the advertising world. By 1965, the ad lineage of *Ebony* was comparable to many general-market magazines. In 1964, the magazine grossed a record $5.5 million from the sale of advertising space alone.

A cause and effect of our new status was the series of ads we ran in major media on the new Black consumer market and the new *Ebony*. Bill Grayson and I worked with the Redmond, Marcus and Shure agency in creating the provocative titles (EBONY IS RUNNING THE BIGGEST BLACK MARKET OPERATION IN THE U.S.A./WHEN WAS THE LAST TIME YOU SAW A COTTON-PICKIN' NEGRO?/ ALL HEADACHES ARE CREATED EQUAL/WE THINK THAT WHITE IS BEAUTIFUL, TOO) which some critics called one of the most brilliant advertising campaigns of the sixties.

# 41

## *Celebrating on Two Continents*

E D Sullivan said it was "the greatest show going on anywhere in the world."

Arthur Godfrey, Lena Horne, Duke Ellington, and Muhammad Ali agreed.

They were among the eight hundred CEOs, ad executives, and celebrities who filled the Starlight Roof of the Waldorf-Astoria on Monday, November 29, 1965, for the twentieth-anniversary celebration of *Ebony* magazine.

Never before had so many certified Black and White legends gathered under one roof. Among the guests were NAACP chief Roy Wilkins, Whitney Young of the National Urban League, U.S. Solicitor General Thurgood Marshall, U.S. housing chief Robert C. Weaver, Dorothy Height of the National Council of Negro Women, Sammy Davis, Jr., Cab Calloway, Ossie Davis, Carl Rowan, Frederick O'Neal, Louis Gossett, Brock Peters, Diana Sands, Langston Hughes, Jim Brown, Roy Campanella, and Jackie Robinson.

Clifford Alexander represented the White House and read a special greeting from President Johnson, who said, "Your publications have been important vehicles in keeping Americans aware of the major occurrences of our times." Vice President Humphrey, eloquent as always, toasted *Ebony* in a moving ten-minute film which was shown on two big screens.

"What a remarkable success story this is," he said. "Starting out in November 1945, as little more than a dream in Johnny Johnson's eye, *Ebony* today is a leader among national magazines. With a circulation which has grown from 25,000 to almost one million copies, it is interesting that the growth of *Ebony* parallels almost precisely the awakening of the American people to the generation of racial injustice and prejudices which have plagued the country.

"John Johnson, I salute you and your associates for your remarkable contribution to building a more just and free America. Happy birthday on this wonderful occasion."

Sammy Davis, Jr., one of our oldest and dearest friends, was impressed by the concrete example of progress.

"No one," he said, "knew my name until I appeared in *Ebony*. I remember when *Ebony* started you couldn't get a room at the Hotel Theresa [in Harlem]. And now *they've* taken over the Waldorf-Astoria."

I was literally struck dumb by the outpouring of tributes. Calling the names of CEOs, public officials, and celebrities took so much time that I thanked my wife, mother, friends, and supporters and sat down, abandoning a prepared speech, that was distributed to the press. The next day, major newspapers printed my prediction that "by 1985 we will probably have Negro mayors in two or three of our ten major cities, Negro congressmen from the South, and perhaps even a Negro vice president."

Two out of three—not bad, especially since Jesse Jackson has proven that the third prediction is within the realm of possibility.

I left that night for Paris, where on Tuesday a second party was held to celebrate our twentieth anniversary and the opening of our Paris office. The new branch office was on a front street across from the Hotel George-V, the site of the celebration.

More than four hundred diplomats, industrialists, and dignitaries descended on the hotel for the party. The guests included Hazel Scott, conductor René Leibowitz, Marpessa Dawn, and Memphis Slim. As one Frenchman put it with typical Gallic extravagance, the whole affair was one *succès fou* (a fantastic success).

There have been many times when I've had to pinch myself to make sure I wasn't dreaming. This was one of those times. I just couldn't imagine a poor boy from Arkansas and the welfare rolls of Chicago throwing a big party at New York City's Waldorf-Astoria and Paris's George-V almost simultaneously. I finally said to myself, "John Johnson, you've made it." It hadn't hit me until that moment that a man who had offices in Rockefeller Center and on Michigan Avenue and Pennsylvania Avenue and Wilshire Boulevard and Avenue Georges V—such a man must have made it.

The next year I received two major awards that pointed in the same direction. At the NAACP convention in Los Angeles, I became the fifty-first recipient of the coveted Spingarn Medal. The medal is given annually "for the highest and noblest achievement by an American Negro during the preceding year or years."

On Monday, May 23, I was one of twelve Americans who received the Horatio Alger Award, which is given annually by the American Schools and Colleges Association to the "living individuals who by their own efforts have pulled themselves up by their bootstraps in the American tradition."

I was the second Black (following Ralph Bunche) to receive the award. Also cited at the Waldorf-Astoria dinner were Roy L. Ash, President of Litton Industries; actor Walter Brennan; William E. Grace, president and CEO of Freuhauf Corporation; and Leslie Worthington, president of U.S. Steel.

Dr. Norman Vincent Peale, national chairman of the Horatio Alger Awards committee, said my career had done "a greal deal to convey to the Negro youth of America that opportunity still knocks for them as it does for all Americans willing to listen and act."

This season of triumph peaked in October 1967 when we sold more than 1 million copies for the first time. West Indian leaders and the Schomburg Collection on Black culture were featured in this issue, which brought to a conclusion one of the hardest campaigns of my career.

In the course of this campaign, I tried fourteen different approaches, including a school program, a church program, a direct-subscription campaign, and a "Send One to Your Friend" program. I've said many times that if I'd been president of a public company with a board of directors, I would have been fired after the ninth or tenth try. I honestly believed each approach was going to do the job. In the end, it was not any one of these efforts—it was all of them.

In January 1968, in the midst of all this excitement, I turned fifty, and reporters asked how it felt to be face-to-face with the big zero. I told them I was reminded of singer Sarah Vaughan, who said she handled fifty a lot better than forty. I was worried about forty, which seemed to close a door on my youth. By 1968 I was comfortable with the whole thing. Comfortable, but not ecstatic. I didn't jump up and down and shout about it. I simply accepted it in the spirit of Dinah Shore's publicist, who rejected all questions about her seventieth birthday, saying, "Dinah doesn't do birthdays."

Like Dinah, I don't do birthdays. I mean, they come and go. And I forget them unless I'm reminded by a reporter. I feel the same way today that I felt when I was thirty or forty. I have the same interests and the same energy, and I've only panicked once. I noticed one day that my hairline was receding, and I went to all kinds of treatment places and sent off for magical oils and salves. Nothing worked, and I decided to relax and enjoy it. I told people, "Love me, love my receding hairline."

In all seriousness, we Americans, Black and White, are too hung up on age. There are seasons in life and history, and some autumns, and even some winters, are more glorious and warming than some springs.

That's why we don't have forced retirements at Johnson Publishing Company. Some people are born fifty, and some seventy-year-olds are and always will be twenty-nine years old in their glands and their hearts. I've always liked the statement of the late Mayor Washington, who answered an age question with an impromptu poem: "I'm sixty, feel like fifty. Nothing hurts and everything works."

# 42

## "The King of Love Is Dead"

IT was Eunice's birthday.

I was rushing home to take her to dinner when I heard the message on the car radio.

Martin Luther King, Jr., had been shot on the balcony of a Memphis motel and was being rushed to a local hospital. Nobody, the announcer said, knew what his condition was.

I knew.

I drove on, trying to see the street through my tears, praying, cursing, hoping against hope, but something in my body, something cold and clammy, knew that it was over. After an interval that went on forever, the radio told me what I already knew, that a friend and leader and conscience was dead.

At that moment—April 4, 1968—lights went out in the hearts of men and women all over the world. At almost the same time, the cities of America started burning.

I drove around aimlessly for a while and then went home for a birthday party that became a memorial to a dream and a hope. It was almost as if you'd heard that God was no longer in heaven. And you began for the first time to worry about America and Black and White people.

Of all the people who spoke and cried after the shots of Memphis, perhaps Nina Simone said it best: "What are we going to do now—now that the King of Love is dead?"

There then followed a national outpouring of grief and concern and the unforgettable image of that river of people following the mule-drawn wagon through the streets of Atlanta. I was there, along with most of my editors. We went to grieve and to pay homage to a brave widow and to make sure that no one would ever forget. One of our photographers, Moneta Sleet, Jr., won a Pulitzer Prize for his photograph of Coretta Scott King holding her daughter Bernice at the funeral.

We went through the motions but somehow it didn't seem real. It was almost as if we were living in a dream world and that we would wake up and find out that none of this really happened. But this was no dream. It happened again, to Robert Kennedy in Los Angeles, and you had the feeling that all of the people we hoped would lead us out of the wilderness were being killed.

In the aftermath, Americans of all creeds and colors mobilized to save themselves and the Dream. Slowly but surely the idea dawned that it was "not just Negroes," as President Johnson said, "but it's all of us who must overcome." Universities started recruiting Black students, and corporations started recruiting Blacks for fast-track programs. I was involved in one of the most creative of these programs, the Chicago United organization launched by the CEOs of the biggest Black and White corporations in Chicago.

It worked for a while. For the first time Whites went out of their way to increase the number of Blacks in colleges and corporations. For the first time we got unsolicited advertising from decent, caring Whites who felt ashamed and wanted to reach out and say in some way that they were sorry.

There was a feeling all over America that we were going to work our way out of the American Dilemma. We lived for a short time in a kind of fantasyland, believing that Christmas was going to come and last forever. Instead of Santa Claus, Vietnam came, wrecking the Great Society programs and pulling men and institutions away from the imperatives of the Dream. The grand outcome was a period of benign neglect which continues to this moment.

These were the peak years of the Dream deferred. And in our attempt to create new programs for the new century we need to go back and think deeply about the lessons of the sixties.

This was a time when men holding the highest ofice of the land said bigotry was wrong and equality was right. For most of this period, we had a powerful moral force in the White House, saying, "Let's be fair. Let's give people a chance. Let's live up to the Constitution."

There was a period before Vietnam when I thought we were on our way to a Great Society. But Lyndon Baines Johnson and the Great Society got bogged down in Vietnam, and we lost our way. And if we hope and intend to complete the unfinished business of the sixties, we must grapple now with the central imperative—and opportunity—of the twenty-first century, the changing color of America. For the old urban majorities are rapidly becoming minorities and the old urban minorities are quietly and undramatically becoming the new urban majorities.

For some strange reason, there's been little or no discussion of this demographic revolution in the press. But the statistics and the realities behind the statistics are not going away. And what we need to do now is to start getting ready for the new century by dealing with our No. 1 economic challenge.

This challenge doesn't come from abroad. It doesn't come from the invasion of Japanese or Korean or German goods. Our No. 1 economic challenge is internal. It is the task of creating a common American market based on a free flow of goods and ideas across all American barriers, regional, social, racial, and sexual.

This is the challenge—and the hope—of the American future. And we can't deal with that challenge without dealing with the increasingly large number of Black and Hispanic consumers, who already constitute the new majority in cities like Chicago, and who will be the new majority in key cities and areas in the twenty-first century.

The Black and Brown presence is real, and it is growing. When the cannons fire to signal the beginning of the twenty-first century, Blacks will be 73 percent of the population of Atlanta, 72 percent of the population of Detroit, 69 percent of the population of Washington, D.C., 62 percent of the population of New Orleans, and more than 50 percent of the populations of Baltimore, Birmingham, Memphis, Newark, and Oakland.*

In that year, Hispanics will be 38 percent of the population of Los Angeles and 23 percent of the population of Houston. By that time, the Hispanic population, according to current projections, will have reached 25,223,000 million, and the Black population will be 35,753,000 million.

In significant contrast, White Americans will be in the minority in four of the five largest American cities: New York City, 45 percent; Los Angeles, 38 percent; Chicago, 37 percent; and Houston, 44 percent.

The consumers in the old minority market are important today and they will be even more important in the twenty-first century. For despite unequal opportunity, despite poverty, *despite everything*, the Black American consumer market is the ninth largest consumer market in the free world. It is, in fact—measured by national market prices of 1985 in current market prices—larger than the gross national product of Saudi Arabia, Sweden, India,

*Decision Demographics, 1988.*

Australia, Spain, Mexico, the Netherlands, Switzerland, Belgium, Nigeria, and Austria.*

We're not talking here about a marginal minority market. We're talking about a major world market with a disposable income of $261.2 billion that will grow to at least $659.4 billion in 2000.

The meaning of this is clear: The color of the market is changing, and corporations can no longer avoid the two tasks that the forthcoming century has put on our agendas.

The first task is tapping the underutilized potential of Black and Brown consumers. Because of discrimination and arbitrary limitations on free market forces, these consumers have never had a chance to participate on an equal basis with other consumers. If, acting in our own self-interest, we made it possible for them to fulfill their unfulfilled needs for housing, transportation, and personal care items, we could double and even triple our income and production schedules.

That's the first task. The second is to utilize the skills, ideas, and energies of previously excluded entrepreneurs, including Blacks, Hispanics, and women. We're paying a big price, in dwindling market shares and balance-of-payments deficits, for arbitrarily limiting our entrepreneurial and technical pool. One of our most urgent duties is to use all our skills, all our energies, Black, White, and Brown, male and female, to revitalize the American market.

The new industries and institutions of the New South are concrete examples of what good men and women, Black and White, can achieve by tearing down the foolish barriers that segregate money and ideas and skills.

Our economic future, then, is in our own hands.

We have the power and the potential *in* America to solve our own problems. For we can solve the balance-of-payments deficit and meet the challenge of foreign competi-

---

*The World Bank Atlas, 1987.

tion by tapping the underutilized and undervalued potential of minority consumers.

And I'm reminded of the famous Booker T. Washington story about a ship that was lost at sea. The captain of the unfortunate ship sighted a friendly vessel and sent a signal, "Water, water, we die of thirst." And the answer came back, "Cast down your bucket where you are." A second and third time, the signal was sent out, "Water, water, send us water," and the answer came back: "Cast down your bucket where you are." The captain finally heeded the injunction and cast down his bucket and it came up full of fresh and sparkling water from the mouth of the Amazon River.

We can extend those words to those who seek salvation in mergers and untried ventures:

"Cast down your bucket where you are."

Cast it down into the neglected markets surrounding your factories and offices and cities.

Cast it down into the underutilized markets of minorities whose unfulfilled needs hold the key to our economic salvation.

Cast it down into the deep well of the millions of Black and Brown consumers who constitute the new majority in an increasing number of American cities and who hold the key to the American twenty-first century.

If the decade of the sixties still has a hold on our imagination, it is because it gave us a glimpse of the hidden possibilities of this dream.

I remember vividly that President Johnson had an organization called Plans for Progress which encouraged businessmen to give Blacks a piece of the action. He'd call businessmen to the White House and challenge them to be fair, to open up and give opportunity to deserving people.

As a result, Blacks started moving into the mortgage lending field, and new partnerships were forged by Black and White insurance companies. But these programs never really worked. Black corporations were thrown the scraps, or programs were organized with minimal Black participation.

Supreme Life Insurance Company, to cite a personal example, participated in a program which called for major corporations to direct their insurance companies to reinsure some of their business with Black-owned firms. But they never allowed us to receive income from reserves. It was a phantom arrangement in which a large White corporation would expose us to so much risk and then tell us at the end of the year whether we had gained or lost on the risk.

In a way it was like the old plantation system where you settled with the plantation boss, who kept the books and told you at the end of the year whether you'd made money or not. In five years or so Supreme Life was exposed to only $10,000 in profits. But when the airlines had a major disaster, the company wrote us a letter and told us our exposure was $100,000. That's when we withdrew.

There were similar problems with most of the fast-track programs, which were not very fast and which were not connected to the main highways. I was talking a little while ago to a young man who was recruited from Harvard for a fast-track program at a major corporation. He'd been on this program for six years, and he had watched, dismayed, while his White colleagues were placed in different divisions. He finally quit in disgust, saying he couldn't recruit other Blacks for the same dead end.

A major problem in the sixties and seventies was that talented Blacks were shunted off into the detours of vice presidencies in public relations or community relations or affirmative action. Some corporations, however, promoted on merit, especially Philip Morris, which elevated Thomas Shropshire to vice president and treasurer of Miller Brewing Company and George Lewis to the position of vice president and treasurer of Philip Morris Companies, Inc.

There were others, including Joe Black, a vice president of the Greyhound Lines, a major division of the Greyhound

Corporation, and Otis M. Smith, the general counsel of General Motors.

In the eighties we have the persuasive examples of Clifton Wharton, Jr., president of Teachers Insurance Annuity Association/College Retirement Equities Fund; A. Barry Rand, president of Xerox Marketing; Jerry O. Williams, president and chief operating officer of AM International; Roy Roberts, head of the main truck division of Navistar International Corporation, the leading maker of medium and heavy-duty trucks; and Forest J. Farmer, president of Acustar, the component parts subsidiary of Chrysler Corporation.

These men invite us to a future that can only be realized by dealing creatively with the lost lessons of the sixties.

A complicating factor in the story of the sixties was a historic shift from the Democrats to the Republicans, who had few Black supporters and who had lost the knack of appealing to Black voters. Richard Nixon tried to help Blacks get a piece of the action with his Black college and Black capitalism initiatives. But his Watergate-shortened administration was hampered by controversies over the advice of aides like Daniel Patrick Moynihan, who recommended a period of "benign neglect."

Nixon and I were old friends and we maintained our personal relationship. In fact, he invited me to more social affairs than any other president. He also appointed me to the committee for the celebration of the twenty-fifth anniversary of the United Nations.

Nixon made a mistake in his handling of the Watergate controversy, but he had redeeming qualities that didn't always come through in his public appearances. Interestingly and significantly, he seemed to be more relaxed and personable at Black-oriented affairs.

I saw him in Chicago shortly after his 1968 election, He told me he was planning a big affair for Duke Ellington's seventieth birthday and that he wanted me to come. After his inauguration, I got an invitation to a dinner for Chief Justice Warren.

I knew his secretary, Rosemary Woods, a Chicago woman, and I called her and said, "The president said he was going to invite me to the birthday celebration for Duke Ellington, and I have this invitation to the dinner for Chief Justice Warren. The dinners are only six days apart, and while I have enormous respect for Chief Justice Warren, if I had a choice I'd rather go to the dinner for Duke Ellington."

Rosemary said, "The president knows that you're coming to the Warren dinner and he wants you to come to the Duke Ellington dinner, too."

The Warren dinner was moving, but the Ellington celebration on Tuesday, April 29, 1969, was one of the great cultural events of the sixties. The White House has never jumped the way it jumped that night. Duke, elegantly attired as usual, with a little ponytail hanging down his back, was in the receiving line with the president and Mrs. Nixon, and he was greeting and kissing everybody.

"John," he asked me, "do you believe all this?"

I said, "It's hard to believe, Duke, but it's true."

Almost all of the jazz greats of the era were on hand. One of the high points of the evening was Earl ("Fatha") Hines's tribute to the Duke. I mean, he really rocked the place, and everybody was clapping and shaking. President Nixon, the country's most famous amateur pianist, played "Happy Birthday" and gave Duke the Medal of Freedom, and the music and merriment went on to the wee hours of the morning.

After Nixon was driven from office by the Watergate crisis triggered by Frank Wills, a Black night watchman at Washington's Watergate apartment complex, I was one of several Black leaders invited to the White House to confer with the new president, Gerald Ford. On Tuesday, November 12, 1974, I was one of several guests who dined at the White House with the Fords.

One of the astonishing consequences of the Black Revolution was the election of a president from the Deep South. I met Jimmy Carter early in the game when he was traveling around the country as "Jimmy Who?" trying to drum up support. At his request, I convened an early-morning editorial board meeting. I sat him in a big easy chair in my office that was later dubbed "the president's chair." After sitting in that chair, Jimmy Carter and Ronald Reagan were elected president. (Since we never held a formal question-and-answer session with Jesse Jackson, the power of the chair was not tested.)

Carter walked in cold on that morning and captivated us. The first thing he said to me was, "Mr. Johnson, I'm glad to meet you. We're both Morehouse Men." He was technically correct, for both of us had received honorary degrees from the predominantly Black college that produced Martin Luther King, Jr. More importantly, he was politically correct in stressing his identification with a tradition and a dream. I knew then that the peanut farmer from Plains, Georgia, was going far, and I was not surprised when he walked away with all the marbles.

During his presidency, I was invited to numerous meetings, receptions, and dinners at the White House. One of the great moments of the era, according to a *Jet* story, was a gospel extravaganza where the president of the United States of America took off his shoes and sat down on the grass and ate fried chicken with his guests.

When, shortly before the election of 1980, I went to the White House, I noticed that a painting had been removed. I asked about it, and Carter said he had ordered it moved. I told him that I didn't know presidents could move White House treasures. "Mr. Johnson," he said in that warm and comforting Georgia drawl, "a president can do any damn thing he wants to do." With, of course, one exception. He cannot, as the 1980 elections proved, ensure his own reelection.

# 43

## *The Loop,
the Gold Coast,
and Palm Springs*

IN three hectic years, from 1968 to 1971, I changed my
personal and corporate addresses and bought a house on
a mountain peak in Palm Springs. In the process, I moved
from South Michigan to the Loop, and from the heart of
Black Chicago to the heart of Chicago's Gold Coast.

These moves, which changed my relationship to myself
and to time and space, were neither planned nor willed.
They were the product of a series of isolated events that
came together, almost as if they were orchestrated, and
picked me up and carried me along.

Which proves, once again, that life is, in part, an accident or, at least, a movement that you don't entirely control.
That's why I would be afraid to live my life over again.
There were too many near-misses, too many happy accidents, and I'm not at all sure that I would make it the next
time.

My headquarters building in Chicago's Loop is one of

those happy accidents. I was happy in my old building at 1820 South Michigan, halfway between downtown Chicago, where I had to sell ads, and the South Side, where I had to sell my magazines. But one day in 1959 I got a letter from the mayor's office which said that an expressway was going to cut through Eighteenth Street and that I would have to move. City officials said they were sorry for the inconvenience and that they would give me a fair price for my property and pay my relocation costs.

Prodded gently by fate, I walked backward into a life-long dream. I'd already remodeled five places, and I didn't want to go that route again. When the letter came I started thinking seriously about my old dream of building a structure from the ground up. Eunice was not working full-time for the company then, and I gave her the special project of finding a place on a front street north of 1820 South Michigan. She finally found a vacant lot at our present location of 820 South Michigan, precisely ten blocks north of our old building.

We tried to buy the land, which was three doors from the Conrad Hilton Hotel and two doors from the Standard Oil Building. To our surprise and disgust, we ran into the same problems we had run into in the old location. As soon as the agents discovered that I was Black, they started backtracking.

Ten years had passed, from 1949 to 1959, and yet nothing really had changed. The real estate industry hadn't changed, and, as it turned out, John Johnson hadn't changed. I went to the same White lawyer who bought 1820 South Michigan in trust, and he bought 820 South Michigan in trust, paying $250,000 in cash.

Then things began to get complicated. Without warning, the city changed its mind and said the expressway was going through Twenty-fourth Street instead of Eighteenth Street. This threatened the old and the new sites, for I'd planned to use money from the sale of one to help finance building on the other.

Faced with this new challenge, I made the profound but understandable mistake of trying to finance the new building the conventional way. It was customary for corporations and developers to sell leases for a proposed building and then use the leases to get interim financing at a bank. I decided to build a thirty-story structure using this method.

To facilitate the plan, I put a sign on the property saying that leases were available and that I would build to specifications. It was a good idea, but unhappily the drift of the times was against it. I got a lot of telephone calls. But when the callers found out that I was Black, they remembered previous plans.

I then flirted with the idea of a joint venture with a rabbi who wanted to build a school in the area. There was only one small problem: We had dramatically different ideas about the final product. Every time we talked about the building, he saw it as a school with some offices for a publishing house, and I saw it as a publishing house with some space for a school.

After floundering around for almost ten years, going from one bank to another, I decided to go it alone. To get seed money, I closed the Paris and Los Angeles offices—the Los Angeles office was later reopened—and made other economies. Before the end of the decade, I'd saved aproximately $2 million. This would have been enough, under normal circumstances, to get interim financing on a $6- or $7-million building. But these were not normal circumstances.

One problem was that my architect, John Moutoussamy of Dubin, Dubin & Moutoussamy, was Black. The bankers didn't say they were opposed to the plan because the architect was Black. They kept saying that the proposed building was too much of a luxury structure and "your architect has never built an office building before."

"He's built schools, apartment buildings, many kinds of structures," I replied, "and the only reason he hasn't built an office building is that he's Black. Most of the people building office buildings are White, and none of them have been willing to let him build their building. And if a Black man doesn't let him build *his* office building, he will never get the experience."

This went on for ten years and would have continued for another ten years if I hadn't forced history's hand. Without consulting anybody, I deposited $2 million in the First National Bank and hired a contractor, Corbetta Construction Company. I told Corbetta to break gound and continue building until I could arrange a mortgage at an insurance company. If I couldn't arrange a mortgage before he used up the $2 million, he was to stop building where he was. Under our agreement, at least 40 percent of the workers had to be Black.

Construction began in February 1970 and continued until there was only enough money in the bank for another week of work. At that point, eight or nine months after the groundbreaking, I went to a United Negro College Fund banquet in New York City and sat next to a senior executive of Metropolitan Life Insurance Company. While other people were talking about the dinner, I pulled out the plans, which I always carried with me, and tried to interest him in my building. When it became clear that I was prepared to spread the plans out on the dinner table, he said, "We can't talk here. Come to my office tomorrow morning."

This was a Thursday night. I went to see him on Friday morning and he decided, after conferring with other executives, including a Black executive, that Metropolitan could probably do it.

"That's great," I said, pressing my luck. "The only problem is that I need the commitment today."

"You got to be kidding," he replied. "We *never* give a mortgage commitment in one day."

I looked him in the eye and said, "You're in charge of this department. Maybe you ought to just try and see if you have enough power in this company to do it in one day."

He smiled and said, "I know you are putting me on, but I'm going to try."

He tried, and what his executives said couldn't be done was done.

This was a true cliff-hanger, almost like the movies. I returned to Chicago hours before my money ran out with the Metropolitan Insurance Company commitment that made it possible for me to go to the First National Bank and get the interim financing.

Life was not presenting its problems in manageable packages in these frantic years.

For all the while, we were going through the trauma of moving from the heart of Black Chicago to the Gold Coast.

I liked Drexel Square, but Eunice has always been an adventurer in searching for homes and office sites. She's always searching, even today, for new and promising locations.

One day, in the midst of the maneuvering over the new office building, a friend told her that the Carlyle, a new condominium at 1040 Lake Shore Drive, was taking applications. There was one Black family in the building, but we didn't want any misunderstanding. We went directly to the builder, Al Robin, who said we met all the qualifications and would be a welcome addition.

We bought an apartment, and another problem developed. The White woman who lived on our floor—there are only two apartments on each floor—told several people that she didn't want to live on a floor with a Black family. We sent word through the grapevine—although we lived on the same floor, almost all of the negotiations were carried on by intermediaries—that we would be glad to buy her apartment.

Word came back that she didn't want to move out of the building. We asked management if it could find her another apartment in the building. When these arrangements were completed, she asked for moving expenses and reimbursement of $15,000 she had just spent to decorate her apartment.

We bought the apartment and reimbursed her for decorating and moving expenses, and she moved. Here again a disadvantage and an embarrassment turned into an advantage. For we got five bedrooms instead of three and the added security of having an elevator that can only stop on our floor if we want it to stop.

Most apartments in the building had been designed by Richard Himmel, a celebrated Chicago interior designer, but we wanted a different, perhaps a California, touch. Friends on the West Coast recommended Arthur Elrod, a Palm Springs–based expert, who'd decorated homes for Frank Sinatra and Bob Hope, among others. We visited some of the apartments and homes he'd done and decided that no one else could give our place the color and pizzazz that we wanted.

Elrod, who was killed later in an automobile accident, was a great artist and a great human being. We hit it off from the beginning, and he created, if I can express a modest and objective opinion, a fabulous apartment.

He told us up front that he wouldn't take the job unless we agreed to leave all of our old furniture in the old house. Two weeks before the job was completed, he made us promise not to visit the apartment again until he was satisfied with the arrangements.

The big night came and he called and said, "I want to invite you to dinner in your new apartment."

It was strange and enchanting. Eunice and I and Linda and John Harold got dressed and went to dinner in our own home. When the door opened, I couldn't believe my eyes. It was like something out of *Dynasty,* or something out of Hollywood. Elrod took us on a tour and we sat down to dinner, prepared by a caterer. It was almost like visiting a rich relative, except it was our own place.

People who visit our apartment ooh and aah over the dramatic color schemes and the Picassos and Chagalls and the paintings by Black artists like Horace Pippin and Edward Bannister. But the thing that impresses me most about the Carlyle is that it has indoor plumbing and steam heat and it's on a front street.

\*    \*    \*

It's eerie how everything came together in this period.

Even before Elrod completed the apartment, he said he wanted to do the new office building. He said he'd never done an office building and that he would give me a reduction in price if I would give him a free hand.

I didn't have any preconceived ideas about the interior, and I said yes. He then shocked me by asking for a $50,000 consultation fee so he could spend three months in Chicago getting to know our key people.

"You are not going to do any work?" I asked.

"No. Not work in the way you think about work. I simply want to get to know your key editors. I want to know what they do, how they dress, what colors they like."

I gave in. After studying the situation, he designed with architect John Moutoussamy a great and colorful office space.

Elrod and I disagreed on some details, but we always worked our way to common ground. When we came to certain things I wanted that were not necessarily a part of his plan, he would say, "But, Mr. Johnson, that's in Alabama."

And I would say, "Send somebody to Alabama to get it."

Then something else would come up and he'd say, "But it's in Paris and I've got to have it day after tomorrow."

I would say, "Send somebody to France and they'll be back in two days."

Finally, he said, "All right, what you are really trying to tell me is that if it's in the world, you want it. Right?"

I said, "Right. That's what I'm trying to say."

The final product was an eleven-story showplace that cost $11 million. Rob Cuscaden, the architecture critic of the *Chicago Sun-Times*, said the building "has been boldly structured by its architects, Dubin, Dubin, Black & Moutoussamy of Chicago. And from its broad, forceful horizontals of sleek Travertine marble to its wide expanses of glass, this building says—quietly, simply but unequivocally—success."

The all-electric building was the first Chicago Loop

building exclusively designed and constructed by a Black-owned corporation.

There were some minor delays in finishing the building, and I decided to move in before the work was completed. I'd promised employees that we were going to be in the building before the end of 1971, and I called the contractor one day in November 1971 and asked if any floors were ready.

"Yes," he said, "five or six."

"Is the water running? Do the toilets work? If so I'm moving."

We moved on Tuesday, December 5, 1971, and celebrated Christmas in the tenth-floor assembly area. My mother, who always made a major statement at these Christmas assemblies, was at her best on that day, giving a prayer of joy and blessing that brought tears to our eyes. The next year, on Tuesday, May 16, 1972, we held the official grand opening with a ceremony in front of the building and an open house.

Michigan Avenue was closed off for the ceremony, which featured a moving address by Mayor Richard Daley. The mayor picked up the keynote theme of master of ceremonies Lerone Bennett, Jr., and said it was significant that a company headed by a Black man had constructed a build-ing near the site where a Black man had founded Chicago.

Pulitzer Prize–winner Gwendolyn Brooks read a poem she wrote for the occasion:

## AN ARRIVAL

In honor of John H. Johnson, a Pioneer and a
Station. And to the Blacks who helped him
reach and range.

*A tribute to Ourselves. And to the will,*
  *the precise will,*
  *the full will*
  *that manages Arrivals through the fire;*
*that manages revisions of the wave.*

*Beyond*
*the genuine crucifixions, and the sleep,*
   *the steep*
*flint, the high*
   *howl of the hurricane,*
*the wide*
   *ice,*
*across our self-recovery and redress—*
   *we look at one another.*
*And we love.*

I thanked the advertisers, subscribers, and supporters who'd made "the miracle on Michigan Avenue" possible. Perhaps more than on any other occasion, I was thankful for the warmth and support of my mother and wife and children, all of whom sat on the platform and gave added meaning to the greatest day of my life. You could tell this was the seventies, for both Linda and John had big "Afros."

"Thirty years ago," I said, "when we started this company, there were few markers on the road, and the way was piled high with obstacles. Back there, thirty years ago, we were surrounded by dangers, and it would have required a building twice this size to house all the creditors and cynics. But we continued to work and dream, for we believed then, as we believe now, that Emerson was right when he said that 'every wall is a door.'"

The new building, I said, was an expression of that faith.

"The horizontals, the glass, the marble, the fabrics, the warm colors: All these elements integrated into one grand design express the essential meaning of our firm ... openness: openness to truth, openness to light, openness to all the currents swirling in all the Black communities of this land."

The opening of this new building, I said, in conclusion, is proof that "the cities of this country, transformed by the challenge of new citizens and new demands, are on the brink of a new era of service and creativity."

Many leaders of Chicago's corporation community attended the grand opening. Chairman and publisher H. F. Gramhaus of the *Chicago Tribune*, President Ferd Kramer of Draper and Kramer, chairman Earl B. Dickerson of Supreme Life, and Chairman George E. Johnson of Johnson Products attended. So did Chairman John E. Swearingen of Standard Oil of Indiana, who brought his charming wife, Bonnie.

Assisted by Mayor Daley and my wife and mother, I cut the ribbon and conducted a guided tour for the dignitaries. Among the distinguished guests were Gary Mayor Richard Hatcher, Jesse Owens, and a young Jesse Jackson sporting a huge Afro and a colorful dashiki.

The building is as modern and functional today as it was on the day we dedicated it. The two-story lobby, punctuated by the sculpture of Richard Hunt and Geraldine McCullough and eighteen-foot walls of bronze and Mozambique wood, is a dramatic invitation to a structure that stuns and pleases. Every floor is different, and every floor has surprises.

Among the unique features are a $1-million collection of Black American and African art and a special library of more than fifteen thousand volumes on Black life and history. There is an employee dining room on the tenth floor and a private dining area that can be partitioned into five different dining rooms or opened up for a meeting room for two hundred persons.

The eleventh floor is reserved for my use and contains office space as well as a kitchen, dining room, living quarters, and an exercise room with a private barber chair.

The building has an indoor-outdoor feeling. Even when you're inside the building, you have the feeling of being outdoors, especially on the tenth- and eleventh-floor balconies.

Perhaps the most unusual feature of the building is the driveway that permits me to drive into my private basement parking lot from Michigan Avenue. When I took this idea to the city Building Department, a guy said, "Johnson, we haven't done that since 1896, and there's only one man in town who could change the regulations, and that's Mayor Daley."

I called the mayor's office and made an appointment. When I arrived, Daley already knew the details of the plan. This was one of the secrets of his success. He always did his homework. Before you could get an appointment, you had to tell an aide what you wanted to see him about. When you entered his office, he usually knew more about the subject than you did.

On this day, he studied the plans and said he would look into it. Like Franklin Delano Roosevelt, he would never give you an answer on the same day. Even if he wasn't going to do anything, he would never tell you no—he just would never say yes.

"Let's see what we can do," he told me. "I'll be back in touch with you."

This was about three o'clock in the afternoon. Early the next morning, the guy from the Building Department called and said, "Johnson, I've been up all night thinking about this thing, and I finally figured out a way to do it. Even though we haven't had anyone entering from Michigan Avenue since 1896, everyone with a basement has a right to go out of the back door. Under city ordinances, there must be two ways out. So why don't we make your back door your front door—and I'll leave it to your discretion as to which door you'll use."

I called Mayor Daley and thanked him for working it out legally and for making it possible for me to enjoy something that hadn't been done in seventy-six years.

I didn't always agree with the mayor, but I respected him. One of the reasons it took so long for a Black to be elected mayor was that Mayor Daley held the IOUs of so many important Blacks. It was impossible to do business in Chicago at that time without dealing with Mayor Daley. You couldn't cut a deal with underlings; you had to see him personally. Which meant that you were personally obligated to him and to a system which let you win sometimes.

Because of Daley's intercession, the Building Department approved the driveway and certain revolutionary features of one of the first all-electric buildings in the city of Chicago. These features have stood the test of time. People come from all over the world to study the building.

The most important visitors, however, are not the artists and architects but the schoolchildren and subscribers who have never been in a building in downtown America built and owned by a Black.

Sometimes tears well up in my eyes when I see the pride on the faces of people walking through the building. A teacher told a touching story about a boy in the sixth or seventh grade who sat in the big chair behind my desk on the eleventh floor. He moved from side to side in the chair and said, "Teacher, I want to grow up and own a building like this."

The teacher told him, "It's possible, for the man who owns this building is Black." After that experience, the boy, who had been unmanageable, changed. When he flared up, all she had to do to quiet him down was to say, "If you want to own a building like that and sit in a big chair like that, you've got to quit playing and study hard."

After Arthur Elrod finished our Lake Shore Drive home, he asked us to spend a weekend with him in Palm Springs. We fell in love with the place and started spending our Christmas holidays there. On one of our visits we heard that a house in South Ridge, an exclusive area on the top of a mountain, was for sale. The house was about a block from Bob Hope's home, and Steve McQueen and William Holden had houses nearby.

The owner of the house had died, and his children were asking a ridiculous price. Several Hollywood personalities looked at the place and told them that the price was outlandish. This angered the heirs and the executor.

Eunice, who handled the negotiations with Linda, used the art of gentle persuasion. She told the executor that it was not a price we could afford but that it was worth it, and we'd keep in touch.

This went on for six months or so. Every month, Eunice would call the executor and tell him, "We can't afford it at the price you are asking, but if you ever go down, please consider us."

When the price went down, Eunice was the only buyer talking to the new owners. Since she was also the only buyer who'd given them respect and courtesy, they sold it to us.

Perhaps the best description of the house was in Norma Lee Browning's column in the *Chicago Tribune* (January 9, 1974).

> It is a spectacular, million dollar manse (give or take a few hundred thousand) that once belonged to the late Ralph Stolkin, a Chicago millionaire (he made it in oil, furniture, and a mail-order business) who retired to Palm Springs and spent most of his time tossing parties in this fabulous house, which he had designed precisely for that purpose. It nestles precariously on a ledge of the picturesque San Jacinto Mountains, just up from Steve McQueen's mountain pad, and down from Bob Hope's [home].
>
> In a resort area liberally sprinkled with millionaires' mansions, the Stolkin house, as it has become known, is unique—with its ever-flowing pools and waterfalls, famed circular bedroom with "his" and "her" boudoirs, complete with bidet and beauty salon in "hers," electric washer and dryer in "his"—and such things as imported *objets d'art* from baronial castles and French chateaus, and a color TV set in every room. The house came complete with two live-in servants. It was the Johnsons' Christmas present to themselves....

One of the highlights of this season of transition and triumph occurred on Friday, September 22, 1972, four months after the dedication of the building, when I was named

Publisher of the Year by the Magazine Publishers of America. New York Mayor John V. Lindsay, Manhattan Borough President Percy E. Sutton, and major media magnates attended the awards ceremony at Manhattan's Plaza Hotel. In my acceptance speech, I called for new vision to deal with the changing colors of the day.

"We must learn now to think in *living* color. We must see not only blacks and whites but also women and youth. We must reflect all the modalities of the pluralistic world in which we live.

"Let me say in conclusion that there is no need for despair. I believe responsible men working together can solve all problems, and I believe we shall overcome in this land.

"I believe, in short, in the silent power of the possible.

"I believe in risk and daring and public responsibility....

"I believe finally in the power of persuasion, in the power of truth. I believe the word is mightier than the sword and, in the end, will prevail."

# 44

---

## *Season of Sorrows*

THERE'S no way you can avoid it.

Rich or poor, Black or White, male or female, you've got to pay the price of being human by dealing with pain, separation, sorrow, death.

The fact that it's inevitable doesn't make it any easier to bear.

On the contrary, the signs and warning of mortality only intensify a pain no human can avoid or prepare for.

I saw the signs in the middle seventies. But my mother and I had been through so much together, had triumphed over so many odds and defeated so many dragons, that it was hard to believe that our partnership would ever end.

For fifty-nine years, from 1918 to 1977, we saw each other or talked to each other almost every day. No matter where I was—in Russia, in Africa, in France—I called her at least once a day. Once, on a trip to Haiti, I climbed a telegraph pole to make my daily call. They laughed at me, but my mother understood.

She was the inspiration and the initiator of the Johnson Publishing Company success story. She provided the furniture I pawned to get the $500 to start the company. And I provided an office on the sixth floor of our new building so she could watch her investment grow. She came to the office to call her friends and to pursue her activities as a leader of her church and the club women's movement.

She had some official duties, including delivering checks to churches involved in our church subscription programs. She liked that, for she had, like all Johnsons, a feeling for the language, and she made a good speech. I always asked her to say a few words at our Christmas celebrations and other company affairs. She always said more words than I had in mind, but she always said them with eloquence and spirit.

My mother and stepfather, James Williams, who served as superintendent of the Johnson Publishing Company Building, traveled extensively, visiting California or New York at least once a year. After he died in 1961, she was attended by a woman friend, who lived in the house with her.

I'm glad she lived long enough to enjoy the fruits of her faith in me. She always had a car, a chauffeur, and a maid. I visited her several times a week and sent flowers twice a week.

She was a tough woman, physically and spiritually, and she was in good health until about three months before she died. From that point on, she was in and out of Michael Reese Hospital, where I visited her every day and sometimes twice a day.

I never will forget the strange vibrations that made it possible for me to reach her before she lapsed into a coma. I had an early-morning board meeting at Zenith that day, and I couldn't, for some strange reason, find the way. I knew where I was going, but the car wouldn't follow the road. I kept going down the wrong street and ending up in the wrong place. I finally said, "To hell with it, I'll go see Mother."

I got there just in time. As soon as I walked into the room, she said, "Son, I just can't fight anymore."

It was almost as if she had been fighting to stay conscious so she could say her last goodbye to me. She later slipped into a coma and died on Sunday, May 1, 1977.

My mother was eulogized at her funeral by historian Lerone Bennett, Jr., who stressed her historical significance.

"She was," he said, "one of the last survivors of a select band of strong Black women who could not be blocked or stopped by anything.

"She was of and in the heroic tradition of Mary McLeod Bethune and Maggie Walker. Like them, like tens of thousands of unsung Black mothers and grandmothers, Gertrude Johnson Williams, vice president of Johnson Publishing Company and mother of publisher John H. Johnson, rose above the scourges of her environment and testified to the indomitable tenacity of the human spirit."

Testified also to the indomitable mother spirit that still lives in me and in the corporations and magazines founded on her dream.

"It was her custom," Bennett concluded, "to speak at least once a year to the employees, and it was her custom to note that the years were hurrying by and that God had seen fit to bless her by giving her another year. 'I'm still here,' she used to say. 'He must be leaving me here for something.'

"It was with this faith, and in this spirit, that she lived her last days, attending church meetings, club meetings, luncheons, conferences, following the paths she believed He directed. She was following one of those paths one day last May in Chicago's Michael Reese Hospital—strong in the faith, serene and unafraid—when the great heart stopped. She was eighty-five and had warmed both hands well at the fire of life."

Not a day passes that I don't feed off the bread of her

spirit. Her office on the sixth floor of the Johnson Publishing Company Building has been left exactly the way it was on the day she died. I've left instructions that the office is to be left that way as long as Johnson Publishing Company lives. I've also given scholarships in her name and grants to the club women's organizations she supported. A chapel at Chicago's Harris YWCA perpetuates her memory.

Throughout all this and on into the early eighties, my son, John Harold, fought his brave and doomed fight against the incurable sickle-cell scourge. On Sunday, December 20, 1981, he died at the University of Chicago's Wyler Children's Hospital. He was twenty-five.

We buried John Harold as he wanted to be buried, in a simple private ceremony. Since he liked simple things, he was buried in casual clothes.

After making the arrangements, I locked my office door and sat down and wrote, with tears streaming down my face, a personal message that was read at the funeral.

Many people had asked me about John Harold, and some had felt sorry for me—and I had to set the record straight. I never discussed the matter during his lifetime, but I had to let people know that it was no great burden for me. It was, in fact, a joy.

That's what I tried to say in the handwritten message that was read by an *Ebony* editor:

"I am too overcome with grief and emotion," I said, "to read this message myself, but I do want to share with you some of my feelings about my son, John.

"He was as dear to me as life itself.

"Because John was adopted, and because he had sickle-cell anemia, people sometimes asked me if I ever regretted having him as a son.

"The answer to that is no—never.

"Not once in twenty-five and a half years did I ever feel anything but pride and gratitude in being the father of John H. Johnson, Jr.

"John bore a heavy burden well. He had great dignity. He also had class and style. And because he suffered so much himself, he had great compassion and feeling for his fellow human beings.

"I learned a lot about courage and patience from John. He loved life but knew he was destined not to have much of it. So he lived each day to the fullest....

"John was true to himself, devoted to his family, and loyal to his many friends.

"John's death creates a void in our family that can never be filled. His mother, Eunice W. Johnson, and his sister, Linda Johnson, and I feel privileged to have known and loved John. We shall never, never forget him."

We created a living memorial to John Harold—a waiting room with the latest emergency equipment—at Wyler Children's Hospital. The memorial was endowed by me and my friends, including Princess Grace of Monaco, who sent a personal check. His office, like his grandmother's, has been set aside in his memory.

Both are as real and present to me today as they were on the last day I saw them. I still have my mother's personal effects, two or three fur coats and some jewelry, and I still have my son's last car.

Eunice and I can't bring ourselves to change John Harold's room. This is our way of saying that he is still alive in us and that he will never die.

You are never the same after a season of such sorrows.

Somehow, someway you survive—no matter how deep the tragedy and how much it hurts.

But the grief never leaves you and the music the mother and son left in your heart never stops playing.

# 45

---

# Mainstreaming With Darryl Zanuck, Princess Grace, and Lee Iacocca

MAYBE Elizabeth Taylor and Richard Burton had something to do with it.

They were the explosive on-screen and off-screen lovers in the making of *Cleopatra,* one of the biggest financial turkeys in the history of the movies.

The movie's runaway cost of $40 million triggered a chain of explosions that rocked the corporate offices of the film's producer, Twentieth Century Fox. The studio went on to back several other flops and was embroiled in internal struggles for the rest of the sixties. The whole thing came to a boil when the legendary Darryl Zanuck, the Twentieth Century Fox chairman, fired his own son in a family fight that produced ugly headlines and uglier rumors. In 1969, the corporation lost $36.8 million. In 1970, it lost $77.4 million.

There was thus by 1971 an urgent need for new ideas and damage control in the Twentieth Century Fox empire.

Hill and Knowlton, the studio's PR firm, suggested broadening the base of the board. One of the firm's Black executives, Andrew Hatcher, former associate press secretary for President Kennedy, recommended me.

Whatever the reason, whether it was the financial strain caused by *Cleopatra* and other flops or the heat generated by the continuing internal struggles, the Twentieth Century Fox hierarchy changed, and I was elected to my first national board.

Darryl Zanuck called personally to extend the invitation, which received wide play in the national press. The morning after the announcement, a neighbor congratulated me and said: "John, you know why they did this. They're in deep trouble." I said, "Of course, why else would they ask me to serve."

Chairman Zanuck introduced me at my first board meeting on March 18, 1971, and I received a welcoming round of applause. Not for the first or the last time, I was surprised by the difference between the personal and public images of legends. Like millions of Americans, I had grown up with Darryl Zanuck, whose name was synonymous in some circles with Hollywood. I expected a great big football player of a man, and was surprised to meet a relatively short person, whose power came not from heft but from the spirit. There was a presence about the man that I've only seen in a handful of people. I saw it in Mary McLeod Bethune, I saw it in Earl Dickerson, I saw it in Zanuck—something magnetic, something that said you're in the presence of an original.

It was fortunate that this was my first major board. For Johnson Publishing Company and Twentieth Century Fox were in the same business. We both tried to read tea leaves and identify the stories and people that readers and viewers would identify with in the future.

Twentieth Century Fox was no better than its last movie, and I was no better than my last issue. With every magazine and every movie, we were going out for a vote of confidence. And if we received too many no-confidence votes, we were out of business. It was an uncertain business at best, and only the nimble and the quick of hand and heart survived.

There was another reason why I was comfortable in the Twentieth Century Fox environment. It was, for lack of a better word, a high-wire environment. The corporation was in trouble. It was in danger—and danger sometimes brings excitement.

Whenever I went on a board, I tried to be more seen than heard in the first meetings. Instead of talking, I listened and studied the situation. After this introductory period, I waded in like other board members and made contributions based on my background and experience.

This usually led to the miracle of the transmutation of color. My color didn't change, but its meaning did. I'd been elected, as everybody knew, as a token Black. But when I opened my mouth, my colleagues discovered, perhaps to their surprise, that I had other talents and that these talents were important to the common venture.

Some of my colleagues on major boards said later that I had a unique gut instinct about people and situations. Many of my fellow board members were formally trained and came from legal, financial, or marketing backgrounds. Few had a total business experience. None or almost none had started their own business with little or no money. This was an important distinction. For when you start at the bottom and work your way up with nothing to rely on except your ability to understand people, you have a certain edge.

I'm convinced that our major problem in competing with Japan is not the Japanese incentive system or the number of engineers in Japanese companies—our major problem is that we have lost the Ford-Armour-Field-Watson entrepreneurial edge. Our corporate system and our business schools are turning out technicians and specialists who excel at merging and managing money somebody else made.

What is lacking is the spirit of the great entrepreneurs who made new money and new opportunities because they came up from the bottom and worked on the other side of the old, the safe, the predictable, the quantified.

If we can believe the comments of my fellow board members, I made my greatest contributions in unstructured situations. If there was time for a detailed study, and if the documents and figures could be put on the table for all to see, I had no particular advantage. But if it was necessary to make a quick decision based on personal knowledge and experience, I was in a position to make a critical contribution.

There were many examples of this. At one meeting, we were trying to decide whether to let CBS Recording Company or RCA distribute our records. The studies and figures were inconclusive; both companies were offering pretty much the same percentages and numbers. Some board members leaned toward CBS because it was the biggest in the field and the most successful. I pushed hard for RCA. Pressed to justify my stand, I said:

"I would go with the company that loves and respects us most."

"What do you mean by that?" somebody asked.

"First of all," I said, "CBS sent a vice president to negotiate, and a vice president can always be overruled by a CEO. On the other hand, the CEO of the RCA division is negotiating with us. He has the power to speak for the company because he *is* the company until the next board meeting. So I would trust what he says more than I would trust what a vice president says. I also believe that a company with fewer options will give more attention and better service than a company with more options. In other words, RCA needs us the most and will try hardest."

The argument made sense, and carried the day.

I was later elected to the five-man executive committee that determined company policy between board meetings. When the company went private under Marvin Davis, I was the only member of the old board to join the new board, which included former President Ford and Henry Kissinger.

Perhaps the most complimentary business letter I ever received came from Chairman Dennis Stanfill, who succeeded Zanuck.

"I cherish my memories of you at the Board meetings," he wrote. "You understood the problem more quickly than anyone else. You enlivened the meetings with a great sense of humor. You injected a remarkable vitality."

When Princess Grace of Monaco joined the board, she and I became allies of sorts and jokingly called ourselves the board's minorities. She was the first woman on the board and I was the first Black. Minority status, whatever its basis, usually brings about a certain kinship, and we were usually on the same side in the votes. There's a certain poetry in the fact that Princess Grace was elected to the board at one of the meetings held at the corporate head-quarters of Johnson Publishing Company.

The former Grace Kelly, whose acting career ended with her storybook marriage to Prince Rainier III of Monaco, was impressive on- and off-screen. Always friendly and gracious, she was forced by circumstances to play three contradictory roles: the role of a real-life princess, the role of a tough corporate overseer, and the role of a beautiful woman. She earned Oscars in all three categories, partici-pating in tough corporate decisions and charming stock-holders in public meetings.

The Twentieth Century Fox Film Corporation met in different cities around the country. As the senior board member in Chicago, I was asked to make arrangements for the two meetings we held in Chicago. Because of the securi-ty problems surrounding the princess, we thought at first that a private club would be the best site for the meeting. LaDoris Foster, my vice president for personnel and other services, and I visited the most elegant private clubs. We rejected the Carlton in the Ritz Carlton because it was in the basement; we rejected others because they were not plush enough or because they posed other problems. After we had exhausted all possibilities, we looked at each other and said, almost simultaneously, "We have the best private club in town. Why should we go anywhere else?"

The meeting was held on Thursday, July 29, 1976, in the Johnson Publishing Company Building, which has private dining facilities and a large screening room. Princess Grace, Prince Rainier, and their two daughters, Princesses Caroline and Stephanie, attended the screening of *Silent Movie* the night before the regular board meeting. Gregory Peck and other celebrities attended the private party we gave for seven hundred at Zorine's, a local nightclub.

There was only one flap, a minor one. Precautions were taken in case the princess or her daughters decided to visit the ladies' room of the nightclub. The frontal male nudes in each stall were covered at strategic locations by fig leaves spray-painted silver.

The menu at the Johnson Publishing Company luncheon included lobster and fried chicken and French-fried sweet potatoes. A southern board member and I reluctantly passed up the fried chicken in deference to the princess. To our surprise and delight, she asked for the fried chicken, and we changed our orders.

Major boards pay from $15,000 to $50,000 a year and provide a certain number of perks. It was rumored that in the old days each member of the Twentieth Century Fox board was assigned a personal starlet. Either the practice—if it ever existed—had been discontinued by the time I was elected or my board briefing was incomplete.

Fortune 500 boards are like olives. Once you get one out of the bottle, the others follow as a matter of course. There's an old boys'—an old *White* boys'—network at this level. If you're elected to one board, you meet people who recommend you to other boards. After you get in the pool and after the old boys find out that you talk and act the same way they talk and act, the word spreads.

I was elected to two other boards as a direct result of my membership on the Twentieth Century Fox board. Gerald H. Trautman, a fellow Twentieth Century Fox board member, asked me to join the Greyhound Corporation board. Don Frey, another member of the board, asked me to join the Bell and Howell board.

I served on the executive committees of both boards. When Bell and Howell went out of the consumer business, I resigned but remained friends with Frey and other board members. I'm still on the executive committee of the Greyhound board.

I was elected to the Zenith board after Chairman Joseph Wright and President John Nevin read interviews in which I said that I had forty-two Zenith color television sets in my headquarters building in grateful remembrance of Commander Eugene McDonald, who gave me my first major advertising schedule.

I serve on other boards, including Continental Bank and Dillard's Department Stores, but my position on the Chrysler board is perhaps my most exciting and visible Fortune 500 post. I was recommended by J. Paul Sticht, who was then chairman of RJR Nabisco, formerly R. J. Reynolds Tobacco Company, which has been one of the primary sponsors of Ebony Fashion Fair for twenty-seven years.

Lee Iacocca came by later with a personal invitation. The first thing I noticed about him was that he was taller than I had expected—six-one or six-two. He was friendly, charming, and tough, and it was easy to understand why he'd become an American folk hero. He'd picked an automobile company everyone had counted out off the floor and put it back into the race. That endeared him to Americans, who admire any man who can translate defeat into success.

Since then, I've learned a lot from Iacocca and the blue-ribbon board he assembled. For the Chrysler experience is a reaffirmation of my experience of winning despite the odds. And it underscored the lessons I'd already learned, that a leader has to lead and keep his options open.

From the first I was impressed by the Iacocca management style, which is, like all viable management styles, more than technique. For what he is saying, above style, above technique, above numbers, is that the car industry must diversify and bring back the competitive spirit that made American industry world-famous.

We are indebted to Iacocca for straight talk and straight action. He has demonstrated that Americans can compete with the Japanese on an equal basis by making a quality car that sells at a competitive price. He has signs all around the plants, saying "We just want to be the best." As you move around these plants and talk to the workers, you get a feeling that you are part of a movement to prove that American workers can bring the pride back.

As a publisher and salesman, I am especially impressed by Iacocca's creative use of advertising. More than any other CEO, he has proven how effective advertising can be in selling simultaneously a company (Chrysler), an idea ("The pride is back"), and a country ("the old-fashioned competitive spirit that made America great").

Black board members are board members but they are also *Black* board members, who can't escape the task of pressing for a common American market. During my years of service on Fortune 500 boards, I've noticed increasing sensitivity to the demands of minorities. Chrysler, for example, has increased the number of Black dealers. Forest J. Farmer, the president of Chrysler's component parts subsidiary, is one of the few Blacks at the top in American industry. Leroy C. Richie is a vice president and general counsel of Chrysler Motors, and assistant treasurer W. Frank Fountain makes financial reports at board meetings. The corporation has also hired a Black advertising agency.

Working on this level for the last seventeen years has renewed my faith in American industry.

I've seen Black men and women and White men and

women working together at the top to create a bigger pie for everybody. The task of the nineties is to increase the number of Black and minority men and women who operate at this level.

I've seen the Black and White future, and it works.

While expanding my business and social contacts on that level, I continued a campaign of diversification that changed the contours of Johnson Publishing Company.

I'd been trying for years to get in on the early bidding for choice FM radio and TV properties. I tried to buy WNUS, which later became WGCI, the No. 1 radio station in the Chicago market. The station was owned at that time by Gordon McLendon, who was honored with me as one of the ten outstanding young men of 1951. McLendon said he would keep me in mind, but even as we talked, he was negotiating to sell the station to others.

The same thing happened with another FM property, WBMX. I called Egmont Sonderling and told him I wanted an opportunity to bid on the station if he decided to sell it. The next message I got was not from him but from a newspaper item which reported that the station had been sold.

There was no need to draw a map or a diagram. I got the message. I wasn't going to get an opportunity to bid on a choice FM station.

Here, once again, I was confronted with an open violation of the free market principle. For I wasn't asking for special privileges. I wasn't asking for affirmative action or a set-aside. All I wanted was an opportunity to compete by the same rules that applied to other entrepreneurs. But in this case, as in so many others, the rules were changed when I got to the one-yard line. One of the biggest challenges we face in the nineties is to create a level playing field and one set of rules for Blacks and Whites, males and females.

If the rules are good when White males are winning,

they ought to be good when Blacks and women are winning. What happens now in subtle and not-so-subtle ways is that Blacks especially are denied the critical information and opportunities they must have if they are going to compete on an equal basis. We aren't told about impending deals. We aren't offered the same opportunities as our peers.

Since I couldn't break the FM barrier, I bought WGRT and created WJPC, the first Black-owned radio station in Chicago. The station had changed hands two or three years earlier for $900,000, but I had to pay $2 million. There was obviously no future in dawn-to-dusk stations, so I applied for and was granted a twenty-four-hour license.

This created an interesting problem, for I had to buy several acres of land in a predominantly White suburb to build a tower. To avoid any misunderstanding, I repeated the 1949 and 1959 stratagems, hiring a White lawyer who put $500,000 on the table and bought the property in trust.

I next bought WLOU, the No. 2 station in the Louisville market. Almost everyone, from Governor John Y. Brown to Mayor Harvey Sloane, turned out for the big party that welcomed me to the Blue Grass State. I staged a number of razzle-dazzle promotions, including free gas during the oil embargo crisis. The station moved to the No. 1 spot before succumbing to the inevitable onslaught of FM stations with better sound and better market positions.

WLOU and WJPC were transitional investments leading to the FM bonanza. The Chicago market was still closed to me, but there's more than one way to turn a radio dial. Instead of beating my head against a brick wall, I entered the Chicago market by the back door, buying a small suburban FM station that could be heard in Chicago.

The strategy worked but it created a ticklish problem. For WLNR was a right-wing station. The station's leading personality was a talk-show disc jockey who got his kicks by making extreme and provocative statements about Blacks and Jews. After I bought the station, fringe groups tried to create a First Amendment confrontation. But I outmaneuvered them and fired the disc jockey for creating an ugly racial scene on the Oprah Winfrey show. That ordeal over, I changed the color and reach of the station, building a new tower which carried the signal as far north as my Lake Shore Drive apartment.

I also entered the expanding TV market. In association with Black and White producers, I sponsored two major shows, the Ebony Music Awards show and the American Black Achievement Awards show. When the White coproducers fell out, I bought their shares and broadened the format of the annual ABAA show, which is seen today in more than one hundred markets.

In television, as in radio and cosmetics, I concentrated on investments that complemented my *Ebony-Jet* base. I hired independent producers and directors, like Mark Warren and Bob Henry, but the spadework of the shows was done by a special company committee, made up of Lydia Davis, the vice president for promotions, general counsel June Rhinehart, Vice President LaDoris Foster, and senior *Ebony* and *Jet* staffers Robert E. Johnson, Sylvia Flanagan, Lerone Bennett, Jr., Hans Massaquoi, Charles Sanders, Herbert Temple, and Norman L. Hunter.

Another JPC core group, headed by my daughter, Linda, runs the *Ebony/Jet Showcase*, a weekly variety show, which dominates the market and is seen on 101 stations.

When Chicago was wired for cable, I was one of the thirty-nine Black investors who agreed to put up $5 million in a joint venture with Continental Cable. But Continental executives wanted us to invest and leave the operating to them. This was unacceptable to me and other Black investors. The situation ultimately worked to my advantage. For Continental later withdrew from the Chicago market, and I am one of sixteen Black investors who own sizable shares in the company that is wiring the whole city.

Because of bad experiences at Supreme Life Insurance Company, I've always avoided real estate investments. Since the forties, the field has grown increasingly complex and if you don't know what you're doing, you can lose your shirt and your underwear.

Despite my reservations, I reluctantly and grudgingly made some major real estate investments. To protect my flanks, I paid $1.3 million for a deteriorating hotel next door to the Johnson Publishing Company Building, $250,000 for an outdoor parking lot, and $1.5 million for an indoor parking lot across from the Hilton Towers. I also bought two buildings on Wabash Avenue, behind the Johnson Publishing Company Building, for warehouses.

In addition to the homefront investments, I made a major investment in Lawless Gardens, a government-sponsored, middle-income complex which houses 750 families. The general partners—world-famous dermatologist T. K. Lawless, Dr. William J. Walker, and I—put up the major share of the $2-million investment. When Dr. Lawless died, I bought his shares and some of Dr. Walker's shares and now own 97 percent of the development.

# 46

# "Linda's Father": Passing the Torch to a New Generation

**B**Y this time, I had a new employee.

After graduating from the University of Southern California with a degree in journalism, my daughter, Linda, joined the staff, working with her mother in the fashion field and in the production of the Ebony Fashion Show.

Then she realized, I suppose, that I had the biggest job in the company and she asked the key question, "What about training for your job?" I was delighted. I had never pushed her, but obviously I wanted a family member in place to carry on the business.

With my encouragement and support, she went to Northwestern University and got an MBA degree. At the same time, she enrolled in the special training program I created to prepare her for business leadership. The program, which continues to this day, is simple and rigorous. I explain what I'm doing and why I'm doing it. I let her sit in on all major meetings, editorial, circulation, advertising, cosmetics, book publishing. Everything we're involved in and everything we're thinking about going into. I also send her copies of all major policy correspondence, along with my replies, so she can see how I handle things, including speaking engagements and requests for donations to charitable organizations.

From time to time I ask her opinion on decisions I plan to make, to see what kind of decision she would make. In 95 percent of the cases, she'd make the same decision I'd make. Since I believe in myself, I believe in her and the future of the company. To make that clear, I promoted her to president and chief operating officer. Since her promotion, she has established new beachheads in the new generation. She knows almost as many people as I know. I'm always surprised and delighted to run into people who introduce me as "Linda's father."

Linda's marriage was not a part of the training program, but I played a key role in fostering it. No matter who you are or where you work, children will protest if you interfere with their social life or suggest a potential mate. But I was lucky or perhaps subtle.

My future son-in-law, André Rice, was a Goldman Sachs stockbroker, who'd been trying to reach me for almost a year. Although he couldn't get through my secretarial shield, he kept calling. One day, when my secretary was away from her desk, I answered the phone. Since he was so persistent, I gave him an appointment.

It turned out that he was a tall, handsome, well-dressed young man. He was well educated with an MBA degree from the University of Chicago and a CPA charter. And he was unmarried. He was two or three minutes into an excellent presentation when something clicked in my mind.

"Wait," I said. "I want my investment committee to hear this."

I've never had an investment committee and I never

intend to have an investment committee. But I quickly formed one and gave Linda the task of following through with André.

One thing led to another, and they were married on November 2, 1984, in what one writer called "the most elaborate wedding in Chicago history."

That covers a lot of territory and a lot of Palmers and Armours and Fields, but who am I to object? The only thing I know for sure is that it was a big, elegant, expensive wedding that had a warm, personal, family feeling.

There were flowers from countries all over the world, Dom Perignon champagne, and a sit-down dinner for seven hundred at the Westin Hotel. But you can't put a price tag on the feeling I had as I escorted Linda, who was radiant in a gown designed especially for her by Paris couturier Jean-Louis Scherrer, down the aisle.

Special friends came from all over to help Eunice and me celebrate this special occasion. Sammy Davis, Jr., and his wife, Altovise, came from Beverly Hills. Greyhound Chairman John W. Teets and his wife, Nancy, came from Phoenix. *Black Enterprise* publisher Earl Graves and his wife, Barbara, flew in from New York. So did UNCF President Chris Edley and his wife, Zaida. The Chicago contingent was headed by Mayor Harold Washington and his fiancée, Mary Ella Smith, and included Jesse and Jackie Jackson, Ann Landers, *Playboy* President Christie Hefner, Irv and Essee Kupcinet, Jay and Cindy Pritzker, Oprah Winfrey, and Chicago Urban League President James Compton.

What I remember most about the wedding is that a brand-new Rolls-Royce got Linda to the church on time and then stopped and had to be towed away. Which didn't matter at all, since the church was directly across the street from the Westin Hotel. One of the biggest moments of the wedding was when traffic on the Magnificent Mile stopped for the grand procession of the bridal party and dignitaries, who walked from the Fourth Presbyterian Church to the Westin Hotel.

Four years later, a daughter, Alexa Christina, was born to Linda and André. The proud grandfather did almost as much celebrating as the mother and father.

# 47

---

# *The Second
Time Around*

THEY said it couldn't be done again.

They said the *Ebony* miracle happened in another era and that I was too old, too tired, too rich.

I decided to show them.

I decided to put myself to the test and answer the doubts and questions.

Could I do in the seventies and eighties what I had done in the forties and fifties?

Was my success based on principles that transcended race and time or was it the accidental product of a particular situation?

The proof and the answers were in the pudding of a five-year marketing campaign that covered two continents and the islands of the sea.

Starting from scratch, with an idea and twenty bottles from a chemist, I created the largest Black-owned cosmetics company in the world.

This was not a lark or a contrived case study. I was playing with real money, and I lost a million dollars a year for five years before I pulled it off. Things got so bad that friends told me I was endangering the whole company. But I had so much invested I had to see the hole card. Beyond that, I wanted to know if I still had it. I wanted to know if I could still open doors and accounts and turn negatives into positives.

I was fifty-five years old when I mobilized my forces to turn yet another disadvantage into an advantage.

The disadvantage was the historic neglect of Black women by major cosmetics manufacturers, who refused to manufacture and sell products that met the particular needs of Black women and dark-skinned White women.

Not only did blondes have more fun, according to the ads, but they also had the best shades and tints. This created perplexing problems for brunettes and Blacks who had to mix their own or choose from products that were clearly made with other people and other skin tones in mind.

Despite repeated pleas going back at least fifty years, major White manufacturers had refused to change this policy. Some said frankly that they didn't want to alienate White women customers by marketing a line for Black women. Other manufacturers said there was no market for Black-oriented products and that Black women were comfortable with the hand-me-down products made for the White market.

I'd been arguing against this policy since the first issue of *Ebony*, but the Ebony Fashion Show made me act. I watched our models as they mixed different shades, trying to find the right blend to bring out the unique beauty in their skin, and decided that somebody had to do something. I had no intention at that time of starting my own company. I simply wanted White companies to meet a pressing and potentially lucrative demand.

I took this idea to several manufacturers—including

Charles Revson of Revlon—and they literally laughed me out of their offices.

Angered by this response, I went with Eunice to a private lab which created permanent formulas out of the mixtures the models had been putting together. We experimented with the models and put out a mail-order package, the Capsule Collection, in 1969. The response was overwhelmingly positive. People kept saying, "Gee, those models really look beautiful. What kind of makeup are they using?"

It was clear that there was a market for a Black cosmetics line, and I organized the cosmetics company in 1973. I financed it primarily by the cash flow from *Ebony* and *Jet*. Since the fashion show was the inspiration, we named the line Fashion Fair Cosmetics. We ran our first ad ("A Private Collection Goes Public") in *Women's Wear Daily*.

There is a high road and a low road in the cosmetics field, and the roads seldom if ever meet. You either market your products in high-line department stores or in mass merchandising outlets, such as drugstores and discount houses. I decided from the beginning to go the high-line route. The line was named after the Ebony Fashion Fair show, a high-line fashion show, and a low-line strategy would have diminished the importance of the inspiration.

That decision made, I faced the big question of how I was going to get a Black-owned cosmetics line into major department stores like Marshall Field's and Neiman-Marcus. There were, by this time, two or three Black-oriented lines but none had made a major breakthrough.

Before doing anything, I surveyed the field and made a surprising discovery. The world had changed, but it hadn't changed that much. And I still had to rely on the hard-bought truths that made *Ebony* and *Negro Digest* successes.

This meant, among other things, that I had to first break through the insider barrier. In every industry, there are certain arrangements known to every insider. The first task of an outsider who wants to become an insider, no matter what his color, is to break into the circle of secret knowledge. How did I break through? I did the same thing in the seventies that I had done in the forties. I asked experts. I made friends and influenced people who gave or sold me information that made me an insider or, at least, a potential insider.

Based on this insider information, I trained myself and then trained others. Despite *Brown* v. *Board of Education*, despite Montgomery and the marches and riots, there were no Blacks at the top in White-owned cosmetics companies or high-line department stores, and I had to invent my own experts. I was lucky here, for I had already created a management staff at my hair-care company, Supreme Beauty Products. This company was housed in a suite of offices in a North Loop building, and managed by Shirley Calloway.

It was relatively simple then to retool for a new industry. If you can sell one thing, you can sell anything. If you can manage one thing, you can manage anything.

I transferred the whole division to our headquarters building. When Shirley Calloway left the company, I made Lance Clarke, the Supreme sales manager, vice president and general manager of Fashion Fair. In the takeoff year of 1974, the staff increased from thirty to fifty.

Assembling a staff was one thing; selling stores was another. Everything, in fact, depended on our approach to Marshall Field's, the old and prestigious Chicago department store. No other high-line department store was going to take our products until we were in the high-line store in our own city. But it quickly developed that nothing much had changed in this area, either. Buyers and middle-management people in the department store refused to give our salesmen a fair hearing.

So there it was again, a challenge from the forties. I dealt with it by going back to the lessons of the forties and learning everything I could about the Marshall Field's executive who was responsible for new cosmetics accounts. I discovered that he was active in various organizations, and I joined the same organizations and worked on him indirectly. When I knew him well enough, I said, "I have a business idea I'd like to talk to you about." He said okay and I went to his office.

It was generally believed at the time that Marshall Field's didn't want a Black cosmetics line and wasn't all that choked up about attracting large numbers of Black customers.

I therefore approached him indirectly, saying, "The business I want to go into is a cosmetics line for Black women. I know Marshall Field's doesn't have a Black line. I even know the reason you don't have one."

That seemed to make him uncomfortable, and I hurried on.

"The reason is that there's never been one good enough for Marshall Field's."

He pounced on that.

"That's the reason," he said. "That's the reason."

I said I didn't know if my line was good enough, and I wondered if he would have his people check it out.

"I believe you are fair," I said, "and that you'll put it in the store if it's good enough. If it's not, I'll just go away and not bother you anymore."

Not long after that, a buyer called and said, "You are in."

I was in, but not over, for store executives asked me not to advertise. They were afraid that a Black line would offend White women customers. They didn't want me to make a big thing out of being in Marshall Field's.

But how are you going to sell a line if no one knows you are in the store?

I answered that question the same way I answered the unspoken doubts of Joseph Levy in 1942. I found out from store sources that the average new line sold approximately $1,200 in a six-day week. I asked female employees, a different one every day, to go down to Marshall Field's and buy odd amounts averaging $200 a day. In the meantime, we hired a makeup artist who visited Black women organizations, made up the members, and told them they could buy the products at Marshall Field's.

After three months, the line was established at Marshall Field's, and I moved on to Bloomingdale's in New York. I took Vice President Lance Clarke with me so he could learn by watching me turn indifference into excitement for the line. This is a basic rule in my management program. I believe a good general leads his army not only by giving orders but also by going out into the field and fighting and selling. In the days of Alexander the Great and other famous military leaders, generals became generals because they were the best fighters. It was important in that day, and it's important today, for top managers to lead by example. I never ask employees to solve problems I can't solve. I never ask them to sell people I can't sell.

I realize there's a certain amount of curiosity about me and that I can get in to see people my salesmen can't see. A lot of people know the story of how I rose from poverty to wealth. I can trade on their curiosity about me, at least to get into the door. But when I get in, I'm on my own. The advantage I have then is that I have a lifetime of experience in changing nos to yeses. And I love to sell. I sell even when there is no monetary advantage to be gained. I sell for the sheer joy of selling.

I sold Bloomingdale's, not by selling my product but by selling the bottom line, Bloomingdale's bottom line. I also sold the power that made Fashion Fair viable, the drawing power of ads in *Jet* and *Ebony*.

The result was that executives saw Fashion Fair not only as a vehicle to sell cosmetics but also as a vehicle for bringing affluent new customers into the store, customers who would buy cosmetics and other things.

Always, everywhere, I talked in terms of value to the store. Not what the line could do for me, not even what it could do for Black women, but what it could do for Bloomingdale's.

My next target was Neiman-Marcus, which was the key to the South. The buyers had already said no, and my only hope was Chairman and CEO Stanley Marcus. While I was planning my strategy, I read in the newspaper that Marcus was coming to Chicago to push his book, *Minding the Store*. I bought a copy of the book, read it, and showed up, uninvited, at a luncheon in his honor.

The host, *Chicago Daily News* society writer Peg Zwecker, spotted me and gave me a seat next to the guest of honor, who autographed my book and shared some of the secrets of his success. Before leaving, I told him that I wanted to come to Dallas to talk about my cosmetics line. He said fine and gave me an appointment. Since the Ebony Fashion Show was going to be in Dallas on the same day, we decided to make an evening of it. The Marcuses invited Eunice and me to dinner, and we invited them to the fashion show.

The evening began in the incredible Neiman-Marcus palace in Dallas with Marcus leading a personally conducted tour that ended in an upstairs showroom, where buyers and account executives had gathered around a rack of Chinese gowns.

When Marcus started talking about the beauty of the gowns and what a lovely Christmas present they would make, I sensed that he intended to sell me. And that if I intended to sell him, I had to buy. So I raised a few objections about the price, which was $5,000, and the fact that I didn't have my checkbook. No problem. He said he would give me an immediate charge card and put it on my account. I finally let him sell me and we went to dinner and the Ebony Fashion Fair without discussing the sale I wanted to make.

There was a mix-up at the fashion show, which was held in the Dallas Civic Center. For some reason, the show started ten minutes early and we missed the dramatic opening. I went backstage and told the staff to start the show over and announce that Mr. and Mrs. Stanley Marcus of Neiman-Marcus were in the audience. Marcus, who was involved in several projects in the Black community of Dallas, got a big ovation.

As we left the hall, he said, "Oh, by the way, tell your man to stop by the cosmetics counter tomorrow morning and there will be an order for $20,000 for Fashion Fair Cosmetics."

The hardest sell of all was at Trimingham's on the overwhelmingly Black island of Bermuda. I used everything I'd learned in thirty-four years of selling on DeForest Trimingham, who kept nodding his head and saying, "No, we can't take it. We don't have space."

At the last moment, I tried my fallback position. Every good salesman should have a fallback position, something he pulls out of his briefcase at the last possible moment as the last possible weapon.

"Mr. Trimingham," I said, "I'm not going to leave this island today without being in a store in Bermuda. You have the best store on the island, I have the best cosmetics line, and we should be together. But if you turn me down, I'm going next door to your main competitor, Smith's."

That didn't sway him, but what I said next opened his eyes.

"I have here," I said, "letters from thirty prominent Bermudians who have bought Fashion Fair in New York and want to buy it here. Do you know any of these people?"

He looked at the letters and nodded.

"I know all of them. Most of them are my customers and have been for years."

"Now, Mr. Trimingham, I bet some of these customers have never been in Smith's in their whole lifetime. And now you are going to force them to go there to buy a cosmetics line they need because it's compatible with their skin tones.... While they're there some of them will see and buy other things—and you might lose a customer. Mr. Triming-ham, do you want your customers to go to Smith's?"

"Hell, no!" he said. "Let's go downstairs and look at some space."

That was thirteen years ago, and we are the No. 1 cosmetics line in Trimingham's today.

This little incident is interesting not only because it illustrates the importance of advance planning but also because it throws a revealing light on one of the hidden mechanisms of selling. To sell effectively, you must tap into the deepest emotions of your client. It's also important to keep an emotional crowbar in reserve so you will have something to pull out and use at the right psychological moment.

One image stands out in my mind as a clear example of this. A representative of a Tennessee company came through Chicago selling a new cosmetics line, and I bought 100,000 items. The man went on to New York and sold at least one order for 3 million items.

When he returned to Tennessee, he didn't have time to fool around with my little order, which he had promised at a certain time. Based on his promise, I had made commitments for shelf space in the stores. Yet whenever I called him, he responded negatively. I said to myself, I've got to find a way to persuade this man to keep his word. I can't do it with anger, I can't do it by cursing. What will move this man? Then it hit me: *honor,* a big word in the South, where Whites have one idea about honor, and Blacks have another.

The next time I called him he kept trying to make me fall out with him. And I said, "You can't make me angry. I'm not going to fall out with you—I need you too much. You are a southerner, and I'm a southerner. I deliberately bought this item from a southern company, even though the same item was offered to me by several Italian companies. When I was in the South, White men wouldn't promise Blacks much, but if they ever gave their word you could rely on it.

I've been away from the South more than forty years. Have White men changed that much?"

There was a long silence on the phone, and then he said, "Johnson, when do you need this stuff?"

I told him next week.

"What about this week?" he said.

The vulnerable spot: Over and over again in this campaign, I proved that selling is a matter of finding and touching the M (for money) spot and reaching that part of the person that will make him say yes, whether he likes you or not.

To be fair, I should add that some department store executives welcomed the new line. Ironically and significantly, the most supportive owner was William Dillard of my home state of Arkansas. He welcomed me to his office and told me how proud he was that an Arkansas native had made good. What he said then and what he has said repeatedly since then is that "your achievement is greater than that of any other person I know, when you consider where you came from."

As for Fashion Fair, he said, "I have thirty-five stores, and you can be in all of them."

To make sure there was no misunderstanding in stores that had never dealt with Blacks on that level, he assigned one of his chief aides to take Lance Clarke around. Whenever a store manager raised a question, the aide would say, "All I knew is that Mr. Johnson and Mr. Dillard made a deal. Do you want me to call Mr. Dillard and tell him you don't want to take the line?"

Nobody wanted to dispute the authority and business judgment of William Dillard, who is one of the most brilliant and genuine persons I know. He now owns more than 130 stores, and is our largest single account. Since our first meeting, I have been elected to the board of directors of the corporation.

All through 1974, a crucial year, we went from department store to department store, selling the idea and creating new common markets. In one year, we opened three hundred high-line department stores, a record that has never been matched before or since. In all that time, I never called on a client more than one time, and I never missed a sale or an order.

After securing my home base, I entered the lucrative post exchange military market—we're now the largest Black vendor in the military—and laid the groundwork for expansion into the European market. And it may be observed at once that the same principles that worked in Chicago and Dallas worked in Paris and London.

The clearest example of this was my whirlwind London campaign, based, like the American and West Indian campaigns, on the peculiar needs of that market.

Before approaching a single store, I surveyed the territory and identified vulnerable points. To help in this effort, I hired a British publicist named Mercia Watkins. After touring our offices, she said she didn't know whether she could sell Fashion Fair but that she was relatively sure she could sell me and the Johnson Publishing Company success story.

"The English," she said, "respect achievement. They respect success. They respect royalty and champions. You're the champion in your field, and the best way to sell Fashion Fair is to sell achievement and a man who succeeded against the odds."

The easiest way to do this, she said, was to bring some of England's top fashion writers to America and expose them to the Johnson Publishing Company–Fashion Fair environment.

All right. But how were we going to get their attention? How were we going to persuade busy and important writers to cross the Atlantic for interviews and briefings?

The solution we came up with was the *Concorde.* The British super-plane was new then, and few journalists could afford the super-fare for the three-hour flight to the States.

We made it affordable, paying all expenses for a group of fifteen writers and editors, Black and White. We flew the group to New York City and put them up at the Helmsley Palace. We got them tickets to the Shubert Theater where they not only saw Broadway's hottest show, *Dreamgirls*, but went backstage to meet the show's stars.

This was the appetizer for a twenty-four-hour extravaganza in Chicago, where they lived at the Ritz Carlton and were carried by limousines to the Johnson Publishing Company headquarters for a tour, luncheon, and interviews and to my Lake Shore Drive apartment for dinner.

The results—a series of glowing stories on the Fashion Fair Miracle—surpassed our expectations and provided the backdrop for a London luncheon that introduced the line to English and French buyers. One writer said that Fashion Fair provided "a foundation shade to blend over every skin from pale to the darkest Caribbean Brown."

We flew the Ebony Fashion Show to London for the luncheon, which was held at the Dorchester Hotel. The theme of the luncheon, "Ebony and Ivory," was reflected in a black and white piano and Black and White models who emphasized that Fashion Fair was for everybody.

This brought immediate orders from London's Harrods and Paris's Printemps, followed by commitments from other high-line stores, including Dickins & Jones and Selfridges in London and Galeries Lafayette in Paris.

While masterminding the Fashion Fair campaign, I was also directing the day-to-day affairs of an insurance company, three radio stations, and three magazines. And although I spent most of my time in this period on Fashion Fair accounts, I had to put on my fireman's hat from time to time to put out fires in other divisions of the company.

One of these fires, a serious one, developed at Supreme Life Insurance Company, where I had installed a master salesman and marketing expert as president. Under his leadership, sales increased. So, unfortunately, did administrative and financial problems. Before things got completely out of hand, I assumed the position of president as well as chairman of the board and reorganized the staff.

This was a delicate operation involving not only the board but the State Insurance Department. To save and preserve the legacy of Pace and other Supreme pioneers, I pulled out all stops and invested additional funds. When the business was reestablished on a sound basis, I named Lloyd G. Wheeler president and installed controls to prevent a recurrence of the problem. Since then, the company has regained lost ground and established new records.

In the midst of this crisis, I confronted and solved two editorial problems. The first was the declining circulation of a new magazine, *Ebony Jr!* The magazine, designed for children between the ages of six and twelve, hit a peak circulation of 100,000 before dropping to 40,000. The major problems—identification of parents with children in the target age groups and city-by-city sales campaigns focused on boards of education—were solvable, but required more time and money than I was willing to give at the time. After investing more than $2 million, I decided to cut my losses and concentrate on the profitable divisions.

The second problem was the *Ebony* format. When I started *Ebony*, the standard picture-magazine size was 13¾″ by 9¾″, the *Life* and *Look* size. After *Life* and *Look* went out of business, all major magazines—*Esquire, Ladies' Home Journal, McCall's*—reduced their sizes to 10⅞″ by 8¼″. *Ebony* bucked the trend and became the last of the big commercial magazines.

This created major advertising and circulation problems, for the whole industry was geared now to the new standard size. I was emotionally tied to the big book. But I couldn't buck the tide of advertisers, who refused to prepare oversized ads. When we lost Ford, Campbell Soup, and General Motors ads in one issue, I bit the bullet, reduced the size, and increased the price.

I was prepared for adverse reader reaction, but circulation increased. It turned out that it was more convenient to handle the standard-sized book. The new *Ebony* also received better display space on the newsstands. All of a sudden, circulation exploded, going from 1.2 million to 1.5 million to the 1.8 million we sell today.

To take up the slack created by the discontinuance of *Ebony Jr!* I created a new magazine, *EM*, addressed to the Ebony man. At the same time, I bought 20 percent of the outstanding stock of *Essence*, a New York–based magazine designed for Black women.

The upshot of all this was a stronger personal and corporate profile, as *Forbes* magazine pointed out in 1982 when it named me to its list of the 400 richest Americans. The magazine said my net worth was $100 million. Two years later, the magazine said I was worth "at least" $150 million.

I've never counted, but I don't quarrel with the figures listed in the Forbes 400—and I don't apologize. Whatever the correct figure, whether it's the $175 or $200 million some analysts cite today, I earned it, and I'm still earning it. I work harder today than I did when I started out. I make more presentations, I call on more clients, I make more speeches and public appearances. In fact, if I were young again, and if I knew then what I know now, I could be even more successful. Young or not, if I get a few more years, I'm going to create a bigger company despite age, despite race, despite the odds.

The Forbes 400 honor was one wave in an unprecedented tide of personal and corporate recognition. There was, to begin with, the national outpouring of acclaim that followed the fortieth anniversary of *Ebony* in November 1985. The company grossed $154,860,000 in that year and was No. 1 for the second straight year on the *Black Enterprise* list of the top one hundred Black businesses. In 1987, when *Black Enterprise* named me Entrepreneur of the Decade, Johnson Publishing Company grossed $173,500,000 from publishing, broadcasting, and TV production and cosmetics, and employed 1,828 persons.

In the same period, the Better Boys Club of Chicago named me Chicagoan of the Year, the first Black so honored. Governor James Thompson and Mayor Harold Washington were among the civic and corporate leaders who gathered to celebrate what I called a Chicago and an American triumph.

There was also a sentimental trip to my Arkansas City hometown—my first visit in fifty-three years. I don't know what I expected, but I was brought to tears by the Blacks and Whites who hugged and kissed me and welcomed me home. This was the New South, and it took some getting used to, White men and women hugging Black men and women and sassing each other and sharing yesterdays and tomorrows.

What a wonderful thing it was, they said, for a native son to come home in glory after showing the world what Arkansas City folk could do. People who were old enough remembered Miss Gert, as they called my mother. They said it was a shame that she didn't live to see the sun of this day.

In the blinding hot Arkansas sun, remembered from decades ago, I relived the lost years with Dorothy Moore, widow of former sheriff Robert S. Moore, and Nathaniel Hayes, an old friend and former captain in the sheriff's department. We talked about old times and old places and called back the flood and the first picture show and the bakery shop, where my stepfather worked. Then we went into the integrated high school for a Black and White welcoming ceremony attended by every major official in Arkansas City and Desha county, led by Mayor R. C. Bixler, Sheriff Ben Williams, and State Representative Bynum Gibson.

I had no illusions about the meaning of the turnout. The people, Black and White, came to see not a man, not a personality, but a dream and a faith. They had perhaps doubted the dream in their hearts. They had said perhaps that it no longer worked. They came on this day to see with their own eyes that it could still happen and that it could happen to a boy from Arkansas City. And if it could happen to a Black boy from Arkansas City, it could happen to anyone.

After the ceremony, I visited the shotgun house where I was born and the St. John Baptist Church. Before leaving town in a motorcade arranged by Governor Bill Clinton and his aide, Rodney Slater, I walked one last time down the great levee and looked across the Mississippi River with eyes misted by the dreams and hopes and fears of my youth.

All the themes and stations of my life—the Mississippi River, Goin' to Chicago, the welfare roll and the roll of the 400 richest Americans and Gertrude Johnson Williams and *Negro Digest* and *Ebony* and *Jet*—came together when I was inducted into the Junior Achievement's Business Hall of Fame, along with, among others, John E. Swearingen of Standard Oil Company of Indiana, Hyatt hotel magnate A. N. Pritzker, and, posthumously, Gustavus F. Swift (1839–1903), Philip D. Armour (1832–1901), Marshall Field (1834–1906), Colonel Robert R. McCormick (1880–1955), and Julius Rosenwald (1862–1932).

As I sat in Chicago's Museum of Science and Industry, listening to the citations, I had a sudden and unbelievable vision of the great names entombed in this Business Hall of Fame, the Armours, the Rosenwalds, the Fields, marching in the same procession with a Black boy who had walked barefooted in Mississippi mud and dreamed an impossible dream.

When I got up to acknowledge the award, I looked beyond the immediate audience and said to Blacks, to Hispanics, to Asians, to Whites, to dreamers everywhere, that long shots *do* come in and that hard work, dedication, and perseverance will overcome almost any prejudice and open almost any door.

That was my faith then and it's my faith now.

I believe that the greater the handicap the greater the triumph.

I believe that the only failure is failing to try.

I believe that Black, Brown, and White Americans are chained together by tradition, history, and a common market and that what helps one group of Americans helps all Americans.

And if my life has meaning and color and truth, it is because millions of Americans, Black and White, have proved through me that the Dream is still alive and well and working in America.

# *Index*